Praise for *The New Arab Wars*

"*The New Arab Wars* is a useful book for this moment."

—*New York Times Book Review*

"A cool but meticulous account."

—*New York Review of Books*

"Lynch, a prolific and keen observer of the Arab world, has written the leading title in what amounts to a second wave of analyses of the Arab revolts of 2010–11."

—*Foreign Affairs*

"A keen observer of the violent upheaval in the Middle East since the Arab Spring, [Lynch] makes a strong assertion: there is no returning to the old autocratic ways. . . . An excellent, clear distillation of recent events in the Middle East."

—*Kirkus Reviews*, starred review

"This is an unblinking, unsparing. and un-put-downable account of the anarchy and ruin that have engulfed the Middle East since the 'Arab Spring' dawned five years ago. Marc Lynch offers no easy answers or escapes: The Arab uprisings had deep roots and they won't be suppressed by the   rats in Egypt or Saudi Arabia; US intervention couldn't have p   ture of Syria; Islamic extremism is only going to get w   honest book that will peel the varnish off conven   who disagree with some of Lynch's conclusion   must-reading."

—David Ignatius, columnist, *Washington Po.*

"This is an important work, full of sharp insi   er analysis. Marc Lynch is an exceptional guide to the deeper driver. ..ange across the Middle East. Anyone looking to understand the roots and trajectories of the Arab uprisings, and their implications for the future of a crucial region, will benefit enormously from this terrific book."

—Ambassador William J. Burns, president, Carnegie Endowment for International Peace, and former deputy secretary of state

"*The New Arab Wars* is a compelling, accurate, and comprehensive overview of our turbulent region's very mixed condition at this historic transitional moment. Lynch succinctly captures all the nuances, strengths, weaknesses, actors, dangers, and promises that define the Middle East today. I strongly recommend this book for anyone who seeks to understand what is going on in our region, how we reached this situation, and how to appreciate the changing roles of the many regional and global players."

—Rami G. Khouri, senior public policy fellow, Issam Fares Institute for Public Policy and International Affairs, American University of Beirut, and internationally syndicated political columnist

THE NEW ARAB WARS

UPRISINGS AND ANARCHY IN THE MIDDLE EAST

MARC LYNCH

PUBLICAFFAIRS

New York

Published by PublicAffairs™, an imprint of Perseus Books, LLC, a subsidiary of
Hachette Book Group, Inc.

First paperback edition published in 2017 by PublicAffairs.

The Hachette Speakers Bureau provides a wide range of authors for speaking
events. To find out more, go to hachettespeakersbureau.com or call 866-376-6591.

Library of Congress Control Number: 2016931932

ISBN 978-1-61039-609-7 (HC)
ISBN 978-1-61039-610-3 (EB)
ISBN 978-1-61039-772-8 (PBK)

First Edition

10 9 8 7 6 5 4 3 2 1

For Sophia Faith and Alexander Reyes

Contents

Preface

"We are coming tonight. There won't be any mercy," warned Libya's Moammar Qaddafi on March 17, 2011, as his troops pushed relentlessly towards Benghazi, the beleaguered base of the month-old rebellion. As Qaddafi's forces advanced, rebel leaders appealed desperately for the international community to intervene to protect them. The coming catastrophe unfolded on live television in the midst of a regionwide tidal wave of popular protest and furious regime crackdowns. The streets were watching, and the fate of the Arab uprisings seemed to hang in the balance.

The world's response was extraordinary. The usually divided Arab League spoke with a single voice, calling for international action against Qaddafi. The United Nations Security Council, against all odds, passed a resolution authorizing military action to protect the Libyan rebels. NATO jets began bombing almost immediately, halting the regime forces and soon driving them back.

The airstrikes did not lead to a rapid victory, however. Six months of long, difficult stalemate followed, until a sudden rebel move into Tripoli overthrew Qaddafi's regime. On October 20, Qaddafi himself was killed by rebels in Sirte. The National Transitional Council, the political leadership of the uprising that took control as the new Libyan government, announced an ambitious road map for a transition to a democratic Libya. By the spring of 2012, Libya seemed to vindicate the hopes of the Arab uprisings, the American strategy of limited military intervention, and a better Middle East.

But then, it all went wrong. The new Libyan state struggled to establish security, find political consensus, or build effective institutions despite holding democratic elections. The armed groups that had fought for the revolution refused to disarm, evolving into militias that controlled the streets. On September 11, 2012, the Islamist militia Ansar al-Sharia Libya launched a brazen military attack on the US consulate and CIA station in Benghazi. Only a month earlier, US Senators John McCain, Lindsey Graham, and Joe Lieberman had pushed for an American intervention in Syria by pointing to Libya, where "profound gratitude for America's help in the war against Moammar Qaddafi has laid the foundation for a bright new chapter in relations between our two countries."[1] The killing of US Ambassador Chris Stephens and two others in the heartland of the Libyan revolution by a jihadist militia amidst chaotic anti-American protests put a cruel face on that new chapter. For many, it offered a disheartening epitaph for the Arab uprisings themselves.

In the aftermath of the Benghazi attack, Libyan politics and society polarized dangerously, while jihadist groups took advantage of the security vacuum to rebuild themselves. In Washington, the smoldering ruins of Benghazi's consulate turned Libya overnight from a tentative sign of a hopeful future into a blisteringly partisan nightmare. As America recoiled in horror and militia violence rapidly spread, the Libyan state rapidly crumbled. Oil production and the rest of the economy collapsed. The government recognized by the international community controlled only one part of the country, while a rival government dominated the rest. The country degenerated into a civil war between two heavily armed coalitions, each receiving significant financial and military support from external powers. Jihadists established new strongholds in the fractured terrain.

The Obama administration's decision to join with NATO and its Arab allies to intervene militarily in Libya stands today as a crucial turning point in the Arab uprisings—one with effects far beyond that country's borders. The lessons of that intervention remain deeply contested. The intervention succeeded in its short-term goal of protecting Libyan civilians by preventing a near-certain massacre, and helped to remove one of the nastier of the Arab dictators. Had Obama not acted, America would certainly have been blamed for allowing the uprising to end in bloodshed. But acting, in turn, caused a whole set of other unintended problematic outcomes. Some now argue that the real problem was not the intervention but rather America's failure to provide for post-war stabilization. But Libya's new political leaders had firmly rejected any such international peacekeeping force. Even had they not, the dark history of the occupation of Iraq ensured no such forces were forthcoming... and suggests that it would not have helped.

Why begin this story with Libya, rather than with the crisis in Syria or the challenge of the Islamic State? Because Libya was a decisive turning point in the transformation of the Arab uprisings from domestic peaceful uprisings into a regional proxy war. Libya's war offered the first violently cautionary tale against seeking democratic change after the dizzying success of protest movements in Tunisia and Egypt. The NATO intervention showed Arab protestors and autocrats alike that armed insurrection could succeed by attracting external assistance. It showed Arab powers that they could convince the West to back their ambitions with military might, but led Russia to block further such United Nations resolutions. Its subsequent collapse into civil war then became an object lesson in the dangers of intervention and state failure. Libya in many ways set the stage for Syria's descent into catastrophic civil war.

Libya's failed promise is personal to me. When these events were unfolding, I was writing as a columnist for *Foreign Policy*, meeting regularly with Obama administration officials, and appearing frequently in the media. I argued for the US to intervene to support the Libyan protestors, both to protect civilians from extreme state violence and to sustain the momentum of the Arab uprisings by deterring armed repression of protestors elsewhere. Libya was the first American war since Bosnia that I supported. That this intervention failed led me to publicly rethink many of the arguments for American intervention in the Middle East.[2] It baffles me that the lesson which most of Washington learned from the tribulations of the Libya intervention was that Obama should also have intervened in Syria.

I began writing this book in part to continue rethinking the assumptions and arguments that shaped my initial analysis of not only Libya but also of the broader Arab uprising. I hope that it encourages others to do the same. Political scientists, journalists, and participants in the momentous events of the last five years have produced an enormous amount of real-time analysis. Much of it has been absolutely first-rate, and I draw heavily in this book on the collective scholarship of hundreds of thoughtful, deeply informed, and brilliantly analytical individuals. What, in the heat of the fray, did we tend to underestimate or exaggerate? What problems did we miss, or fail to propose adequate solutions for what we correctly diagnose?

One thing we most certainly did not get wrong was the epochal and fundamentally transformative nature of the Arab uprising. It's true that the five years since that historic eruption have been cruel to those who hoped for positive change in the Middle East. Only a few years ago, the Arab world seemed poised to escape decades of autocratic misrule and state violence. Today, the hopes of millions of Arab citizens who heroically took to the streets demanding change have faded.

The entire regional order appears to be in freefall. Egypt's democratic transition ended in a military coup, mass arrests, and political stalemate. Syria, Libya, and Yemen are mired in grinding civil war. Millions of refugees live in tenuous conditions, their lives shattered and their homes destroyed with little prospect of a return to normality. The Islamic State is holding tenaciously to its Syrian and Iraqi strongholds, spreading into Libya and other shattered states, and inspiring terrorism globally. The very idea of democracy has been discredited among large swaths of the Arab citizenry. The major short-term effect of the Arab uprisings has not been democratization, but rather a dramatic increase in regional interventionism, proxy war, and resurgent repression.

These struggles should lead to sober reflections, but we must not take away the wrong lessons. It is far too soon to conclude that the uprisings have failed. The deep economic, social, and political failings that drove Arabs to rise up in 2011 have only grown worse in the intervening years, the frustrations of ever more empowered youth more intense. Policymakers and pundits may find it comforting to contemplate a return to stable and friendly authoritarian regimes. It is a myth.

Many wrong lessons currently dominate the conventional wisdom. The failure of the transitions does not prove that Arabs are not ready for democracy. Obama could not have saved Mubarak or stopped the Arab uprising if he had tried. There is no monarchical exception protecting the Gulf regimes from popular discontent. The resurgence of jihadist groups does not mean they were the real, hidden face of the uprising all along. And stronger states are not the solution to the region's woes. Autocratic regimes, in their single-minded pursuit of survival, are the root cause of the instability and have fueled the region's extremism and conflicts. The region's autocrats, from Damascus to Riyadh, are the problem and not the solution.

These are grim times, but it is far too soon to give up hope. The Islamic State is unlikely to survive in its current form. The civil wars will eventually end. The nuclear agreement between Iran and the United States offers a historic opportunity to establish new foundations for regional order. The current morass is no more likely to be the final endpoint of the region's political development than was the February 2011 revolutionary delirium or the 2012 Muslim Brotherhood electoral victories. 2016 is not the endpoint of a five-year-long process. It is the midpoint of a decades-long process, driven by deep structural changes in the region's politics, economics, and society. Attempting to rebuild the old order through closer cooperation between the United States and Arab autocratic regimes in the name of stability is a recipe for disaster. Autocrats may have clawed back their power in most Arab countries, but none of the underlying problems have been solved and most have gotten worse. We might not know exactly when and where the next eruption of mass protest appears, but another wave is almost certainly coming.

There is an emerging consensus in Washington DC that the blame for these many failings lies with the Obama administration. This too is a myth. American policy disputes tend to exaggerate the role of the United States and to filter events through a partisan lens. This has little to do with the realities of today's Middle East. US influence on the Arab uprising was far less than most Americans or Arabs believe. In part, this was intentional. Obama tried to support the Arab uprisings, but he also believed, correctly, that the best hope for the uprisings' success would come with less American involvement. Few of the Arab protestors looked to Washington for signs, and none would have left Tahrir or Change Square at Obama's request. When Secretary of State Hillary Clinton came to Cairo in early 2011, activists refused to meet with her; when she came to Alexandria in 2012, Egyptian activists pelted her with tomatoes.

Still, Obama's strategy towards the Middle East poses a profound test of America's role in the region. Determined to reduce the American footprint in the Middle East and focus instead on Asia and global issues, Obama pursued a determined strategy of minimalism. He withdrew US military forces from Iraq, refrained from direct military intervention in Syria, and concluded an unprecedented nuclear agreement with Iran. By the end of his second term, however, he faced a vocal elite consensus that this policy of restraint had failed the region, and that American inaction had become as damaging to the region as the Bush administration's overreach. American military forces had returned to Iraq, and a major American-led air campaign was pummeling the Islamic State in both Iraq and Syria. If even Obama could not enduringly reduce America's military presence in the Middle East, could anyone?

In my 2012 book, *The Arab Uprising*, I argued that the verdict on the Libya intervention and on the entire process of change remained unclear. The Arab uprising marked a fundamental rupture in the status quo, an epochal event whose ramifications would take years to fully manifest. The changes reflected in those synchronized, massive protests rendered a return to the old ways inconceivable. These were generational changes that could not be judged by the momentary vicissitudes of an electoral outcome or a constitutional gambit or a coup. They would be measured in the new attitudes and expectations and behavior of the millions of Arabs suddenly able to act politically in ways previously inconceivable.

But that, I warned, did not guarantee that the new order would necessarily be better. Every earlier wave of popular mobilization in modern Arab history, I noted, had ended in the reassertion of an even more intensely repressive autocracy. The public being so powerfully mobilized had been shaped by generations of autocracy, corruption, patronage, and a smothering state security apparatus. Old elites had not gone anywhere. Public culture had been deeply molded by decades of Islamist activism which had cultivated deeply held new behaviors and belief systems. The conflicts of the previous decade, especially in Iraq, had unleashed frightening new forms of sectarian hatreds and left behind a generation of refugees. The new public sphere, so gloriously unified and optimistic in the glory days of the uprisings, already harbored the seeds of populism and division. The uprising could lead to a new despotism as easily as a new democracy.

Both the hopes and the fears in the conclusion of *The Arab Uprising* have been amply manifested. The generational change was real. Young Arabs across the region are wired, mobile, restless, and keenly aware of their own potential. Even the regimes that have survived were profoundly changed by the process of confrontation and co-optation. The Arab media and the socially-mediated information environment will never again resemble the dismal days of the 1970s and 1980s when states could control the flow of information and ideas and individuals lived in political silence out of fear of state surveillance. Arab politics today is fundamentally different than it once was, and Arab citizens have dramatically new expectations, capabilities, and experiences.

For now, those hopeful long-term trends have been overwhelmed by the catalog of horrors that has befallen the region. Since late 2012, almost everything has gone wrong. The uprisings have proven to be far more successful at breaking the status quo than at building better alternatives. Uprisings shattered Libya, Yemen, Syria, and Iraq beyond repair. In Egypt, they transformed a decrepit autocracy into a new, more repressive, internationally illegitimate and politically unstable form of personalistic direct military rule. They unleashed a wave of sectarianism and radicalism that has profoundly reshaped national identities. Even ISIS might best be understood as appealing not to religious devotion but to the profound attraction of a movement that fundamentally breaks the old order and replaces it with a new utopia.

Optimists about the Arab uprisings failed to appreciate just how far the region's autocrats would go to prevent positive change. Bashar al-Asad was famously willing to burn Syria if that's what it took to stay in power. Most of his fellow Arab leaders thought exactly the same way. With only a few rare exceptions, Arab leaders have proven that they would do virtually anything to hold on to power. They pushed back popular uprisings through violent repression, political and economic co-optation, and the manipulation of identity politics. They fought their battles for political survival not only at home, but across the region's many new battlefields.

That is why this book tells the story of the subversion of the Arab uprising from a regional perspective. It emphasizes the connections between the many complex, local political battles and places them within a broader political war over regional order. This is not to downplay the primacy of local politics or the responsibility of domestic political actors for their own failures. But their choices, and the challenges they faced, cannot be understood outside the context of the new Arab wars. Local politics could not escape the long struggle between Iran and Saudi Arabia, the battles between Turkey, Qatar, and Saudi Arabia for Sunni leadership, the conflict between the United Arab Emirates and the Muslim Brotherhood, and the persistent challenge to international order by small, violent jihadist groups.

Wherever possible, I draw on Arabic sources for this book's narrative: my own conversations, social media, the vast wealth of published articles and television broadcasts available online. I try to highlight the views of local voices wherever possible—but also to situate those local voices within their own hotly contested and politicized context. The debate over the Arab uprisings has been poorly served by the reliance on a small number of interlocutors to translate and explain complex internal debates. The sheer intensity of the polarized political debates that raged in almost every transitional country should be taken seriously. Any invocation of what "the people" want should be immediately seen for the political claim it is. "Syrians" or "Libyans" or other populations going through divisive civil wars did not collectively want anything. Uncovering those internal debates will offer a better understanding of the region's new politics than adopting one side's narrative—even if it is far easier to sympathize with some than others.

I draw frequently on social media as a window into these debates. Today's social media platforms, where millions of Arabs offer their thoughts on a daily basis, present an unprecedented window into those internal debates, if approached with methodological rigor and analytical caution and supplemented by experience on the ground and historical perspective. Social media offers researchers an unprecedented source of evidence and insight, breaking the long-cultivated monopoly over information claimed by regimes. I supplement this wealth of social media data with a wide variety of more traditional sources, including the media, survey research, and many personal interviews and conversations with policy-makers and activists in Washington, Europe, and across the Middle East.

This book draws on political science as well. Both sources are essential to an effective understanding of regional politics. Political science alerts us to structural drivers of events, comparative perspectives, and the expected operation of distinctive mechanisms. Local debates and arguments give essential insights into the lived experience and the informed choices of the people most affected by and most driving the events. Neither alone is sufficient. Relying solely on the views of people caught up in events can lead to analysis distorted by the passions and misconceptions of the moment. We must always be sensitive to local context without adopting the partisan perspective of preferred interlocutors on the ground. Many Egyptians truly believed that their military coup was unique in the history of military coups. Many Syrians failed to understand the iron logic of external intervention into civil wars. Both were wrong, to disastrous effect. On the other side, political scientists are at risk of misapplying theories by missing local context or particularities, or by inaccurately specifying the expectations and priorities of local actors. That's why I try to draw fully on the insights of both, even if such a synthesis ends up satisfying neither.

This book ranges widely over the greater Middle East, from the tortured transitions in Egypt and Tunisia to the wars of Syria, Iraq, Libya, and Yemen. Rather than offering deeply detailed narratives of each individual country, my goal is to provide a framework for understanding the new politics of the region, explaining what went wrong and suggesting what to expect. Fortunately there is now a wealth of outstanding research and writing on most of these countries, a literature upon which I draw freely and recommend to those hoping to go deeper into the issues touched upon here.

Virtually everyone writing during the heady days of the Arab uprisings warned that change would be a long, hard process with uncertain outcomes. Even during the headiest days of Tahrir, it was clear how difficult it would be to bring about enduring, meaningful political democratization. The activists who drove those hopeful uprisings of early 2011 have suffered terrible defeats. Many have evolved in almost unrecognizable directions, from idealistic proto-democrats into violent radicals or regime apologists. But the underlying forces that drove so many Arab citizens into the streets continue to transform societies, economies, and polities. Autocratic regimes may play at being back in control. They might even believe it. But they are not. Their determined efforts to suppress, co-opt, or divert the forces for change have only succeeded in shutting down the options for peaceful reform. But crushing peaceful protestors and discrediting democratic institutions without addressing real grievances is a recipe for much more dangerous explosions to come.

The appeal to restore the Arab state system in response to this tragedy fundamentally misdiagnoses the problem facing today's Middle East. Like the Islamic State, restored Arab autocrats propose a return to an imagined past. Their vision of an autocratic restoration juxtaposes today's chaos with the supposed stability and predictability of the recent past. Authoritarian regimes might not accord with Western values, they argue, but they do work. Keeping hold of all this chaos requires a strong hand, which can only be offered by traditional forms of Arab leadership reinforced by a fully empowered security state. An absolutist monarchy like the United Arab Emirates or Qatar or a military dictatorship like post-coup Egypt may look appealing when compared with the horrors of a collapsing Libya or an apocalyptic Syria and Iraq.

But that's a mirage. The Arab uprisings erupted precisely because the autocrats could not deliver on the promise of an acceptable life. The decade leading up to the Arab uprisings was not a period of stability, reform, or economic improvement. The autocratic past was one of failed governance, rising sectarianism, and ever more pressing popular discontent. The uprisings did not fail because Arabs are not ready for democracy or because Islamists cunningly exploited the naiveté of hopeful liberals. The Arab uprising failed primarily because the regimes they challenged killed it. This book is about how the crime was committed . . . and what happens next.

| 1 |

THE NEW ARAB WARS

O n September 30, 2015, Russian military forces poured into Syria in response to a formal request for assistance from the government of Bashar al-Asad. The Russian forces immediately began a bombing campaign primarily targeting rebel forces in support of the regime. A regional war became ever more international as Russian aircraft shared operational space with those of the United States and its coalition partners waging an intense bombing campaign against the Islamic State.

Russia had acted to reinforce Asad's military, which faced pressure from a new well-armed Saudi, Qatari, and Turkish-backed hard-line Islamist coalition that had made significant advances in the north against exhausted regime forces. A few weeks earlier, Turkey and the United States had agreed on the use of a key Turkish airbase, which could potentially be used to create protected safe zones for rebels. Russia's intervention predictably prompted a counter-escalation in regional support for the rebels. Arab states rushed new weapons to their rebel allies, who quickly rallied to hold their territory. On November 24, Turkey shot down a Russian jet that it claimed had violated its airspace. As the dust settled, neither Asad nor the rebels were any closer to victory. Within a few months, the

Russian campaign had bogged down, leaving Syria's grinding civil war no closer to resolution.

Syria's war was only one of at least three simultaneous destructive military quagmires reshaping the region. On March 26, 2015, a Saudi-led coalition launched a military intervention in Yemen to roll back the seizure of Sanaa and Aden by the Shi'ite Houthi Movement. The Saudis and their Emirati partners sought to restore to power the deposed President Abd Rabbo Mansour al-Hadi, who had been elected in 2012 in a one-candidate referendum as the culmination of the Gulf Cooperation Council's transition plan. Their allies in Yemen included southern regionalists, the Muslim Brotherhood-linked Islah movement, and, implicitly, al-Qaeda. Arrayed against them, with opportunistic Iranian support, were not only the Houthis, but also forces loyal to the deposed President Ali Abdullah Saleh, a longtime Saudi ally.

The architects of the Saudi intervention viewed the Yemeni political collapse primarily through the lens of Iranian regional ambitions. They heralded the Yemen campaign as a new model for joint Arab military action, with the Gulf states acting independently to confront Iran rather than depending on the United States. But long months later, the campaign had accomplished few of its goals. Months of bombardment caused massive humanitarian suffering but produced little political progress. Nor did the introduction of troops, not only Saudi and Emirati, but also Egyptian and Sudanese and even Columbian. The Yemen war, too, bogged down into a grinding campaign with staggering humanitarian costs and no political horizon.

Libya, too, was embroiled in a multiparty civil war involving high levels of international intervention and little prospect for victory. The regional struggle between the United Arab Emirates and Qatar, not Iran, dominated this quagmire. Two rival governments claimed authority over post-revolutionary Libya. The Libyan state had largely collapsed, riven by political polarization and outgunned by well-armed militias. The UAE and Egypt threw their weight behind the campaign of General Khalifa Haftar to militarily defeat Islamist and regional forces backed by Turkey and Qatar. Indirect UAE and Egyptian support soon gave way to air strikes, as arms poured in despite a formal United Nations embargo. The growing presence of Islamic State jihadists in Libya added urgency as the United Nations mediators painstakingly tried to assemble an acceptable coalition government to end the fighting.

The emergence of the Islamic State hung over the region as these wars ground on. Its emergence reminded the world that Iraq's civil war ignited by the American invasion and occupation had never really ended. The June 2014 capture of Mosul and declaration of an Islamic caliphate by Abu Bakr al-Baghdadi had radically refocused the world's attention. Only a few years earlier, the global jihadist movement had been on the ropes. The May 2011 American killing of Osama bin Laden had been a major symbolic and operational setback for al-Qaeda. The Islamic State of Iraq had suffered severe losses at the hands of the "Sunni Awakening" and the US-led coalition in the late 2000s. The Arab uprising model of peaceful change had initially badly discredited al-Qaeda's ideological vision. But by 2015, al-Qaeda and Islamic State affiliates had surged into prominent positions in Syria, Yemen, Libya, the Sinai, and across North Africa, and their terrorist attacks had become a regular feature of life across the globe.

The jihadist resurgence was rooted in the failure of the Arab uprisings and the openings created by the region's new wars. Egypt's July 2013 military coup had shattered the Muslim Brotherhood, weakening the most powerful competitors to the extremist organizations. The coup had made a mockery of the Brotherhood's strategy of peaceful democratic participation, vindicating long-standing jihadist arguments for violent struggle. State failure in Libya, Egypt, and Yemen had opened space for jihadist groups to reorganize, acquire weapons, and establish new strongholds. Syria's war had mobilized massive financial and military support for jihadist movements that had once been shunned, and had galvanized a resurgence of the Sunni insurgency in Iraq. Libya's civil war had opened yet another new front for the renewed jihadist trend.

Less than three years after heralding the arrival of Egyptian democracy and triumphantly withdrawing US troops from Iraq, President Barack Obama found himself accepting a new Egyptian military regime and launching a large-scale bombing campaign against the self-declared Islamic

State in eastern Syria and western Iraq. While an air campaign and military assistance mission joined by more than a dozen countries had stopped ISIS from gaining territory and faced growing internal and external pressure, it remained entrenched. As ISIS struggled on its home turf, its model posed a growing regional and global threat as terrorists claiming inspiration or affiliation with the IS carried out horrifying attacks in Tunisia, Yemen, Egypt, Libya, Somalia, and Paris.

The Middle East has rarely seen such a confluence of wars and interventions. A new form of regional politics has taken hold, with transnational networks battling politically and militarily across borders and states struggling to hold themselves together. Yemen, Libya, Iraq, and Syria were only the most fully internationalized hot wars in a region increasingly beset by state failure, terrorism, and insurgency. Egypt faced an escalating insurgency in the Sinai Peninsula and, increasingly, in mainland urban centers. Terrorism struck repeatedly at the heart of Tunisia's tourism industry and against Shi'ite mosques in Saudi Arabia and Kuwait. Lebanon and Jordan were barely holding together under the weight of refugees and transnational violence. Bahrain simmered with the effects of its brutal campaign of sectarian repression. These battles overlapped and intersected: Islamic State jihadists left Syria to fight in Libya; Libyan jihadists crossed into Tunisia to attack its tourist sites; Saudis and Bahrainis and Kuwaitis traveled to Syria to fight with or against the Islamic State.

Each of the region's wars and domestic political upheavals is part of a larger story. The failed transitions of the so-called Arab Spring, the rise of the Islamic State, and the various wars that have consumed the Middle East are often treated as discrete events. They are not. Egypt's transition, Syria's civil war, Libya's collapse, the Islamic State's emergence and Tunisia's success are all part of a single story. The Arab uprising was a singular event, uniting the entire Arab world within a single, incredibly potent narrative of the possibility of change. The failure of each uprising has often been explained by local conditions. But these struggles for the Arab future never stopped being fully regional in their nature. In surveys conducted over the last five years, nearly 70 percent of Arabs agreed that foreign interference was an obstacle to reform in their country.[1] As the leading Saudi pundit Abd al-Rahman al-Rashed put it starkly in April 2015, "the region is one playing field, its wars are tied together."[2] He was right—even if the lessons he drew from this observation were almost exactly wrong.

The Arab uprising and its defeat were each a thoroughly international phenomenon. They were shaped by shifting global and regional power dynamics, a series of intense shocks to a brittle and stagnant regional order, and an extraordinarily rapid and deep change in the media and information environment. Actors moved across multiple arenas, taking both cues and material support from supporters and rivals abroad. Networks of like-minded movements and individuals across borders—whether Islamists or anti-Islamists, Sunnis or Shi'ites, liberals or monarchs—supplanted national narratives. Ideas, techniques, hopes, and fears moved quickly and decisively from one protest movement to another and from one government to another. Embattled regimes learned from both the successes and failures of their peers. Protest movements weighed the efficacy of peaceful and violent actions in part by observing outcomes elsewhere, just as did their would-be supporters.

International forces mattered at every level of the region's upheavals, from the outbreak of the uprisings to the struggles over transitions to the proxy wars and insurgencies. There is no way to explain why almost every Arab country experienced a popular protest movement at the same time based on their internal qualities. Nor is there any transitional outcome, with the very partial exception of Tunisia's, which can be explained without reference to external factors. All of the civil wars ripping apart Arab countries have been shaped profoundly by transnational flows of money, information, people, and guns. Protestors and regimes and insurgents all understood their struggles to be part of a unified regional arena—and such perceptions informed political reality. The role of Saudi Arabia, Iran, Qatar, Turkey, and the UAE have in many cases supplanted even the role of the United States as deeply polarizing issues of contention in regional politics.

This new political reality is readily apparent from the Arab media and the rhetoric of policy elites. Many ordinary Arabs saw it that way as well. In the spring of 2012, the Gallup Organizations asked Arabs from across the region whether the uprisings were mostly caused by domestic desire for change or by foreign influence.[3] The results were striking; publics in the revolutionary countries generally thought that domestic factors were at the root of the uprisings: the foreign role was highlighted by only 7 percent of Libyans, 9 percent of Tunisians, 11 percent of Egyptians, and 19 percent of Yemenis. But publics in countries with less protest activity were more likely to point to foreign factors: 29 percent of Iraqis, 37 percent of Algerians, 32 percent of Jordanians, and 31 percent of Palestinians. Roughly 20 percent of the publics in the revolutionary countries said both mattered, compared with approximately 50 percent in the non-uprising countries.

A year later, at the cusp between transitions and their failure, the Arab Barometer asked Arabs in a dozen countries about the influence of neighboring countries on the development of democracy in their country.[4] Across the whole region, only 34 percent overall thought that neighbors had played a very or somewhat positive role. In Tunisia, the first of the Arab uprisings' countries, only 21 percent saw a positive role for neighboring countries, while 55.8 percent deemed external demands for reform unacceptable. In Egypt, 34 percent saw a positive role for the neighbors in developing democracy and 36 percent a negative one—with only 16.6 percent saying "neither positive nor negative"—while 45 percent of Egyptians saw external pressure for reforms as unacceptable. Those two pivotal Arab uprisings' cases do not suggest a warm welcome for regional involvement. But in Yemen, 41.3 percent gave a positive answer on their neighbors and 48.2 percent considered external pressure legitimate. Libyans, liberated by foreign intervention and living through a profound crisis of state incapacity, were even more receptive: 54.3 percent saw a positive role and only 17 percent a negative one, while 56.6 percent welcomed external pressure for reform.

For all the importance of local factors, it is striking how similarly trends unfolded across enormously different local arenas. The interconnection of the Arab uprisings was obvious to those living through them. Events frequently tore through the entire region at once, rather than originating or being contained in any single country. The uprisings themselves were a famously transnational moment. Leadership transitions, from the departure of Hosni Mubarak and the killing of Moammar Qaddafi to the Egyptian military coup, resonated through the wildly diverse national politics. Failed states and wars spilled over to affect neighbors, as in Syria's galvanizing effects on Iraqi Sunni politics or Libya's disruptive impact on Mali. Global moments played out simultaneously in multiple arenas, such as the September 2012 protests over the anti-Islam film *The Innocence of Muslims,* which spanned dozens of countries. Major diplomatic initiatives, such as the drive towards a negotiated resolution of the Iranian nuclear program or the collapse of Israeli-Palestinian talks, shaped all levels of political dynamics throughout the region.

The uprising initially promised change in societies liberated from decades of predatory domination by despotic regimes. Beginning in Tunisia, spreading through Egypt, and then erupting across virtually every Arab country, this uprising brought millions into the streets demanding political, social, and economic change. For all their local particularities, those uprisings shared common themes, slogans, modes of action, expectations, and hopes. They crossed ideological lines, preached nonviolent resistance, and rejected traditional sectarian and religious lines of division. Beholden to no government or singular movement and empowered by ubiquitous communications technology, these movements violated the long-standing experiences of Arab politics.

Regimes responded to this unprecedented challenge by fighting back to protect themselves from the contagion of popular uprisings. This should not be surprising. Every Arab regime had been built around the singular imperative of ensuring its own grip on power at any cost. Those efforts paid off as they faced down the regional popular surge. Egypt's once-proud Tahrir Square revolution ended in a military coup, intense violence, the restoration of the old order, and a suffocating wave of repression and neo-populism. Yemen and Libya collapsed into civil war. Bahrain was suffocated by the forces of its Gulf allies. Syria's grim, horrifying stalemate was disrupted by the emergence of the self-proclaimed Islamic State, which united with its Iraqi ancestors to seize territory and declare a farcical caliphate. The Arabs who had joined the uprisings, often at great personal risk and cost, felt betrayed.

That is not to say that the uprising or its aftermath can be explained by some sinister conspiracy or that events unfolded according to some master plan. Nor is it to deny the importance of national context, or remove the agency of local players. Quite the contrary. The competition between states, social forces, and political movements unleashed forces far beyond their ability to control. Proxies failed to deliver or went rogue. Plans consistently went awry. No actor ever had quite the power to shape events that had been imagined in the royal palaces or peddled in state-controlled media. Local actors in every country careened wildly in the face of extreme uncertainty and a seemingly bottomless well of external support for their local ambitions. Guns poured into unstable conditions tended to produce violence, chaos, and radicalism rather than influence. Revolutionaries failed to translate their mobilizational capacity into enduring political parties. Militias seized local power with little regard for the national good. Islamists overreached in their bid for a stake in the emergent systems. Liberals opted disastrously for renewed alliances with militaries and Gulf monarchs in defense against the Islamists. The failures of the Arab uprising are a catalog of unintended consequences and misjudged strategies.

Efforts to control events in these transitional countries, whether by the United States or by regional powers, have followed a predictable trajectory. Almost all proxy interventions by regional powers have failed to achieve their objectives, and have usually made things significantly worse at great cost. Iran's support for Shi'ite militias in Lebanon, Syria, and Iraq had strengthened its hand militarily, but consistently sparked sectarian backlash. Arab and Turkish regime efforts fared even worse. Their intense efforts in Syria had failed to overthrow Bashar al-Asad. The transition plan for Yemen they had overseen had collapsed in ignominious failure. Libya following international intervention against Qaddafi had collapsed into a deeply divided, failed state. The Egyptian military regime they had helped reinstall seemed unable to restore stability or come to terms with its economic and governance catastrophe despite billions of dollars in assistance. And the sudden rise of the Islamic State had revitalized a jihadist movement that they had thought was under control, and that seemed to appeal dangerously to their own people. Again and again, these regimes found their plans going awry, their control over their proxies wanting, and their assumptions overturned.

The resurgence of autocratic regimes, rampant militarization, and proxy warfare, and the explosion of virulent new jihadist movements was not how the Arab uprisings were supposed to go. None of the participants in the great Arab uprising in early 2011 called for the expansion of monarchical power, more violently repressive autocratic regimes, or greater military intervention in their domestic struggles. Nor did they call for jihad towards a new caliphate, sectarian polarization, or the violent repression of mainstream Islamists. Indeed, it would be fair to say that the dominant voices within the major protest movements rejected every one of those things. But events spun out of the control of their makers.

The Arab uprising's impact on regional order intersected with that of the international push towards agreement with Iran over its nuclear program. Preventing Iran from acquiring a nuclear weapon had been the primary focus of American and international diplomacy for more than a decade. Israel had long taken the lead in warning of the devastating consequences of an Iranian nuclear arsenal. But for most regional actors, the nuclear issue was only one manifestation of a deeper struggle with Iran over regional power. The nuclear program might help to justify the elaborate web of sanctions against Tehran and proxy battles against Iranian surrogates across the region, but it was not the primary concern. The nuclear deal, no matter how effective at countering proliferation, threatened Arab regimes because it removed the foundation of a regional order built around countering Iran's role.

The simultaneous disruptions of regional order posed by the Arab uprising and the Iran nuclear deal powerfully intensified the new Middle Eastern proxy wars. Saudi Arabia, the United Arab Emirates, and other Gulf regimes projected an aura of confidence that belied their profound feelings of insecurity. Gulf leaders in 2015 boasted of a new model of military and political campaign breaking with decades of dependence on the West and regional timidity. Their assertive language could barely mask the profound insecurity behind their swagger. As they flexed muscles across the region, these regimes seemed to believe that they had beaten back the wave of popular protest and taken the lead in reshaping the region. But their military efforts had failed to achieve the desired results in Syria or Yemen, their diplomacy had failed to prevent the Iran nuclear deal, their critical alliance with Washington had been badly strained, and the plummeting price of oil had threatened the very foundation of their domestic stability.

The new Arab wars were driven by the frantic efforts of the old order to sustain itself against these inexorable changes. The effects of those interventions had proven catastrophic. Egypt's coup installed an unstable, violent, and unpredictable military regime that promises years of turmoil. Regionwide repression of the Muslim Brotherhood has discredited strategies of peaceful participation and removed a major obstacle to the spread of extreme jihadist ideas and organizations. External involvement in the wars in Syria, Libya, and Yemen has destroyed those states, caused untold human suffering, and fueled the rise of ISIS. The Saudi-Iranian competition has unleashed virulent new forms of sectarianism. In the end, the determined refusal by entrenched elites to allow for progressive change has likely doomed the region to something far worse—not just the Islamic State, but the much more significant forces that will emerge in its wake.

REGIONAL ORDER ON THE EVE OF THE UPRISING

The Arab uprising, which began in Tunisia in December 2010, erupted at a distinctive moment in regional history. When President Barack Obama took office in January 2009, he enjoyed broad public and international support for his promise to turn the page on a decade of war. Obama focused on restarting Israeli-Palestinian peace talks, extricating American troops from Iraq, and reframing relations with the Muslim world.

Obama's hope for change directly challenged the regional order that had consolidated following the Bush administration's invasion and occupation of Iraq. Regional politics were locked in an enduring divide between two blocs, a "Resistance Bloc," led by Iran, and a "Moderation Bloc" of Sunni autocrats, led by Saudi Arabia. The two blocs fought their proxy wars across multiple arenas, including Iraq under occupation,

Lebanon, Yemen, and Palestine. The region's autocratic regimes, while seemingly firmly in control, were struggling with mounting economic problems and novel forms of political protest.

Despite the deep unpopularity of the Bush administration's policies, the Middle East of the 2000s was a profoundly American regional order. The region's vast oil reserves and strategic location had always made it an area of disproportionate interest to the superpowers during the Cold War. The United States was further drawn into the region by its unique relationship with Israel. For decades following the second World War, superpower competition, access to oil, and the Arab-Israeli competition structured the region's politics.

That changed with the collapse of the Soviet Union at the end of the 1980s. The removal of Soviet global competition allowed the United States to establish a new structural order in the Middle East, one in which all roads led through Washington. The formation of an Arab coalition in support of the liberation of Kuwait from Iraqi occupation in 1990 decisively marked the passage from the Cold War order to an American-dominated regional system. Operation Desert Storm united traditional American allies such as Egypt and Saudi Arabia with adversaries such as Syria and (quietly) Israel. The absence of any meaningful alternative to the United States forced regional players to choose between inclusion in the American-dominated international system or isolation as rogue states. Public opinion largely defined itself against this American-led regional order, leading to occasional hand-wringing in Washington about the problem of "anti-Americanism." This popular hostility rarely affected the foreign policy of the autocratic regimes, though, which felt secure in ignoring public hostility.

America's leadership of this unwieldy coalition required constant maintenance. Over the course of the 1990s and 2000s, America led endless but inconclusive Israeli-Palestinian and Israeli-Syrian peace talks, which kept Washington at the center of ongoing diplomacy. It maintained "dual containment" against Iraq and Iran, which required a significant increase in its regular military presence in the Gulf. Permanent American bases took root in the small Gulf states after popular antipathy led to their removal from Saudi Arabia. The enforcement of the no-fly zones and sanctions against Iraq required a near-constant level of military attention, and provoked an endless series of political crises at the United Nations and across the region. The mounting humanitarian toll of the sanctions against Iraq, blamed primarily on the United States, became a major popular issue across broad sectors of the Arab public. Mounting public hostility to the United States only helped Arab dictators to justify their repressive ways, and Washington generally proved willing to look the other way.

America's approach to this dominant structural position differed profoundly between the 1990s and the 2000s. In the 1990s, the US worked with its autocratic allies to sustain the status quo. The September 11, 2001 terrorist attacks against Washington, DC and New York provoked the Bush administration into adopting an aggressive new revisionist strategy in the region. The autocratic status quo, which had been deemed acceptable for decades, was now seen as an incubator of extremism and violence that required drastic change. The administration and its supporters viewed the toppling of Saddam Hussein as the single most crucial catalyst for such regional transformation. In this at least they were right, though not in the ways they had intended.

The invasion of Iraq, the highly intrusive global war on terror, and the "Freedom Agenda" to promote democratic change altered the regional balance of power in ways that could only be sustained at an unprecedented cost to the United States. Saddam's fall significantly increased Iran's regional power, removing its primary military rival and allowing Iranian proxies to seize commanding positions in the politics of the new Iraq. Frightened Gulf states escalated their efforts to combat Iranian influence, seeking ever greater American security assurances and moving ever closer to alignment with Israel as the only power capable of balancing a rising Iran. Hundreds of thousands of American troops took up seemingly permanent residence in Iraq and Afghanistan while the archipelago of military bases across the Gulf region expanded dramatically in both size and function. The global War on Terror expanded American intrusion into Arab lives, politics, the economy, legal system, judiciary, educational system, media, and formal religious sector. All of this coincided with staunch US support for Israel despite the absence of any serious peace process and highly contentious wars with Palestinians and Hezbollah. It is no coincidence that this was a decade of both radically increased American interventionism and dramatically intensified anti-Americanism.

This new regional order over time took root. Arab regimes became accustomed to this high level of American interventionism once they understood that it did not threaten their personal survival. They eagerly embraced an alliance structure based primarily on the containment of Iran and the prioritization of counterterrorism over democratization and human rights. They proved able to live with the lack of Israeli-Palestinian progress. By 2010, only Iran and Syria remained outside this American-led order, and both were actively seeking a way in. Syria, which had joined the US-led coalition against Iraq and peace talks with Israel in the 1990s, was actively exploring diplomatic cooperation with Washington. Most significantly, even Iran now saw nuclear negotiations as not just an obstacle but as a vehicle for changing its relationship with the United States and the broader international community.

How one feels about the Arab uprisings and the Iran nuclear deal largely depends upon how one feels about the regional order of the previous decade. The 2000s are today rather oddly presented as a time of relative stability in the Middle East, a period in which Washington worked closely with its regional allies rather than constant friction. But this retroconning of regional politics is, frankly, bizarre. The 2000s were in fact a deeply violent and unstable time marked by the occupation of Iraq, successive Israeli wars with Palestinians and Hezbollah, and rapidly evolving sectarian tensions and jihadist violence. Iran, far from being contained, had vastly expanded its influence in Iraq and was making steady progress towards a nuclear weapon. The false stability enjoyed by the autocratic regimes was starkly exposed by the Arab uprising.

To illustrate the falsity of the nostalgia for this pre-upring order, it is useful to take a closer look at those regional politics. The long-running cold war between blocs led by Iran and Saudi Arabia, combining elements of both geopolitics and sectarianism, structured the region's politics. But there were also extremely important struggles inside the "Sunni" camp that complicate any simply sectarian narrative. The competition between

Qatar and Saudi Arabia and the battle between Islamists and regimes often mattered more directly than the Sunni-Shi'ite conflict. Furthermore, the decade also featured a steadily rising wave of popular opposition and a stunningly rapid transformation of the regional media environment, which challenged autocratic regimes from all sides.

The regional balance of power had been basically stable throughout the 1990s. The 2003 US-led invasion of Iraq, which had been meant to break the "axis of evil" and empower pro-American moderates against radicals, instead tilted the regional balance of power decisively in favor of Iran. The overthrow of Saddam Hussein removed Iran's only militarily capable Arab neighbor, leaving the Gulf states with few viable alliance options to balance Tehran. The United States significantly expanded its military and political commitments to the Gulf, but was increasingly bogged down in epic counterinsurgency quagmires in Iraq and Afghanistan. With all resources dedicated to those campaigns, the Bush administration lost its appetite for expanding its wars to Syria or Iran. At the peak of the 2007-08 troop surge, the United States had more than 160,000 combat troops deployed in Iraq. While this massive military deployment in some sense balanced Iran's power, it also came in the service of protecting a central Iraqi government dominated by Shi'a politicians. Democratic elections under rules designed primarily by Washington empowered Iraq's Shi'a majority, which many Sunni Gulf leaders interpreted as inevitably aligning Baghdad with Tehran. Saudi Arabia and other Gulf states thus felt an urgent need to balance against rising Iranian power.

The Arab world polarized into two broad coalitions: a "moderate bloc" of Sunni dictators allied with the United States (and, indirectly, Israel) against a "rejection bloc" including Iran, Syria, Hezbollah, and Hamas. In that cold war, the leading players rarely fought each other directly. Instead, they waged their struggle for political influence through proxy wars and competitive interventions in the region's weak states.[5] The cold war was fought in the pan-Arab media, transnational networks and easily penetrated Arab political systems. In Lebanon, the Saudi-backed March 14 coalition faced off against the Hezbollah and Syria-dominated March 8 "resistance" coalition. In Iraq, every neighbor from Iran and Syria to

Saudi Arabia, Jordan, and Turkey, backed armed factions, tribes, political parties, and individual politicians. In Palestine, regional powers demonstrated their power by supporting Hamas or various factions of the Palestinian Authority.

The broader public was rarely fully aligned with either bloc. Unifying issues such as hostility to Israel and the push for greater democracy counterbalanced the top-down push towards sectarian polarization. Hezbollah's war against Israel in 2006, for instance, attracted near-universal enthusiasm among Arab publics. The disconnect between the official stance of most Arab regimes and the attitudes of the vast majority of the Arab public became ever more visible in this period. Arab regimes permitted a steady stream of media criticism and even public protests against Israel or the United States as a way to let off steam, divert attention from domestic affairs, and to prove to Washington that they could not risk taking more assertive actions.

This bipolar structure provided order and meaning for a wide range of regional alliances, initiatives, and policies. The growing intensity of the Iranian-Saudi rivalry and the new pattern of alliances were primarily driven by realpolitik calculations, but soon took on sharper sectarian overlays. Iraq's degeneration into a brutal sectarian civil war spread Sunni-Shi'a hostility to quarters where it had never before had significant purchase. Saudi Arabia found it particularly useful to exploit this rising sectarianism, for both domestic and regional reasons. Highlighting the Sunni-Shi'a divide could undermine Iran's appeal to Arabs otherwise sympathetic to the ideas of resisting Israel and the American-led regional order. Sectarianism also helped to legitimate the internal repression of Saudi Shi'a citizens in the Eastern Province by portraying them as a potential vehicle for Iranian subversion. The attempt to use sectarianism against Iran was crystallized in popular discourse by the 2004 warning by Jordan's King Abdullah against a "Shi'a Crescent" threatening the Middle East.

A regional order defined by moderate Sunni autocrats united against a radical Shi'a threat masked considerable internal competition, however. Saudi Arabia aspired to lead a unified Arab world against Iran, but faced multiple challengers. Some traditional powers were, by the 2000s, largely out of the picture. Iraq was completely broken, an arena on which the real powers fought their battles rather than a player. Egypt, despite its pretensions to Arab leadership, was consumed by internal disarray over its impending presidential succession and largely subservient to Saudi policy preferences. Syria was a power in its own right, but had become an object of competition for the region's powers. In 2005, popular protests following the assassination of former Prime Minister Rafik Hariri had forced it to withdraw from Lebanon after a decade and a half of occupation. The Saudi-backed March 14 movement rose to the fore of Lebanese politics, while Syria faced mounting sanctions and the threat of prosecution by the Special Tribunal for Lebanon. By 2008, however, Saudi Arabia, Turkey, and the United States were each actively cultivating a new relationship with Syria in hopes of luring Asad away from Iran.

With those traditional Arab powers on the sidelines, new players rose to the forefront. Qatar, flush with natural gas wealth and enjoying the popularity of the al-Jazeera satellite television station, challenged Saudi domination in multiple arenas. Its diplomatic initiatives in Yemen, Afghanistan, and Palestine explicitly challenged Saudi patronage over those processes, while offering an alternative source of funding for a wide range of transnational movements, journalists, and politicians. Qatar enjoyed a particularly close relationship with Muslim Brotherhood networks, but also cultivated relations with a diverse array of liberal and leftist activists. The Saudi-Qatari rivalry provided a second channel of regional competition which disrupted the dominant Saudi-Iranian narrative.

Turkey, too, made a noticeable bid for Arab influence in the late 2000s. Then-Prime Minister Tayip Recep Erdogan portrayed his government as a model for democratic participation by moderate Islamists, implicitly challenging the many Arab regimes which defined themselves against movements such as the Muslim Brotherhood. Turkey's thriving economy, robust democratic institutions, and NATO membership all offered attractive counterpoints to the dysfunction of Arab states. Even Turkish soap operas were more popular than Arab television shows. Erdogan's Turkey, like Qatar, presented itself in regional diplomacy as a third-way bridge between

Iran and Saudi Arabia. It attempted to broker a bridging agreement with Iran over its nuclear stockpile, actively involved itself in Iraq, and cultivated a close relationship with Syria's Bashar al-Asad. Erdogan also appealed to Arab public opinion with his outspoken denunciations of Israel, a campaign which spiked with the controversy surrounding the May 2010 violent boarding of the Turkish ship Mavi Marmara en route to Gaza with humanitarian assistance.

Israel's position by the end of the 2000s had also changed in significant ways. The decade of peace talks overseen by the Clinton administration in the 1990s ended in a failed summit at Camp David. The extreme violence of the Second Intifada which followed fundamentally changed Israeli policy thinking and public opinion. Israel's unilateral withdrawal from Gaza and the fallout from Hamas's electoral victory entrenched deep Palestinian political divisions, which regional powers rushed to exploit. Israel worked ever more closely, if still privately, with the Gulf states and Egypt not only against Iran but also against "resistance bloc" members Hamas and Hezbollah and for Salam Fayad's Palestinian Authority institution-building efforts in the West Bank. Israel was delighted by a regional order in which it enjoyed tacit alliance with most Arab regimes against Iran without making any meaningful progress towards a Palestinian state.

But this Israeli comfort with the regional order could hardly be equated with stability or security. Israel fought multiple wars in this decade, at enormous political and human cost. The reoccupation of the West Bank during the second Intifada had been extremely bloody and set back a decade's worth of Palestinian institution building. The 2006 war with Lebanon had been fought to a draw, which translated practically into a strategic and political victory for Hezbollah. The pummeling air wars against Gaza in 2008-09 and again in 2012 had achieved few strategic gains while galvanizing unprecedented levels and forms of international condemnation. The stagnation of the peace process and continued settlement construction, along with the lobbying against the Iran deal, sharply strained relations with the Obama administration.

In short, the regional order at the time of the uprising was predictable in its own way but could not be sustained. A regional order built around

counter-terrorism and containing Iran nurtured its own internal contradictions and consistently failed to produce genuine stability or security.
Arab autocrats were firmly in charge, but they were rotting from within.
States struggled with massive economic problems, including growing inequality, corruption, and unemployment. A young, well-educated generation chafed at the absence of opportunity and at stagnant political
systems. Information and communications technology was rapidly eroding
the domination over opinion and information long exercised by oppressive
states. For years, Arab regimes confidently dismissed such problems, assur-
ing the world and themselves that they had things under control. They
did not.

AFTER THE UPRISING

The Arab uprising reshaped the terrain for all of these battles. It challenged
America's position in novel ways, exposing the contradictions in its policies and the limits of its power. It first eclipsed and then accelerated sectarianism and the Saudi-Iranian conflict. It dramatically expanded the
intra-Sunni power struggles into a greater variety of fractured states, potential allies, and adversaries. And it sharply exacerbated the threat perception of Arab regimes by revealing that popular challengers could actually
overthrow them.

The occupation of Iraq and the endless wars against terrorism had
exhausted the United States, while the 2008 financial crisis had battered
its economic foundations. Obama responded to these structural realities
with a pragmatic policy of "right-sizing" America's overextended Middle
Eastern presence. Obama hoped to decrease the American military and
political footprint in the region in order to pivot away from the Middle
East towards the more vital strategic challenges in Asia. This did not
mean immediate diplomatic disengagement or the abandonment of the
region. Moving towards a reduced presence required resolving (or at
least dispatching) long-standing issues such as the occupation of Iraq,
the war on terror, the dispute over the Iranian nuclear weapons program,
and the Israeli-Palestinian peace process. Obama invested an enormous

amount of political and diplomatic capital on vain efforts to restart the Israeli-Palestinian peace process and a successful bid to negotiate a deal with Iran. But he did so on the basis of a grand strategy designed ultimately to reduce America's presence.

This American grand strategy was in part premised on the underlying reality that there still remained no serious strategic competitor at the global level. The US remained the dominant power in the region. For all of Russia's posturing and China's economic growth, there was still no alternative to the American order, even if that order looked weaker and more vulnerable than ever before. China's dramatic economic rise, which entailed massive energy interests in the Gulf, had yet to translate into any remotely serious political or military presence in the Middle East. Russia, despite the opportunistic adventurism of Vladimir Putin, remained a fading economic power with few allies or assets in the region. Europe was beset with its own economic and political problems, and continued to work primarily to shape policies from within the US-led alliance. In short, then, despite the declining American power projection there had not yet been a clear structural change in the global balance of power.

The uprising and its aftermath would graphically reveal the limitations of US power, however. The Arab order against which these millions rebelled was embedded within an architecture which the United States had crafted and which broadly serviced its core interests of protecting Israel and the flow of oil. American leaders spoke often about promoting democracy, but it was widely understood that they had little real interest in undermining the control of friendly autocrats who protected their core interests such as the flow of oil, the security of Israel, and the combatting of terrorism. The argument was between those who thought the existing autocracies would do perfectly well to serve American interests and those who viewed them as insufficiently stable or legitimate to do so.

The Arab uprising operated in an entirely different key: it sought to smash the system, not to fine-tune its mechanisms of control. The greatest impact of the Arab uprising may ultimately prove to be the dismantlement of the American Middle East regional order—an outcome which terrifies the regimes protected by that order but of which almost all the original protestors, whether secular or Islamist, would likely approve. Their hopes of changing this system had not anticipated the traumatic costs of such a transformation. Were Syria's killing fields and Egypt's prisons an inevitable outcome of challenging the regional status quo?

Obama's careful diplomacy presented a sharp, unsettling contrast with the assertive, militarized posture of his predecessor. Arab regimes and Israel had grown accustomed to Bush's willingness to pour unlimited resources into the Iraqi quagmire, eagerness to fight a cold war with Iran across every available theater, and cheerful hypocrisy about democracy. For all their complaints about Bush, the regimes had found his eagerness to use military force and expend massive financial resources on their behalf quite congenial. They profoundly distrusted an American president committed to easing the confrontation with Iran, extricating from Iraq, and avoiding the invitation to a new quagmire in Syria. They could hardly believe that the United States might be serious about supporting democratic movements, even Islamist ones. "Abandoning friends and rewarding enemies" was a potent sound bite against Obama. But as much as it captured those perceptions, it had little to do with a reality in which Washington continued and even expanded its close diplomatic and military coordination with all of those supposedly abandoned allies.

The American diplomatic restraint that the region's leaders and publics had long demanded won few friends in practice. US clients and allies were furious over their supposed abandonment during the uprisings and by American failure to support their ambitions in Syria. The activists and youth upon whom Washington placed such great hopes were mostly scornful or suspicious of what they viewed as a hypocritical empire. Protestors of all sorts, from the democrats of Tahrir Square to the grim jihadists of ISIS, therefore defined themselves against the United States. Similarly, Israel and the Gulf states lobbied so hard, publicly and privately, to shape American policies precisely because they understood that despite all their posturing of independence they had no place else to go. Even if American policies over the years had been unpopular, their predictability had allowed local players to formulate their own policies, survival strategies, and even identities. The pattern of erratic behavior and catastrophic policies could be considered Obama's fault only in that others planned for a different American policy.

American policy will always matter in a region deeply shaped by the legacy of its imperium, of course, but there is no reason to believe that a more assertive American posture would have made a positive difference in the unfolding politics of the Arab uprisings. It is easier to blame Barack Obama's weakness for Syria's catastrophe than to examine the contributions of a diverse range of actors to the radicalization and fragmentation of an externally-fueled, ill-conceived insurgency. It is easier to accuse Obama of failing to lead on Egypt than to assess the domestic and regional drivers of Cairo's hotly contested politics. But that doesn't make the critique correct. The failure of the 2003 occupation of Iraq, which so deeply informed Obama's approach to the use of military force in the region, should have fully revealed the limitations of American power. One of the most commonly repeated mantras in Washington has been that "everything which opponents of intervention in Syria warned would happen has happened anyway." These pundits refuse to notice that thousands of American troops are not dying while vainly patrolling the streets of Damascus.

America's long policy of aligning with unsavory but cooperative regimes would become a crippling liability after the Arab uprising. A key vulnerability of the American imperium in the Middle East was the absence of any major ally which shared its fundamental values or goals. The assembly of kings, generals, and presidents-for-life which ruled American-allied regimes did not even make the pretense of valuing democracy, human rights, or liberal values. Their survival depended on heavy-handed repression, patronage disbursed through state and non-state channels, and, in some cases, electoral institutions designed to distribute resources among elites. Most depended heavily on the demonization of external and internal enemies to legitimate their rule—Israel, Iran, Islamists, and America. This challenge has only become more acute as America's putative allies spiral in ever more violent and repressive directions.

American right-sizing afforded an unusual degree of autonomy to regional powers, since they had little fear of American punishment as the

U.S. tried to downsize its commitments and hand off more responsibility to its local partners. Conventional wisdom has it that the Gulf states began to go their own way because of growing doubts about American commitment to the region. Fearful for their security and doubting the Obama administration, the Gulf states cast out to guarantee their own security in new ways. In fact, even without those policy initiatives or the Arab uprising, the past few years would have likely seen greater self-assertion by the wealthy and secure Gulf states—precisely because they did not really believe that they would pay significant costs for their defections.

The compliance of Arab regimes combined with the hostility of Arab publics made American rhetoric about promoting democracy somewhat puzzling. Why would the United States want to weaken its friends and empower its enemies? Prior to the Arab uprisings, this confusion was easily resolved as both regimes and publics quickly came to understand that the US had no intention of actually pushing for serious political change. At best, it might push its friends for marginal increases in public freedom, which could serve as a pressure valve to stabilize—not undermine—their stability. The bargain of America's imperium had always been that Washington would tolerate the domestic behavior of its regional allies, no matter how acute or embarrassing, so long as the oil flowed and they cooperated on anti-Communism, counterterrorism, and the containment of Iran or war in Iraq. The regimes knew from experience that they could safely ignore the public lecturing about democracy.

The Arab uprising introduced the possibility of real change, forcing the United States, its allied regimes, and the broader Arab public to seriously confront what it truly wanted. Obama did far better with this challenge than did his predecessors, proving at considerable cost his willingness to accept victories by the Egyptian Muslim Brotherhood or Tunisia's Islamist party Ennahda in the course of democratic transition. Obama's pursuit of a diplomatic track with Iran and his resistance to intervention in Syria threw this bargain into question. His rhetorical embrace of the Arab uprising as the right side of history, his willingness to accept the removal of Mubarak, and his support for Egyptian democracy, even if the Muslim Brotherhood won elections, cut to the very heart of the survival guarantee which Arab regimes wanted from the United States. If Obama would allow Mubarak to be overthrown, Arab elites fretted, what guarantee did other equally unpopular and corrupt US allies have that he would come to their support?

Those regimes might have embraced the administration's advice to embrace change and commence democratic reforms. Meaningful reforms would have helped to make them into better, less morally offensive allies while enhancing their stability and regional order. But instead, they doubled down on repression and embarked on a series of hastily conceived and poorly implemented independent foreign policy initiatives. Their authoritarian restoration involved intense new forms of nationalistic domination designed to meet the challenge of highly mobilized and thus dangerous populations.[6] Militaries and security services took on significantly new roles in the economy, internal security, and direct rule, while ruling coalitions often narrowed in potentially consequential ways.[7] And several key countries, including Saudi Arabia and Qatar, managed controversial generational leadership transitions in the midst of this all.

That those reckless policies typically came against American advice, at the least, and often directly against American preferences, only exacerbated the growing divide between traditional allies. The divide between the US and its traditional allies was not due to Obama's personality or his lack of engagement. It revealed a serious divergence in preferences. This was a bargaining game, not a reassurance game. Most of the official rhetoric and punditry on the topic should be understood as lobbying for one view or the other—mostly, as it happens, in support of the Gulf views which were aligned with those of the Israeli government. The Obama administration, broadly speaking, wanted to see a democratic transition in Egypt, a nuclear deal with Iran, serious Israeli-Palestinian peace talks, and a political solution in Syria. Saudi Arabia, like Israel, wanted the opposite—restored autocracy in Egypt, rigid containment and regional cold war with Iran, and an escalated military campaign in Syria (it could live with lip-service to the Palestinian cause).

The diplomacy of the Arab spring revolved around each side's efforts to force the other to its way of thinking: futile efforts by the United States to restrain Saudi adventurism in Syria and win support for the nuclear deal, persistent lobbying by the Saudis to scuttle the Iran deal and force America into the Syrian quagmire. The popular image of Obama is that he has been a weak and feckless steward of foreign policy, but the opposite is actually the case: these regional powers and their American political allies were repeatedly surprised and infuriated that they could not roll him. Obama stuck to these ambitions in the face of relentless pressure on Syria and Iran, while making compromises in arenas where he had few vital interests at stake and no other good choices. I long ago lost track of how many times pundits and officials aligned with these competing policy viewpoints confidently predicted publicly or privately that Obama would soon change American policy in their direction. They were almost always wrong. It was Obama's strength, not his weakness, which drew their ire.

Arab regime pressure typically found strong support within the American policy elite, but failed to persuade the Obama administration. This intra-alliance conflict proved consistently counterproductive. From arming Syrian insurgents to bombing Yemen to overturning Egyptian democracy, the Gulf states consistently made things worse for America. As Vice President Joseph Biden publicly observed in October 2014, "Our allies in the region were our largest problem... [They] were so determined to take down (Syrian President Bashar) Asad and have a proxy Sunni-Shia war, they poured hundreds of millions of dollars and thousands of tons of weapons into anyone who would fight against Asad. Except that the people who were being supplied were (Jabhat) al Nusra and al Qaida, and the extremist elements of jihadis coming from other parts of the world."[8] He was right.

For Obama, the agreement with Iran over its nuclear weapons remained the highest strategic priority. Iran's steady accumulation of nuclear materials created a looming deadline for diplomacy. If negotiations did not succeed before Iran reached a vaguely defined "point of no return," many believed (and even hoped) that the United States and/or Israel would feel compelled to launch military strikes to set back the nuclear program. Such a war would have been devastating for the region, and yet by 2010 many in the Middle East policy world had come to see it as virtually inevitable. Obama avoided such a disastrous war by finalizing a comprehensive agreement which lifted sanctions in exchange for blocking Iran's route towards a nuclear weapon.

The implications of the nuclear deal extended well beyond the realm of disarmament. For most players in the Middle East, the nuclear deal represented a potential transformation of the regional order itself, on par with 1979's Iranian revolution and Egyptian-Israeli peace agreement. Their fear had less to do with proliferation than with the possibility that the nuclear agreement would end the containment of Iran and lead eventually to an American realignment away from its Gulf Arab allies towards Tehran. Arab leaders generally feared such a strategic realignment more than they did Iranian nuclear weapons.

The Obama administration did change US strategy in significant ways, and struggled with the tenacious regional resistance to those ambitions. American allies did not need reassurances or fear US retreat so much as they resented its changing priorities. The Arab uprising left the United States with few real allies in the Middle East, except perhaps for loyal and utterly dependent Jordan. Virtually every important regime in the American alliance structure disagreed with American strategies and goals, and most were actively working against them. It is therefore not quite right to suggest, as the current conventional wisdom would have it, that the region's chaos was caused by American disengagement.

The political struggles between Washington and its traditional allies, not American retreat, best defines the structural context for the new Arab wars.

THE NEW ARAB PROXY WARS

How did power politics work in this new regional structure? The balance of power in the region thus shifted dramatically in the wake of the uprising. The implosion of the traditional powers favored the tiny principalities of the Gulf, which enjoyed vast wealth and fewer domestic political threats. The traditional great powers of the Middle East have almost all fallen into disarray, losing their leading position in regional order to internal failures, economic lethargy, corruption, and misrule. Egypt, with its eighty-five million people and traditional cultural leadership, has become a dependent basket case, reliant on Gulf financiers to remain solvent. Iraq and Syria, the traditional powers of the Arab heartland, have virtually ceased to exist after years of brutal civil war, state failure, and massive population displacement. Large populations, high levels of urbanization, strategic location, and industrialized economies became sources of weakness, not strength.

Of the traditional Arab contenders for regional leadership, then, only Saudi Arabia remained. It continued to be challenged by exceptionally small and wealthy Qatar. The United Arab Emirates, far more regionally active than ever before in its history, generally closely aligned itself with Saudi Arabia but had different priorities and a sharply different perspective on Islamist movements. Non-Arab powers on the periphery such as Turkey, Iran, and Israel were inexorably drawn into the Arab political wars through the same combination of threat and opportunity which motivated their Arab counterparts.

At first, the Arab uprisings defied the logic of proxy war. Certainly, networks aligned with external players could be found within oppositional coalitions, but for the most part the protestors who seized the streets of Tunis and Cairo aggressively rejected efforts by any state to co-opt their struggles. Bahrain's fearless protestors worked to distance themselves from Iran, while Yemen's broad-based activist coalition sought to position itself against the long history of regional (especially Saudi) penetration. None of these mobilized activists viewed themselves as anyone's proxy, and most thought that they had found ways to counteract familiar regime tactics designed to label them as dangerous subversives.

This could not, and did not, last long. Libya's uprising was the first to invite external intervention. Syria's would soon follow, to disastrous effect. But no Arab country escaped completely from the rapidly emerging competition between regional powers. The sudden opening of these states invited competitive intervention by powers keen to advance their interests and block the advances of their rivals. Even if regimes had not wanted to get involved, they could hardly cede influence to their rivals.

And some regimes had far more offensive motivations, seeing in the uprising a rare opportunity to revise the regional order in their favor and establish their control in new ways. Regimes saw the opportunities, and knew that their rivals saw them, too. And thus a classical security dilemma took hold in which ever greater intervention only left everybody less secure. Given this array of threats and opportunities, Washington found it almost impossible to restrain or influence its putative allies or to deter its adversaries. The local stakes were simply too high, the perceived threats too intense, and the opportunities too great, for them to accede to American pressure.

The Arab uprising, by weakening key states and empowering diverse non-state actors, opened the gates to a dramatically new regional politics of proxy war and competitive interventions. The leaders of Gulf states such as Qatar, Saudi Arabia, and the United Arab Emirates, along with regional powers such as Turkey, Iran, and powerful non-state networks such as the Muslim Brotherhood, each moved aggressively in response to the popular mobilization. Money and guns poured in, institutions collapsed, bodies piled up, and hatreds spread. The idealistic, courageous protestors of early 2011 were displaced by hard men with guns, extreme ideologies, and foreign patrons.

Proxy politics drew on both formal organizations and informal networks. A counterrevolutionary network links the rulers of Saudi Arabia, the United Arab Emirates, and Kuwait to the old elites, militaries, businessmen, and frightened cosmopolitans of Egypt, North Africa and the Levant. Qatar and Turkey compete to lead and exploit Islamist networks involving many different national Muslim Brotherhood organizations and other Islamist personalities. The jihadists of the Islamic State have tenacious, small networks of their own, capable of doing great damage, with links to private citizens and Islamist movements across the Gulf. Iran commands a robust network of Shi'a militias and movements with varying degrees of subordination to Tehran's ambitions. Media platforms, access to sophisticated weaponry systems, and effective local proxies became a far more reliable indicator of power than did traditional metrics such as population or the number of men under arms.

These interventions have for now almost completely destroyed hopes for democratic change. The blame for the failure of the Arab uprisings lies primarily with the regional powers that set out to destroy or exploit them—usually in direct opposition to the policies of the United States and the aspirations of the original protestors. This involved unusual levels of cooperation between regimes better known for their disagreements, competition, and mistrust. What the Egyptian journalist Wael Qandil sardonically called an "International Organization for the Counter-Revolution" was not so far from the truth.[9] Those Gulf regimes did work together to block democratic change and to rebuild the regional order.

Their interventions were rarely so effectively coordinated, however. The Arab states feared each other almost as much as they feared Iran or the mobilized street. Their competition among themselves profoundly shaped the trajectory of many of the Arab transitions. Getting rid of Qaddafi wasn't enough—each wanted to dominate the new Libya. They might all agree on fighting Asad, but each wanted its own allies to control the rebellion. They sought every opportunity to deploy their financial, political, media, and military assets in support of their preferred local proxies. Even when their competition manifestly undermined their own goals, as with the fragmentation and radicalization of the Syrian insurgency, they could not stop.

Proxy warfare has a long history in the Middle East. Regional powers have always waged their battles for influence inside of Lebanon and Yemen or within the institutions of the PLO.[10] What's different today is the sheer number and centrality of the states upon whose territory the wars were now fought, and the new ways in which external powers are able to influence events in those theaters. It was one thing to jockey for influence in marginal states like Yemen and Lebanon. It was altogether different to be fighting them out in central states like Syria and Egypt. Egypt, for instance, had for decades been a major regional power and a key Saudi ally. The January 2011 revolution which overthrew Mubarak put Cairo into play within regional politics, with Qatar bidding to pull the new Egypt into its orbit through financial assistance and close support to the Muslim Brotherhood. The July 2013 military coup ripped Cairo away from Qatar, restoring Egypt to its place within the Saudi-led coalition.

Direct military intervention became normalized as a policy instrument in Yemen and Libya in ways rarely seen before among Arab states. The post-uprisings period also offered innovative forms of cultivated patronage and indirect influence across multiple arenas. Gulf states used their own media, such as al-Jazeera and al-Arabiya, but also funded local media outlets such as the Qatari-backed Libya TV to serve as voices of their preferred factions. Money might flow directly from the state in the form of official aid, but it also could be channeled through private citizens, religious foundations, or transnational organizations. Massive quantities of weapons were sent to armed insurgency factions by states, and huge amounts of money and non-military supplies were sent by non-state religious networks. Videos of military exploits posted on YouTube became a tool for patrons to monitor local clients and for local groups to advertise their services to potential patrons.

Weaker states and local organizations were never fully under the control of their patrons, though. After the July 2013 military coup sponsored by Saudi Arabia and the United Arab Emirates, Egyptian policy towards Syria conflicted sharply with Saudi views. UAE support for Tunisian President Beji Caid Essebsi in his electoral campaign did not prevent a falling-out after he took office. Patrons rarely found their clients to be easy servants. Typically, patrons seek to use proxies to advance their interests, while proxies seek independence by cultivating multiple patrons, then exploit the dependence of their patrons on them for local influence. In the 1980s and 1990s, non-state actors such as the Palestinian Liberation Organization, Hamas and Hezbollah, and the Muslim Brotherhood drew on varying degrees of support from external supporters, some state and some private, but maintained significant independence and played crucial roles in domestic politics. Despite their reliance on financial support from the Gulf, Muslim Brotherhood organizations sided against Saudi Arabia with Saddam Hussein in 1990 and with Hezbollah in 2006. Anti-Islamist forces in Egypt or Tunisia might call the Muslim Brotherhood and Ennahda proxies of Qatar, but this radically overstates the latter's control. Islamist movements may have shared broad ideological aspirations, but differed widely in their organizational structure, strategic vision, and tactical choices. Some, such as

Hamas and Hezbollah, evolved into de facto governments with interests that sometimes clashed with those of their external sponsors.

Shi'a movements were especially open to accusations of being Iranian proxies. Iran's relationship with Bahrain's al-Wefaq, Yemen's Houthi Movement, or Iraq's Mahdi Army or Hashd militias proved exceedingly contentious in the highly sectarian post-uprisings environment.[11] In early January 2016, Saudi Arabia provoked an intense outcry by executing the Saudi Shi'ite cleric and political leader Shaykh Nimr al-Nimr. This execution demonstrated both the potency of sectarian framing, and that even the most closely aligned movements retained their own local interests and concerns. Nimr had carefully worked within a Saudi context, just as Bahraini Shi'ites had evolved a distinctly national politics keeping Iran at arm's length. Hezbollah's need to take care of its Lebanese front first, even when that conflicted with Iranian priorities, would take on great urgency as the costs of its intervention in Syria began to mount. These relationships could also prove malleable in response to changing domestic and regional conditions, of course. Self-fulfilling prophecies of Iranian sponsorship became all too plausible as the regional sectarian confrontation escalated and other options for political participation closed down. The Shi'a militias fighting for Asaad in Syria were often fired with the same intense religious fervor as their Sunni jihadist counterparts.

America faced a unique set of problems in this newly networked region. The Obama administration tried in vain to prevent this descent into proxy warfare. Even had it been willing to embrace proxy war, it had few of its own on which to call. In Iraq, the Sunni "Awakening" fighters which had joined its fight against the Islamic State of Iraq in 2007 had disintegrated a few years later through Iraqi government sectarianism and neglect. The US was extremely suspicious of the armed Syrian insurgent groups, for good reason. In Egypt and Tunisia, the US tried to support the democratic process rather than specific parties or movements, leaving all of these would-be proxies furious that America had not taken their side. For all its very real power, Washington held surprisingly few cards in this game of networks.

The unpopularity of American foreign policy meant that individuals or groups that openly identified with the United States faced potentially severe social stigma, political costs, and even state repression. With its open association becoming a kiss of death, the United States was forced to either covertly cultivate its networks or to support very weak, isolated groups. The kiss of death had always been an issue, especially due to American support for Israel. It spiked during the decade of the 2000s, however, at precisely the historical moment when networks began to supplant states as key actors. The Bush administration's support for Israel during the fierce wars of the Second Intifada, and its general close alignment with Israel, set the stage. But it was the practices associated with the global War on Terror and the 2003 invasion of Iraq, which brought the "kiss of death" to a fever pitch.

The Bush administration's efforts to promote democracy in the 2000s, including aggressive new programs such as the Middle East Partnership Initiative, put a spotlight on the civil society groups supported openly or secretly by its democracy and governance programs. Repressive regimes, whether Bashar al-Asad's Syria or Hosni Mubarak's Egypt, used the pretext of US funding to crack down hard on democracy and civil society NGOs which received American funding. The US's efforts at promoting democracy might have helped to organize and train the activists who fought for the Arab uprisings, but they generally failed to create a reliable pro-American network.

Instead, America's primary network in the Middle East was with precisely the security agencies and the autocratic regimes which the popular uprisings challenged. America's imperium rested not on popular support, but on stolid alliances with the repressive regimes whose illegitimacy and governance failures would drive the Arab uprisings. Generations of Arab officers had trained with the US military, developing both professional affinity and personal bonds—the use of which would become unusually transparent in February 2011 when the Pentagon sought to convince the Egyptian military to exercise restraint against the protestors in Tahrir Square. But for the most part, these military and intelligence networks conflicted with American values and rhetoric. Close association with the security state was a solid foundation for imperium, but a bit embarrassing during a revolutionary moment when history seemed to be on the side of the people demanding democracy.

America's focus on building neutral state institutions rather than supporting specific proxies challenged but ultimately could not overcome the emerging regional game. From Egypt and Tunisia to Libya, the public American posture was one of supporting the democratic transition regardless of who won elections. This was an admirable, and, in my view, correct, stance. But it was poorly suited to a networked politics in which every actor wanted a reliable patron, not a neutral referee. In each case, the US ended up hated and publicly lambasted by liberals, Islamists, and regimes. Each side viewed American neutrality as effective alignment with its enemies. Regional states typically felt no need to pretend at neutrality or to feel embarrassed of their choice of proxies, leaving them free to lavish assistance on whomever they found useful.

The US also, unlike other regional players, sought to hold its potential proxies to a relatively high standard of accountability. Some American agencies had proven to be less picky about their proxies, most famously in General David Petraeus's decision to align US forces in Iraq with Sunni armed factions against al-Qaeda during the 2006-08 "Awakening," which underpinned the "Surge." But in Syria, American insistence on vetting opposition fighters and organizations contrasted sharply with the free-spending ways of Qatar, Turkey, and Saudi Arabia. Syrian rebels complained almost nonstop about the restrictions attached to US funding: "The basic problem is that they give ammunition and weapons to a handful of trainees only. I have 1,200 fighters. But they only armed 54 because of strict vetting," complained rebel leader Col. Hassan Mustafa.[12]

That strict vetting was needed precisely because so many rebel factions worked closely with jihadists, and individuals and brigades moved fluidly between groups. The Obama administration worried deeply, and wisely, about the risks of unintentionally arming Islamist extremists who would eventually use the weapons to attack America, Israel, or its regional allies. Few serious American officials wanted to be the one who signed off on the delivery of surface-to-air missiles for Syrian rebels, which then were used to shoot down an Israeli or Turkish jet. Saudi Arabia may have viewed its support for the Afghan jihad of the 1980s as a model for a successful proxy war, but Americans remembered all too well that the aftermath of that jihad had been a failed state, the rise of the Taliban, and the emergence of al-Qaeda.

As Arab states, Iran and Turkey faced off in these proxy wars, Israel rather remarkably faded into the background. Arab public hostility would spike during Israel's episodic bombing campaigns against Gaza, but the regimes already cracking down hard on public dissent did not show much concern. It could hardly stand up its own local proxies, but it found new opportunities for quiet cooperation with Arab regimes. Revelations of Israeli aid to Syrian rebels, for instance, had virtually no impact on popular support for their cause. The proliferation of traumas crowded the Palestinian issue off the top of the Arab agenda for perhaps the first time in a century. It isn't that Arabs stopped caring for Palestine. Each time Israel bombarded Gaza, the issue surged to the top of the regional agenda and Arabs from all across the spectrum rallied to the cause. But when the immediate crisis passed, attention faded. By September 2015, 80 percent of Palestinians believed that their cause was no longer the principal Arab cause.[13]

Dore Gold, a Netanyahu adviser, occasionally gave voice to a prevalent Israeli sentiment that its relations with the Gulf states had approached a near-alliance level in response to the Iranian deal. This was both true and overstated. Such relations continued to be viewed as shameful in the Arab context, however actively consummated behind the closed doors. In April 2015, leading Saudi columnist Khaled al-Dakhil ignited a fierce debate with a column entitled "Is Israel or Iran the enemy?"[14] His colleague, Daoud Shriyan, pushed back, noting that the broader Arab public would never accept removing the label of enemy from Israel even if geopolitics suggested that they should. But even Shriyan's equation of Israel with Iran as equally demonic represented a substantial revision in its favor. This quiet alignment came about despite the complete absence of a peace process or any real hope for the negotiated two-state solution which had long been held out as the key to Israel's acceptance in the region.

In spite of the obvious alignment of interests between the Gulf states and Israel over Iran, Israel's conflict with Palestine prevented any formal alignment or public relationship. But over the few years preceding 2015, the Arab agenda grew crowded, and the Palestinian issue stalled and ceased to command much consistent attention. Syria, not Palestine, stood at the nexus of the region's fault lines. Libya and Yemen produced near-daily reminders of war, state failure, and suffering. Egypt's dramas commanded the headlines. ISIS demanded attention. Palestine fell down the ladder of concerns almost imperceptibly. Israel, which had long dreamed of such Arab neglect, was ill-advised to take too much comfort from this, though: Palestine retained the ability to surge to the top of the Arab agenda at moments of crisis, and few Arabs had actually switched their allegiances in favor of an increasingly internationally isolated Israel.

Regional power politics therefore took on new forms and dynamics in the years following the Arab uprising. Saudi Arabia took on an increasingly aggressive leadership role over the second half of 2015, reconciling with Qatar and Turkey while leading a fierce campaign to restore Iran's isolation. In addition to its Yemen war coalition, Riyadh declared a new Islamic Coalition against terrorism and asserted its primacy over the organization of the Syrian insurgency by sponsoring a meeting of opposition groups.

The fate of President Bashar al-Asad in the endgame of Syria's conflict became perhaps the most potent symbolic proxy for these regional wars. Syria after 2011 unfolded as a near-textbook example of the logic of competitive proxy war. Any time one side in Syria seemed to be gaining significant ground, external backers of the other would ratchet up support in order to restore balance. When Asad's regime seemed shaky, Russia, Iran, or Hezbollah would bolster it with direct or indirect support. The same played out on the other side. When Asad's forces seemed to be advancing, the insurgency's external backers—including Saudi Arabia, Qatar, and Turkey—would flood in new shipments of cash, weapons, and other assistance to prevent their defeat. But their mutual suspicion ensured simultaneously that the insurgency would remain fragmented.

SOCIETIES AGAINST STATES

The autocrats of the old Arab order were not simply fighting rival contenders for regional power. They were fighting for their political lives against newly empowered publics whom they suddenly feared. Keeping themselves in power against threats from abroad or at home had always been the main preoccupation of Arab leaders. Monarchies, militaries, and old elites alike struggled to maintain a status quo eroded by genuinely fundamental transformations in the nature of politics and society. New technologies and economic trends have shifted power away from the state, allowing multiple transnational networks to seep in to the political landscape. Only a few years removed from the overthrow of Ben Ali and Mubarak, Arab leaders today feel these threats extremely keenly. Their fear inspires domestic and foreign policy responses, which likely have left them less secure in the long run.

A dramatically empowered public opinion forced even the most autocratic regimes to take popular views a bit more seriously. The balance of power between society and state had been palpably shifting for more than a decade. Satellite television and the Internet had revolutionized political communication and societal expectations. It is often easy to miss just how radical the change in the nature of politics and society has been over the course of a single generation. The Arab uprisings erupted within a radically new information environment, and there will be no return to the old ways.

The proliferation of communications technology represented a profound structural shift in the nature of politics in the Middle East and globally. I do not mean to make caricatured arguments like "Facebook caused the January 25 revolution" or "Twitter caused the rise of ISIS." The point is that the entire political environment has changed. In the 1980s, states could control information and could impose very high costs on the sharing of dissenting opinions. By 2011, they could not. In 2016, they are certainly trying to regain control. They will fail.

The flow of information today is at an entirely new order of magnitude, speed and intensity. Social media and smartphones allow for an overwhelming quantity of user-generated content. Virtually every event of any significance in the Arab world today will now generate hundreds or thousands of videos uploaded to YouTube, allowing distant observers to judge events at an exceptionally finely grained level. The absence of video evidence of a battle, a protest, or a speech is almost taken as evidence that it did not really happen. These videos and images can carry an enormous emotional punch, making conflicts far away seem immediate and visceral. The ubiquity and potency of online videos has come to reshape the political and media strategies of movements like the Islamic State and various autocratic regimes.

The sheer volume of content gives considerable power to the curators, those who sort through the deluge and act as gatekeepers for the broader public. Such gatekeepers include traditional mass media, of course, which selects videos to broadcast or link, but they also include a wide array of popular personalities, activists, individual journalists, and others. Information and images on social media tend to flow through dense networks of like-minded individuals. This means that many Arabs today (like people everywhere) experience political life through a heavily filtered lens shaped by the prejudices and interests of their identity group. Egypt's Muslim Brothers and secular activists, members of Libya's dueling coalitions, and Syria's rebels and regime supporters consume entirely different streams of information—which helps to explain why they often seem to be living in entirely different worlds. Information is one of the primary fronts of the new Arab wars.

Few regimes responded by adopting more popular positions or by accommodating calls for democratic reforms. The battlefield of the public sphere shifted irrevocably, but states remained powerful players in the unfolding rhetorical warfare. They proved strikingly effective at manipulating public opinion, selectively repressing discordant voices while deploying sophisticated media campaigns to harness and redirect popular agitation. Their success mirrors earlier historical patterns. Every previous wave of popular mobilization in the Arab world has ended not with liberation or democracy but in the retrenchment of a nastier form of authoritarianism. By 2015, the surviving autocrats in countries such as Egypt enjoyed more active and assertive public support than aging dictators such as Mubarak could have dreamed of commanding. This is likely to prove temporary, however, given the profound generational change in attitudes, expectations, and capabilities of restless and angry publics.

The relentless pull of polarization came from a combination of the deliberate strategy of the old regimes and the absence of settled institutions during the transitions. In lighter-hearted days, I called this "Calvinball," the game invented by Bill Watterson's *Calvin and Hobbes* cartoon, in which the players make up the rules as they go along.[15] What worked for a little boy and his tiger did not work in a violent, chaotic political transition—especially as the stakes grew higher and the blood began to flow. Ennahda leader Rached Ghannouchi once explained this to me in slightly different terms.[16] "Strategy for a transitional period must be different than for a settled democracy," he argued, because a polarized confrontation between a ruling party and an opposition "is dangerous when rules are not settled. A transition can't withstand that kind of conflict."

The Arab protestors in part revolted against states for failing to provide effective governance, economic security, or justice. But the uprisings were unable to replace corrupt, autocratic regimes with stable institutions which would provide predictable rules of the political game. The absence of institutional confidence drove protesters and rebels to retreat to the relative safety of their primal identity groups. Worsening polarization between groups recurred across different contexts, whether between Islamists and their enemies in Tunisia and Egypt, Sunnis and Shi'ites in Iraq and the Gulf, or tribal and local forces in Yemen and Libya. Muslim Brothers and Cairene liberals alike struggled to navigate a treacherous political game without settled rules or norms, not because of their ideological, organizational, or personal pathologies but because that game had been systematically broken. The deeper drivers of Arab political dysfunction lie with the rapacious power-seeking of regimes determined to preserve their own domination at virtually any cost.

One of those methods for retaining power has long been the manipulation of sectarian and ethnic identities. Sectarianism, one of the most disturbing forms of regional identity politics in recent years, has been driven more by power politics and regime survival concerns than by ancient hatreds. The US occupation of Iraq empowered Iran and unleashed a brutal sectarian civil war, which played out across the nascent transnational and social media. Regimes used the sectarian underpinnings of the regional conflict and Iraqi war to divide their citizenry, prevent mass-based popular revolts, and legitimate an otherwise shaky political order.[17] Saudi Arabia uses anti-Shi'ite sectarianism as a weapon against Iran, while also systematically discriminating against its Shi'a citizenry. When protests arise in the Eastern Province against inequality or mistreatment by the government, their claims can be dismissed and contained by designating them as "Shi'a" and thus alien to the identity of the state and, implicitly, Iran-backed subversion.

These strategic uses of sectarianism tend to work all too well in the short term, but over the longer term they backfire by spawning dangerous new tensions and unanticipated blowback. The passions unleashed by the uprising were no less real for having been cynically manufactured from above. Sectarian rhetoric had been useful to the Saudis at home and abroad, but took on new resonance amidst Sunni-Shi'ite massacres and an endless reservoir of online hate speech. Jihadist groups that Gulf regimes found useful against Asad suddenly proved threatening when their ideology appealed to disaffected Saudi citizens. It has proven far more difficult to ratchet these identity-based hatreds back down than it was to inflame them. The virulent new sectarianism ripping the region apart today is one of the most dangerous by-products of the new Arab wars.

ISLAMISTS AMIDST THE CHAOS

The Islamic State and the virulent new forms of jihadism are fully the creature of these political battles and structural changes. The Islamic State itself emerged from the remnants of the Sunni insurgency in Iraq. It inserted itself into the Syrian insurgency early in the conflict and evolved and thrived within the broader jihadist environment fueled by the Gulf states, Turkey, and Islamist non-state networks. It expanded beyond Syria and Iraq in large part because of the setbacks to the Arab uprising. Libya's collapse created an opening for the Islamic State to establish its presence there. The Egyptian military coup and repression of the Muslim Brotherhood removed the most effective competitor to IS-style jihadism. And the

Islamic State itself thrives within a socially-mediated global arena which transmits its images, narratives, and ideas both broadly to mass audiences and deeply to potential recruits.

The uprisings were deeply shaped by the evolution and interplay among divergent strands of political Islam. It is not just the Islamic State. The constellation of Islamists epitomizes the ambiguities of the rapidly changing political environment and offers a glimpse into the underlying transnational networks. Active across multiple regional theaters, Islamist networks complicated the state-centric order by establishing solidarities and identities that spanned multiple countries. They were no monolith: in Syria and Yemen, Muslim Brotherhood networks and Saudi interests aligned even as they clashed in Libya and Egypt. Islamist movements fiercely competed with each other over ideology, strategy, tactics, and (where allowed) votes.

Islamists were rarely a majority in any Arab country. Not all Muslims shared their aspirations to make Islam the foundation of state and society, and many distrusted their motives and methods. But since the 1980s, Islamists typically were the best organized and most powerful opposition and enjoyed a powerful presence in civil society. Most Arab states had made political compromises with the groups, conceding a role in education or public culture in exchange for political acquiescence. In part through their extensive outreach and propaganda efforts, Arab public culture palpably became more religious over the years. Meanwhile, violent extremists waged jihad from the margins, appealing not only to religious motivations, but also to those thoroughly alienated from mainstream society and seeking a violent outlet.

The uprisings and the wars upended virtually all of the assumptions which long guided our understanding of these movements. Before the uprisings, Islamist movements were fairly stable. Mainstream groups like the Muslim Brotherhood built civil society and charitable organizations, eschewed violence, and participated in electoral politics to the extent possible. Salafist movements built parallel religious societies, staying out of formal politics while promoting their rigid religious views through multiple channels. Jihadist organizations fought from the margins of society, organizing their violent campaigns transnationally and cultivating a narrow base of the faithful.

The predictability of these divisions rested upon the basic stability of political institutions and lines of conflict.[18] Mainstream Islamist organizations understood that they could not actually win power through elections and ran their campaigns accordingly. The Arab uprisings created deep uncertainty, which ripped away much that was predictable. The Muslim Brotherhood proved as effective as expected in early elections, but woefully inadequate at dealing with the fluid and polarized political environments which followed. Unmoored, the Muslim Brotherhood careened from one approach to another, making decisions such as breaking a public commitment not to field a presidential candidate and forcing through a controversial constitution, which lost popular sympathy and gave their enemies an opening to move against them.

Islamists did not begin thinking about democracy in 2011. Movements such as the Muslim Brotherhood had spent decades on a long-term strategy of societal and cultural transformation. The previous decades had witnessed a slow, massive wave of Islamization of state and society which shaped the terms of politics in almost every state in the region. The patience of the Muslim Brotherhood was sorely tested by the jihadist eruption of 2001. The decade between September 11 and the Arab uprisings witnessed fierce interpretive and political battles across multiple dimensions: On one front, Western and official Arab views conflating the Brotherhood with al-Qaeda as undifferentiated Islamism; on another, Brotherhood and al-Qaeda figures furiously attacking each other and seeking to differentiate themselves. The enthusiastic endorsement of extreme anti-Islam views by candidates in the 2016 American Presidential election testifies to the enduring effects of those earlier debates.

Muslim Brotherhood organizations in Egypt and elsewhere aligned themselves with democratic reforms.[19] While skeptics denounced the Brotherhood's democratic rhetoric as a fig leaf for autocratic and fundamentalist ambitions, the Islamist organization did everything it could to affirm its determination to play the democratic game. There were obvious tactical benefits to this stance, including the opportunity to align with prevailing international norms against authoritarian regimes and a well-earned belief that their popular ideas and strong organization would enable them to win any free electoral competition. Such tactical considerations were hardly unique to the Brothers—liberals and secular activists rejected democracy in Egypt on similar grounds, boycotting elections when they believed they had little chance to win. But the Brotherhood's commitment to democratic procedures would prove to be a central pivot in the coming wars—and one which would cost them dearly.

The early Arab uprisings played to the Brotherhood's strengths and momentarily sidelined al-Qaeda. An era defined by peaceful uprising and democratic transition seemed to vindicate every aspect of the Brotherhood discourse. Al-Qaeda was left to the margins, no longer able to convincingly claim that violent jihad led by the vanguard was the only path to change. But al-Qaeda was able to take advantage of the uprisings, regrouping while state security forces were distracted and taking advantage of prisoner releases and unregulated weapons markets that had opened in failed states. The Egyptian military coup which overthrew the Muslim Brotherhood-led government in July 2013 abruptly reversed the intellectual trajectory of the uprisings, proving to many Islamists that al-Qaeda had been right all along about the futility of peaceful political participation. This, along with the devastating wars in Syria and Libya, charted the course towards a dangerous new era for Islamism.

Salafi organizations outside the Gulf had been absent from politics, but cultivated their constituencies. In the years leading up to the uprisings, the large Egyptian Salafi community began to emerge more publicly, with inflammatory television broadcasts and a growing Internet presence.[20] After the toppling of Mubarak in 2011, these Salafi networks suddenly jettisoned their ideological opposition to democracy and enthusiastically joined the game of electoral politics, shocking virtually everyone by taking 25 percent of the vote in the first free Parliamentary election. Kuwaiti Salafis emerged as a key support network for the key Syrian Salafi-jihadist armed rebel faction Ahrar al-Sham and a major hub for raising funds for both humanitarian relief and the armed insurgency. Salafis in Lebanon challenged both Hezbollah and existing Sunni parties. Across the region, they mobilized protests against *The Innocence of Muslims* in September 2012, an episode which had especially lasting implications for Libya. Salafi networks could slide imperceptibly into the rapidly evolving jihadist networks such as Tunisia and Libya's Ansar al-Sharia.[21]

Then, of course, there was al-Qaeda, the most important non-state actor of the 2000s. By the dawn of the uprisings, al-Qaeda was a shadow of its former self. Nonetheless, it proved far more resilient than might have been expected. Al Qaeda Central was quickly dismantled and dispersed in October 2001 by the US invasion of Afghanistan, before regrouping in Pakistan. Its ideas rapidly moved from the margins to the mainstream of public discourse. Its ideology took hold with small numbers of intensely motivated individuals across the world. It did not need a mass movement to carry out acts of terrorism and spread its ideas. Instead, it acquired a string of affiliate organizations across a wide range of countries, of widely varying strength and reach.[22]

Iraq became the key to transforming al-Qaeda's fortunes. The direct introduction of US troops in an unpopular war offered unparalleled opportunities to wage war against Americans and to identify the jihad with a broadly popular campaign. In 2003, Abu Musab al-Zarqawi's local jihadist movement pledged allegiance to bin Laden, creating by proxy the most potent and powerful of the al-Qaeda affiliates. Zarqawi proved a difficult affiliate, however. He refused to accept control of his organization by al-Qaeda Central, pursuing instead his own vision of localized jihad. Mainstream Arab public opinion was horrified by how ruthlessly he targeted Shi'ite civilians. Even al-Qaeda leaders worried this would affect the movement's carefully cultivated public image. But Zarqawi was playing a different game than al-Qaeda. He sought to establish territorial control and mobilize foreign fighters into a large-scale jihad. His brutal methods ultimately backfired, at least in the short term, as less extreme factions of the Sunni insurgency turned against the so-called Islamic State of Iraq. By 2008, Zarqawi was long dead, and the ISI driven underground. But the same organization would survive, adapt, and reemerge in Iraq and Syria after the outbreak of the Arab uprisings—vindicating the Zarqawi model of jihad, at great cost.

Faced with these new jihadist trends, the Muslim Brotherhood sought to position itself as a moderate, more mainstream alternative to al-Qaeda's jihad. Publicly rejecting violence while embracing democratic participation opened the door to engagement with the West across multiple arenas. In Egypt, this meant Muslim Brotherhood parliamentarians becoming familiar with Western diplomats and journalists. In Iraq, it meant supporting the realignment of the "Awakenings" with the United States and the Iraqi government against al-Qaeda and the Islamic State of Iraq. The ability of the Muslim Brotherhood to appeal to a long-skeptical West was, in turn, profoundly threatening to the entrenched elites worried about what this could mean for their own hold on power.

Al-Qaeda and other jihadists clearly struggled to adapt to the early Arab uprisings, but did not simply give up in the face of the complexity of the new challenges.[23] Al-Qaeda did take advantage of the chaos, however, and especially of the distraction of key security services. The relentless campaigns waged by the intelligence services in Yemen, Tunisia, Egypt, and Libya faltered during the political chaos, offering rare breathing space to beleaguered organizations. Crucially, the prisons opened up, allowing not only political prisoners but also key jihadists to escape and rejoin the fight. This moment of respite and reorganization compensated for the temporary political losses associated with the hopeful days of the uprising. And then, of course, the narrative of loss began to correct itself as politics turned grim. Jihadists who had seemed foolish and hopelessly out of touch in February 2011 with their denunciations of democracy and dismissal of peaceful protest now began to look prescient and principled.

It was around this time that the "Ansar al-Sharia" phenomenon began to manifest.[24] In newly open territories like Libya and Tunisia, rebranded al-Qaeda franchises and local jihadist cells now sought to govern territory, provide social services, and seek popular support in ways which would have been alien to al-Qaeda only a few years earlier. The open political environment of the day allowed them to operate openly in ways which would have been fiercely repressed under the old autocratic regimes. As Aaron Zelin documented carefully through monitoring of their prolific social media accounts, the Ansar al-Sharia groups actively cultivated an image which maintained their jihadist ideology but incorporated the long-derided Muslim Brotherhood strategies of outreach and service provision.

The Islamic State's declaration in June 2014 accelerated and intensified all of these patterns. The declaration of a caliphate and seizure of a vast territory in the Levant offered a dramatic alternative to either the Brotherhood or al-Qaeda's strategic vision. Its canny use of social media, brazen media spectaculars, and reformulation of al-Qaeda's affiliate strategy created an impression of momentum attractive to many within the jihadist orbit. The broadcasts of the decapitation of American journalists and burning alive of a Jordanian pilot captured the global imagination, while successive terror attacks in Paris reignited a panicked anti-Islamic frenzy in the West last seen in the early days following 9/11. By 2015, al-Qaeda and the Islamic State were locked in a fierce intra-jihadist struggle, with their local affiliates fighting each other on the ground and their ideologues and leaders each claiming ownership over a rapidly evolving global movement.

THE NEW ARAB WARS

The Arab uprising therefore involved at least four different, overlapping lines of conflict. The Iranian-Saudi conflict, reinforced by Israel's priorities, continued to structure much of the region's alliances and interventions. The battle for leadership of the Sunni Arab world between Saudi Arabia, Qatar, the United Arab Emirates, and Turkey often mattered even more. The challenge posed by different Islamist networks, from mainstream Muslim Brotherhood and Salafi movements to the violent extremists of al-Qaeda and the Islamic State, represented a third level of conflict. And, finally, a broader struggle between autocratic regimes and mobilized societies continued to unfold within a context framed by the three regional wars.

Local politics unfolded within this international and regional context. The decisions and perceptions of the Egyptian Muslim Brotherhood and military, the mediating role of Tunisian civil society, the fears and ambitions of Libyan militias, the brutality of Asad, and the burning intensity of the Syrian opposition's determination to end his reign of terror—none of these can be reduced to the machinations of foreign powers. But the regional and international structural dynamics shaped every one of these local battlefields, all of which remained locked within broader narratives which gave local, contingent events their meaning.

All four of those conflicts were, in turn, shaped by questions about America's changing role. The US refusal to intervene in Syria and the nuclear deal with Iran hinted at fundamental changes. Its continued support for Israel and its Gulf allies, accommodation of Egypt's military coup, and escalating military role in Iraq and Syria suggested that, in fact, little had changed. Enduring alliances have been thrown into question, while traditional adversaries negotiate terms for entry into regional order.

In these brutal wars, most of the region became what it said it wanted to fight. The courageous, principled activists were overtaken by hardened men. The vast majority of those honorable souls were killed, arrested, or driven from their homes. Some gave up hope, while others reversed their positions as conditions changed. Tawakkol Karman, the Nobel Peace Prize laureate from Yemen, evolved from a powerful voice for nonviolent resistance to an outspoken backer of the Saudi military campaign in her country. Leading Egyptian activists such as Alaa Abdel Fattah and Ahmed Maher disappeared into the regime's political prisons, their reputations savaged by loyalist media. Syria's courageous citizen activists were imprisoned and tortured by the Asad regime, forced into exile, or killed in the crossfire between rebel groups.

Arab regimes, never paragons of morality in the first place, grew more violent at home and abroad as they lashed out, seeking to restore their stability. It was difficult to muster respect for the humanitarian and moral claims of regimes keen on action in Syria as they simultaneously imprisoned their own dissidents, dispatched troops to crush popular protests in Bahrain, supported Egypt's military coup, and bombed Yemen at tremendous human cost for months on end. There is no morality in supporting an insurgency which necessarily involves fierce, bloody combat.

The Arab uprisings are truly tragic, not because they were always doomed to fail but because they did not need to end this way. The enormous hope unleashed by those early days of revolution reflected a genuine generational change and the prospect of a very different Arab future. But the frustrations and horrors which followed were something equally real. For all the potential of newly empowered publics, the old elites retained enormous power to resist change. Those regimes which survived the initial onslaught bought the time to bring those power resources back into play. The moment of enthusiasm could not last, and the underlying balance of power would inevitably tell. Old elites clawed their way back to power in reconfigured, post-revolutionary systems, with the active support of the regional powers determined to stymie change. States that collapsed under the strain—Libya, Syria, Yemen—became arenas for regional powers to fight their wars.

It is to those wars that we now turn.

| 2 |

THE ARAB UPRISING

The Arab uprising radically transformed the Middle East in ways that will not fully be understood for decades. In today's gloomy, violent, and repressive conditions it is difficult to recall just how exhilarating the protest movements of early 2011 really were—or how fully they challenged the entire regional order.

While the Arab uprising is generally understood as a fully transnational story, what followed has typically been told as a series of loosely related national stories. The various transitions happened simultaneously, of course, but their outcomes tend to be explained by unique internal factors. Egypt's failure is thus blamed on the excesses of the Muslim Brotherhood or the machinations of the deep state. Tunisia succeeded because of its National Dialogue, its strong and organized Left, or its wiser Islamist leadership. Bahrain failed because of Saudi intervention and the sectarianism of its protests. Jordan and Morocco avoided regime change because they had kings. There is much to these arguments, of course. All politics is local, and political scientists and local political analysts have done a tremendous job of unpacking the complex local calculations and structural forces which shaped outcomes. But this misses the deep interconnectedness of those processes.

In today's more cynical and hardened environment, it is too easy to forget the radically revolutionary nature of the Arab uprising. This was an extraordinary moment in world politics. Millions of people mobilized in the streets across more than a dozen countries almost simultaneously. Participation in these protests transcended social class, religious and ethnic differences, and political ideology. They self-consciously constructed their political struggle as one which transcended national boundaries and rejected the existing rules of politics. The rhythms and dynamics of politics across an entire region were synchronized, with intense interaction and demonstration effects moving from one Arab state to another. When individuals tweeted "injustice is injustice whether in Bahrain or Libya or Syria" (@salmaeldaly, March 2011) or "#daraa of #syria is #sidibouzid of #tunisia and #suez of #egypt" (@drsonnet, March 2011), they explicitly constructed a sense of shared struggle and shared fate. And they genuinely expected things to change.

Tunisians were the only ones to take to the streets alone, with no role models, no expectations, no precedents, and few external interventions. Every other uprising took place within this deeply interconnected arena in which both protestors and regimes constantly monitored events abroad. At almost every important point, external players shaped the capabilities and the strategies of domestic political actors. External events shaped expectations about the prospects of success or failure. The Arab uprisings began in transnational diffusion, ended in transnational repression, and birthed transnational proxy wars.

Once they leapt from Tunisia, the uprisings unfolded within a remarkably integrated shared political arena. Egypt's revolution unleashed a genuinely extraordinary protest wave, which mobilized massive crowds almost everywhere in the region. It has become fashionable to dismiss those protests because of their later failures. But they were truly extraordinary. Protests began to roil Algeria in early January, even before Ben Ali fled. Jordanians began protesting on January 14, quickly forcing the king to dismiss the unpopular government. Yemenis held a major protest in Sanaa on January 27, within a week compelling President Ali Abdullah Saleh to announce he would not seek reelection. Omanis too began protesting in January. Smaller protests were already percolating in Libya and Syria.

The success of the Egyptian uprising in forcing President Hosni Mubarak from power took these protests to an entirely different level. Bahrainis took to the streets on February 14, and soon had the largest per capita mobilization of any Arab citizenry. Libyan protests escalated nationally on February 15. Moroccan protestors took to the streets on February 20. Syrians tried to get protests going, albeit with little success in attracting widespread support, until the cataclysmic southern protests in mid-March. The only Arab states to avoid significant popular mobilization in those first few months were the exceptionally small, wealthy, and repressive Qatar, UAE, and Saudi Arabia, and the traumatized quasi-states of Palestine, Lebanon, and Iraq.

While every country had its own issues, nobody at the time considered the protests to be isolated affairs. Al-Jazeera provided a common language, narrative, and imagery across not only the Arabic-speaking world, but also to the West through its successful Al-Jazeera English franchise. The synchronicity of those protests was one of their most striking qualities. In country after country, protestors raised the same slogans and tried the same tactics. They were actively observing and often interacting with each other, learning lessons and formulating strategy based on what unfolded in other countries. They saw what worked and what didn't elsewhere, and tried to apply the lessons. They drew inspiration from successes elsewhere and were sobered by the failures.

There is no exaggerating the integration of these political arenas in their early days. Events in one country immediately inspired reactions in others, while regimes fought for their survival at home and abroad simultaneously. Every uprising needs to be understood within the context of the broader regional political arena. This is not to say that the uprisings were only, or even mainly, sparked by foreign agitators, as threatened regimes would have it. The impulse behind the uprisings was overwhelmingly domestic, with angry and frustrated publics inspired by events abroad to act at home. But regional intervention shaped all subsequent outcomes, even if it took time for the Arab regimes to regroup from the initial shock. The early days of the Arab uprising were uniquely beyond the control of regional powers. The crowds which seized Bourguiba Street and Tahrir Square had little interest in the money or guns, which were the currency of the region's proxy wars. But this indifference would not last.

The story of the Arab uprising has by this point been told many times. This chapter does not attempt to offer a detailed history of those momentous events. Such an account can be found in my 2012 book *The Arab Uprising* or in numerous other excellent books. Instead, this chapter will reframe those first months of regional turmoil through the lens of the deeply interconnected regional political arena in which activists and regimes alike fought their battles—and show how they set the stage for the conflicts to come.

TUNISIA, ALONE

Few expected the protests, which began in the south of Tunisia, to spread to the capital city of Tunis, much less to the broader Arab world. Tunisia's peripheral status was ironically necessary to its ability to ignite the regional uprising. If the first uprising had been in a central state such as Egypt or Jordan, it would probably have been snuffed out forcefully before the wider world had even begun to pay attention. Tunisia, however, existed very much outside the mainstream of Arab politics. Physically located far to the west on the north African coast, Tunisia was closer to southern Europe than to the core conflict zones of Palestine and Iraq. Tunisia's severe repression and running battle with al-Jazeera over critical coverage largely kept the emerging Arab public sphere at arm's length. Its most important public intellectuals, such as the Islamist Rashed al-Ghannouchi or the human rights advocate Moncef Marzouki, lived in enforced exile.

Tunisia also had a long experience with outbursts of protest in its neglected southern towns like Sidi Bouzid. The familiarity of failed protests in Tunisia's south over decades likely lulled the regime and its Arab backers into a false sense of security—an advantage of surprise which no other Arab uprising would share. When the protests began, they initially felt familiar to Tunisians and to those outside observers who paid attention to the country. It was only when the protests suddenly leapfrogged the security cordon and spread across the country that the situation began to feel revolutionary.

Al-Jazeera and social media each played a crucial role in this new trajectory. Facebook had been one of the few largely tolerated Internet sites, primarily because of its seemingly apolitical nature. But social media activists, many of them in exile in France, were able to use Facebook's widespread penetration to rapidly spread information about the protests and to organize actions far outside Sidi Bouzid. Al-Jazeera, despite being officially banned from the country, was able to use footage and news provided via social media activists to offer a compelling portrait of a country suddenly gripped by revolution. It framed its coverage of the uprising within its broader narrative of an Arab struggle for democracy and freedom, which resonated broadly.

That element of surprise momentarily offset the enormous power advantages enjoyed by the Ben Ali regime. The speed, intensity, and magnitude of the protests simply did not leave enough time to mobilize the regime's considerable repressive skills and power resources. The army's refusal to disperse the protests by force left him few cards to play. By the time Ben Ali's external backers grasped the extent of his predicament, it was already too late to save his regime. All Saudi Arabia could offer Ben Ali was safe haven as a political exile. Ben Ali's corruption and weakness had made him indefensible, but that did not mean that the interests he represented would easily give up. Preserving the state, protecting friendly elites from the old regime, building up more effective local proxies, and creating political parties capable of exercising influence through new institutions became the line of defense.

FROM TUNISIA TO THE ARAB WORLD

The Arab debate between Ben Ali's fall on January 14 and the Egyptian uprising on January 25 revolved around whether Tunisia's uprising was a singular event or the harbinger of a regional trend. There were two predominant narratives. Regime elites across the region and activists offered almost diametrically opposed diagnoses and predictions. Caught off guard, the best the defenders of the status quo could muster was a claim of Tunisian exceptionalism: that what was unfolding on the streets of Tunis had no lessons for any other Arab country and should not be seen as any fundamental rupture in the Arab order. Most leaders and elites sought to portray Tunisia's events as utterly unique, inapplicable to their own country, and thus, unlikely to spark comparable challengers. Many political scientists, skeptical of facile comparisons across very different countries, agreed with their analysis.

Al-Jazeera's initial framing of the Tunisian uprising, on the other hand, emphasized its deep similarities with other Arab countries. Rather than covering Tunisia's turmoil as an intriguing oddity on the periphery of the Arab world, al-Jazeera chose to place the protests within a much wider narrative of popular mobilization, which resonated widely. Most activists and engaged publics highlighted the similarities between Tunisia's plight and their own, and predicted that the uprisings would spread. Captivated by the scenes of an utterly unexpected peaceful and successful revolution, most embraced the al-Jazeera narrative. That embrace, in defiance of the signals being aggressively sent by regional and national elites, mattered in no small part because they were the people who were about to make the revolutions.

The massive protests in Egypt on January 25 decisively settled the debate about whether the protests would spread.

The fate of Egypt mattered far more than any other single Arab country for defining the regional trajectory. Egypt's uprising moved the challenge from the periphery to the core of the Arab world, striking at the heart of the American and Saudi-led regional order. By 2011, there was nothing new about political protest in Egypt. Successive waves of protest from a wide array of societal sectors had been challenging authorities for the previous decade. Since early in the decade, the small, ideologically diverse band of activists and intellectuals of the Kefaya movement had creatively challenged the Mubarak regime while pioneering new uses of information technology such as blogs and MMS video sharing. The April 6 Movement in support of a strike in al-Mahalla al-Kubra was only the most heavily publicized of a significant wave of workplace unrest.[1] Student movements, lawyers, judges, and many other professional sectors had mobilized over various issues. The "We Are All Khaled Said" Facebook campaign protesting the unpunished police killing of a young Alexandrian, which became so central to the January 25 uprising, was built upon a decade of activist organization, mobilization, and experimentation.

What made January 25 exceptional was not the fact of protest but its size, speed, and intensity. Egyptian security forces were well-prepared for the protests and would have likely handled even slightly larger than normal crowds with ease. The activists who organized the protests did not really expect much more. The enormous response to the call into the streets overwhelmed the security forces and the protest organizers. Egyptians had been apathetic and alienated for many years without small protests galvanizing large-scale revolution. Why did so many ordinary people now for the first time join the core activists in the streets to demand political change? In large part because Tunisia had proven to them that the once unthinkable had become possible. Egyptians who had been disgruntled for years suddenly believed that they could win, which made the risks of joining the crowds worth taking. Once the crowds took to the streets, the uprising gained its own momentum, sweeping everyone up in a narrative of popular revolution and national renewal.

This is not the place to rehash the exhilerating, frequently told story of the eighteen days of the Egyptian revolution. During that tense period, Cairo's Tahrir Square became the focal point for Egyptian national politics as well as for the regional and international media. The revolutionaries encamped in the square famously included secularists and Islamists, leftists and liberals, and a cross-section of Egyptian society. Through the long days of political gamesmanship, this revolutionary coalition agreed on little besides the core demand of Mubarak's removal. Their persistence, and their claim to speak for the Egyptian people, allowed the protestors to exercise a veto over certain political gambits, but not to dictate the outcome.

The Obama administration quickly understood that Mubarak personally could not survive popular protests of this magnitude and focused its attention on navigating a meaningful transition. Obama aligned himself

rhetorically with the protestors and publicly urged Mubarak to avoid violence and to step down rapidly to allow for an orderly transfer of power.
During the early days of the uprising, Washington had gone to great lengths
to convince the military to refrain from crushing the protests by force.
American officials floated numerous proposals, including the elevation of
intelligence chief Omar Sulaiman to the presidency. While Egyptian protestors were enraged by reports that Obama envoy, former Ambassador
Frank Wisner, had expressed support in a private meeting with Mubarak,
the Obama administration's public message was remarkably forthright in
defending the uprising's core demand for a regime transition.

Mubarak's allies in the region did not see it that way. They could hardly
believe that Obama was cutting off a longtime American ally. They clearly
hoped and expected that he would survive the protests. Allies such as Jordan's King Abdullah and the Palestinian Authority's Mahmoud Abbas offered their support. Saudi Arabia's King Abdullah called Mubarak to denounce the protestors who had "infiltrated into the brotherly people of
Egypt, to destabilize its security and stability... [and] to spew out their
hatred in destruction, intimidation, burning, looting and inciting a mali-
cious sedition."[2] On February 8, Mubarak met with the UAE's Foreign
Minister Abdullah bin Zayed, who reportedly urged him to hold on to
power for the moment, even if that required a promise to not contest the
next election. The fate of Mubarak himself was of great interest to the Gulf
regimes, who fumed at their inability to protect a longtime friend. This
interest was matched by the intensity of the revolutionary focus on
Mubarak, whose removal had perhaps been the only thing on which the
broad revolutionary coalition agreed. This meant that the Supreme Council of the Armed Forces, or SCAF, could not meet Gulf concerns without
forfeiting their fragile post-uprisings legitimacy.

Mubarak's inability to survive despite this regional support revealed the
weaknesses of the region's putative power brokers in the face of exceptional
public mobilization. The instruments of normal politics, from financial
inducements to carefully maintained personal relationships with state leaders, were largely ineffective at moments of extreme popular mobilization.
Mubarak's inability to clear the streets and restore normal politics, which

they blamed in part on American calls for restraint and regime transition, brought their worst nightmares to vivid life. Mubarak's overthrow punctured the image of inevitability which all Arab regimes cultivated, inviting challenges which previously would have been unthinkable. Even worse from the Saudi and Emirati perspective, Qatar stood to gain from Mubarak's fall, given al-Jazeera's centrality to the revolutionary moment and the political opening for both Muslim Brothers and youth activists who had long been cultivated by Doha. This interpretation of the Egyptian disaster would shape their response to the rising protest wave elsewhere.

Still, despite the revolutionary euphoria, it was clearly premature to conclude that Egypt had been lost to the old regional order. The February 11 announcement that Mubarak had stepped down empowered the Supreme Council of the Armed Forces to oversee a democratic transition. This resolution met the core interests of most of the international and domestic players far better than their vocal complaints suggested. Mubarak's departure satisfied the one clear demand of Tahrir Square, which soon emptied despite the fears of activist leaders of a premature demobilization. The promise to move towards democracy satisfied the White House, which viewed democratization as the best hope for a stable Egypt. Doha reveled in the new prominence of the Muslim Brotherhood and the global acknowledgment of the Qatari role. Crucially, however, the leading role of the SCAF reassured the Gulf states and Israel, as well as many in the United States, that the fundamental foreign policy orientation of the new Egypt would not change. While Saudi Arabia and the UAE might have preferred Mubarak, they still had the SCAF as a firewall against real political change.

The US role in the Egyptian transition helped activate a profound existential perception of threat among the Arab leadership class. In another world—and the one in which many of us in Washington hoped to live—this might have triggered a cascade of preemptive reforms and democratic changes in order to better align the regional order with Washington's new preferences. Instead, it drove those leaders to double down on their antagonistic position towards democratic change—at home, and everywhere else in the region—and towards the United States.

"SURVIVE AND ADVANCE"

By mid-February, Egypt and Tunisia were at least for the moment lost to the Gulf powers, and the immediate focus became containing the protests spreading to every corner of the Arab world. In the days following Mubarak's departure, protestors filled the streets demanding the overthrow of the regime in almost every Arab country. Cold rational analysis of the protest dynamics can't quite capture the sheer dizzying enthusiasm of those days. After the peaceful overthrow of Ben Ali and Mubarak, Arabs hoping for change in their own countries had come to believe that success was not just possible but inevitable. Many believed that the old rules simply no longer applied, and that change everywhere had become just a matter of time. In this moment of enthusiasm, mobilized publics seemed unstoppable and democratic uprisings really did seem like the right side of history. Contempt and pity for the regimes had replaced fear.

Yemen's uprising offers an outstanding example of the connections between Egypt and the other Arab countries. Yemen and Egypt have little in common politically, culturally, economically, or geographically. Nonetheless, the protestors who seized Change Square in Sanaa strongly resembled Tahrir's diverse coalition of youth from many different ideological and political trends. Shi'ite Houthis and Muslim Brotherhood-aligned Islahis, slated to become determined enemies in later years, sat together in this exceptional period just as comfortably as did Egypt's secularists and Islamists during Tahrir's eighteen days. Yemeni activists appropriated Egyptian slogans and methods and consciously situated themselves within the al-Jazeera narrative of a unified Arab uprising. The Islah-affiliated activist Tawakkol Karman, who played a key symbolic role in thus situating the Yemeni uprising, was thus an inspired choice for the Nobel Peace Prize in 2012.

The overwhelming importance of this inspiration could be felt in every corner of the Arab world. What else could have convinced Libyans or Syrians to venture into the streets, when decades of experience had taught them that such public opposition meant certain death? Jordanian protests brought together young members of tribes with their Palestinian counterparts along with the traditional opposition parties. While the Jordanian security forces forcibly prevented the establishment of any Tahrir-style encampment, the protest movement would take root among tribes and evolve into an enduring movement known as the Herak.[3] The youth activists of Morocco's February 20 movement proved remarkably resilient even after the co-optation of the Islamist opposition through elections.[4] Kuwaiti activists challenged the regime with unprecedented mass public protests.[5] Omani activists mobilized in the greatest numbers in a generation, demanding economic reforms and political inclusion.[6] Protests even raged in Saudi Arabia's Eastern Province for years.

The surviving regimes understood clearly the magnitude of the threat. If Mubarak could fall to protests, anyone could be vulnerable. They saw how quickly the protest wave had spread and how difficult it would be to disperse entrenched protest camps once they settled in to press demands for political change. They learned diverse lessons from Ben Ali and Mubarak's failures, and hastened to apply them as if their survival depended upon it.[7] After all, staying in power had long since become the primary motivation for most of these regimes, and none had any intention of easily surrendering their grip.

Perception and narrative mattered. Ben Ali's impulsive decision to flee Tunisia and the SCAF's removal of Mubarak horrified these regimes in part because they undermined the belief that leaders would fight to the death to stay in power. Such weakness invited challenge. Their response aimed to restore their image of overwhelming, irresistible strength. As the then-editor of al-Quds al-Arabi Abd al-Bari Atwan noted early in the uprising, "[T]he Libyan regime learned from the experience of Tunis to its West and Cairo to its East that the refusal to use bloody force against protestors is what caused the fall."[8]

The guiding logic in these early months was not complicated. Had they been college basketball fans, they might have adopted the slogan of the late North Carolina State coach Jimmy Valvano, who led his underdog team to an unlikely national championship by winning a series of ugly games against superior teams: "survive and advance." To survive, they mobilized every resource at their disposal, from financial promises and media propaganda to government shuffles and invitations to political dialogue.

If that required violence, then so be it. They would worry about the future costs of these commitments later, after the revolutionary fever had broken. To advance, they moved aggressively into the transitional and failed states to shape the emerging political orders. They cultivated local allies, offered huge financial aid packages, and when appropriate, supplied weapons and military training.

The Arab order's counteroffensive played out very differently for states inside and outside the Saudi-led camp. The surviving regimes inside the good graces of the Arab order closed ranks. Whatever their disagreements, these regimes first and foremost wanted to survive, and they had learned from Tunisia that failure in one could quickly spread to others. This made regime survival a collective, not an individual, project. The wealthy monarchies provided desperately needed infusions of cash to shore up threatened friendly leaders in Jordan, Morocco, and Oman. This support allowed these perennially cash-strapped regimes to co-opt challengers and offer popular economic handouts. The Gulf states could also provide political cover, deflecting any American pressure to make concessions. Their media advanced anti-revolutionary narratives, praising limited reforms, warning of the risks of chaos and civil conflict, and demonizing challengers. When necessary, they would go even further. Saudi Arabia took the lead in managing Yemen's transition, and drove a military intervention into Bahrain in defense of its embattled monarchy.

Regimes went about this common goal of self-protection in a variety of ways appropriate to the local context. Some regimes offered preemptive political concessions, which spoke to the protestors without conceding the core of power. The Moroccan constitutional reform is an excellent example of this method. Faced with the example from Tunisia, King Mohammed VI quickly saw the need to get out ahead of the February 20 protest movement. With considerable financial support from Saudi Arabia to deploy, the monarchy made a high-profile commitment to meaningful reforms towards a constitutional monarchy. It welcomed the participation of opposition parties, including the leading Islamist party, the PJD, and sought dialogue with youth activists.

Jordan's King Abdullah similarly responded with a flurry of political concessions. While he did not offer quite such dramatic constitutional changes, he did fire the prime minister and promise a wholesale house-cleaning. Gulf media showered positive coverage on these minor reforms in order to present them as both the answer and the alternative to popular revolutionary mobilization. This went to the point of offering Jordan and Morocco membership in the Gulf Cooperation Council, a symbolic gesture never likely to materialize. The message was clear: reform without revolution was possible, and could be quite lucrative for countries who chose to remain within the Saudi-led bloc. Such moves were typically sufficient to blunt the popular wave, giving it the time to co-opt different constituencies and bring politics back into the realm of the normal.

Money mattered. With oil prices high, the Gulf states were in a strong position to spend their way out of trouble. The wealthiest Gulf states lavished public spending on their own citizens to deflect any popular opposition. State employees received huge salary bonuses. Subsidies on consumer products and energy were maintained or expanded. Some governments built up new housing projects to alleviate overcrowding. They offered huge new scholarship programs for youth who might otherwise be prime candidates to join protest movements. They did not only spend at home. Saudi Arabia and the UAE doled out billions of dollars to the less well-off GCC states, Jordan and Morocco, to subsidize their own financial survival strategies.

The Gulf powers were still reeling in the early days following Egypt's uprising, though. Their old friends and allies such as Mubarak and his circle were in prison, exile, or disgrace. They were ill-equipped to play the new game of democratic politics or to co-opt the nationalist, revolutionary wave. What they did have, however, was the SCAF, the military rulers who took control of post-Mubarak Egypt with the promise of guiding a transition towards democracy. That firewall preserved the interests of the GCC, but it too was shaky. Gulf states offered a safe harbor for pro-regime elites, dismissively labeled feloul ("remnants") following the revolution, to regroup and prepare to return.

External players drew on different networks. The Muslim Brotherhood proved a primary point of entry for Qatar and Turkey, each of which had long-standing ties and rich existing transnational financial, media, and organizational networks.⁹ This would prove to be a common theme across North Africa and the Levant, albeit with local variations. Qatar and Turkey were competing for these Muslim Brotherhood networks, however, leading to multiple points of competition and an uneven strategy. For the rabidly anti-Islamist UAE, the obvious point of entry was those Egyptians hostile to the Brotherhood's rise. The UAE cultivated old elites from the business community, along with Christians and other anti-Islamist secular elites from Mubarak's NDP such as Ahmed Shafik. Egypt became the UAE's primary interest in the emerging regional wars, as it fought Qatari influence and pushed for the restoration of some form of secular, pro-GCC rule.

Saudi Arabia faced a more difficult trick. Riyadh could not credibly mobilize an anti-Islamist bloc, but shared the UAE's fear of a rising Muslim Brotherhood. Its media empire largely supported the same political blocs as did the UAE's, but this was not a natural fit. The most long-standing and intimate set of relationships for Saudi Arabia was with the Egyptian salafi community. The sudden, shocking rise of the Salafis in the electoral landscape, facilitated by their sudden reversal of long-held ideological positions condemning democratic participation, offered one vehicle for Saudi influence. But the Salafi networks complicated the broader Gulf strategy for mobilizing anti-Islamist, secular elites to restore the old order. It is not an accident that, publicly at least, Saudi Arabia took a backseat to the UAE on the Egyptian front.

None of these networks should be simply dismissed as proxies for their external patrons. Most were fully capable of playing the proxy game, extracting desperately needed financial and media resources while maintaining their independence. Empowered, mobilized publics were not easily manipulated by external powers, especially following revolutions that had been crafted into symbols of national identity and patriotic pride. Qatari, Saudi or Emirati help might have been crucial for achieving the overthrow of hated leaders, but no patriotic Egyptian, Libyan or Tunisian wanted to be reminded of their dependence. Qatar's prestige spiked after each uprising, but then collapsed when it was seen to overreach and try to impose the Muslim Brotherhood on Egypt. The UAE followed a similar, though less extreme, trajectory.

Where backing political parties and building local clients proved difficult, another option was always to try to overturn the playing field through promoting violence or military coups. Trashing of transitions proved a winning strategy for those seeking authoritarian restoration. They won by destroying the process and leaving no options beside a return to strongman rule. Once-optimistic citizens became disenchanted by pervasive insecurity, political stalemate, and unresolved economic problems. The same media ecosystem which had carried messages of hope and possibility in early 2011 could just as easily transmit images of horror, violence, hatred, and despair. In an uncertain and divided region, the media easily whipped up ever greater fears and hatreds. The combination of rage, polarization, and disenchantment proved highly conducive to reversing the democratic tide. It left those new regimes vulnerable, though, as unpredictable new movements took up the mantle of these new campaigns.

Above all, Arab regimes relearned the many virtues of violence. Even where a military response did not succeed in putting down protests, the introduction of bloodshed would rapidly change the narrative. A peaceful uprising with crowds of ordinary people locking hands and singing inspirational songs inspired others to join. Chaos, panic, and bloody corpses could deter such participation by demonstrating the risks and costs of open opposition. Reminding citizens of the brute force underlying regimes might deflate a revolutionary bubble. Publics once thrilled about the prospect of change had second thoughts as they observed the negative trajectories of the revolutionary states. Jordanians might still be upset by corruption and a dismal economy, but pull back from the streets for fear of following Syria into the abyss. Thus even Syria's horror had its uses for Arab leaders keen to show their own citizens the folly of protest.

This strategic use of violence for demobilization was risky, of course. Too much violence captured on video could attract unwanted international pressure. Blood in the streets might also build the protest movement by generating anger and a thirst for revenge, as proved to be the case in Syria. Regimes sought to calibrate their public and private violence carefully as they maneuvered throught these newly complex domestic and international arenas.

Rhetorical violence accompanied the actual killing and beating. Regimes typically sought to demonize and discredit protestors as foreign saboteurs. Qaddafi's descriptions of rebel as "rodents" or Asad's labeling them as "germs" were only an extreme form of a typical line of defense. Regimes, often with the support of Saudi-owned pan-Arab media, painted protests as essentially unpatriotic, using whatever raw material was at hand. Sectarianism was the easiest approach in countries with significant Shi'a populations such as Bahrain, Kuwait, and Saudi Arabia. They drew on long-established stereotypes against Islamist movements to depict them as extremists and fanatics loyal to transnational organizations rather than to the nation. And even though all of these regimes were US allies, they frequently tarred liberals and civil society organizations as American assets.

This demonization also meant a deliberate strategy of social polarization. The Arab uprisings generated considerable power from their ability to harness temporary coalitions across traditional lines of division. The crowds in Tahrir and Bourguiba Street famously included all social classes, Islamists alongside secularists, and a cross-section of almost all political parties and trends. Yemen's Change Square featured tents hosting Houthis, Islahis, and southern secessionists alongside liberals and socialist revolutionaries. Sectarianism was therefore a key weapon in the counterrevolutionary arsenal against the uprisings.[10] Whatever divided the public and blocked the path towards large, cross-sectional crowds served the interests of maintaining the status quo. This hateful logic applied broadly: pitting Christians against Muslims in Egypt, Jordanians against Palestinians in Jordan, and, above all, Sunnis against Shi'ites wherever possible.

These assorted methods and mechanisms for the most part worked. None of the long-term problems had been solved, but the regimes had survived the moment of revolutionary enthusiasm. For the purposes of restoring the regional order, this was enough.

Those outside the "axis of moderates," such as Libya and Syria, had no such external saviors. Instead, Gulf media and money acted as intensifiers, supporting rebels and protest movements, and putting added pressure on already fragile and shaky regimes.[11] In the months following the uprisings, every potential transition became part of the broader regional political wars. The Gulf states defended their allies while working towards the overthrow of targeted regimes. They built international support for action against their adversaries, highlighting their violence while downplaying similar violations of their own. They began to aggressively try to mold the direction of the popular uprisings. Such interventions were often more competitive than cooperative. Qatar, Saudi Arabia, the UAE, and Turkey may have cooperated early in the Libyan intervention, but they had an eye on their place in the post-Qaddafi future. The chance to break Iranian influence in Syria invited offensive moves into suddenly open terrain, but was not enough to keep them together in a collective strategy.

WHEN ALL ELSE FAILS

Saudi Arabia took a more direct role early on in two key cases: Yemen and Bahrain. Each of these Saudi neighbors had long been in its sphere of influence, and Riyadh saw an Iranian hand behind unrest in both. There was nothing novel about an intense, intimate Saudi involvement in either Bahraini or Yemeni affairs. Still, its interventions in each country differed significantly from traditional patterns and set the stage for serious problems down the road.

YEMEN'S MANAGED TRANSITION...

Yemeni politics had long been penetrated by regional networks, particularly Saudi, which would emerge to structure the protest movement and the civil war which followed. Yemen's famously weak state and regional divisions had long meant that real power lay at the local level.[12] Ali Abdullah Saleh and his ruling party had long and deep connections to Saudi Arabia. Multiple Islamist networks exercised authority on the ground and received significant external support, including Salafists and the Muslim Brotherhood-aligned Islah Party. The Ansar Allah movement of the Houthis had a tentative, contentious relationship with Iran, which was typically exaggerated by Saleh and his Saudi backers. The loose coalition of youth protestors in the early days of 2011 strongly identified with their counterparts across the region, adopting many of the same forms and methods. The very diversity of the constituent parts which made the protest coalition so powerful initially also carried the many external connections and resources which would later become sources of division.

Saudi Arabia had long maintained a strong position in its southern neighbor through extensive contacts with tribes and an alliance with the long-ruling President Ali Abdullah Saleh. Tribes dominated local power structures and served as a primary conduit for Saudi influence and funding. There were also an impressive array of Islamist movements. The Al-Islah movement included Muslim Brotherhood affiliates, while Salafi movements enjoyed close relationships and significant support from the Saudi religious establishment. Saleh excelled at balancing the interests of Yemen's regional and local power brokers.

Saleh also excelled at extracting support from the West as a partner against al-Qaeda's terrorism, to the point where many Yemenis accused him of manipulating the threat level to justify support. Al-Qaeda in the Arabian Peninsula (AQAP) had grown enormously inside of Yemen after key members had fled the repression by Saudi security forces inside the Kingdom in 2003.[13] Saudi efforts against AQAP in Yemen accelerated after its 2009 failed assassination attempt against then-Interior Minister Mohammed bin Nayif. The United States escalated its own air campaign following the attempted Christmas Day airliner bombing orchestrated by Anwar al-Awlaki for AQAP. American air strikes depended heavily on Yemeni intelligence, however, which gave Saleh ample opportunity to point them towards his political enemies.

Saudi Arabia viewed Yemen as an active theater in its regional struggles with Iran. Its attentions focused on the Ansar Allah movement, a northern Shi'a movement more commonly known as the Houthis after their charismatic leader. Unlike the US Embassy and most independent observers, the Saudis were convinced that the Houthis were an Iranian proxy. In 2009, Saudi Arabia fought a short, disastrous military campaign against the Houthis, to little benefit, and frequently pushed Saleh towards confrontation with the movement.

Yemen's protest movement erupted at roughly the same time as Egypt's, emulated many of its forms and demands, and sidestepped many of the enduring traditions of local politics. The January 27 seizure of Sanaa's Change Square by a broad coalition of activist youth resembled the occupation of Tahrir, as did the shared slogan "The People Want the Overthrow of the Regime." Within a week, the protests had wrested a promise from President Ali Abdullah Saleh not to run in the next presidential election. He had made such promises before, though, and few protestors were inclined to take him at his word.

The protestors stayed in Change Square, serving as the focal point for a broad range of demonstrations across the country. They included representatives of almost every political trend in the country, including Islamists and secularists alongside southerners and northerners. The early protest movement seemed primed to reject and transcend those entrenched divides. The students and youth who set up camps in Change Square represented a remarkable range of interests, identities, and networks. The protestors coalesced around the same simple demand for the overthrow of the regime, which had resonated so powerfully elsewhere. More than almost any other Arab case, the Yemeni protestors responded to the images and slogans from elsewhere. The Saudis were particularly alarmed by the inclusion of representatives of the Houthi movement, which they predictably viewed as the sharp edge of Iranian infiltration.

This narrative frame which united them was promoted heavily by Qatar's al-Jazeera, which saw the opportunity to contest the traditional Saudi domination in Yemen. Qatar had for years been pushing itself forward as an alternative mediator in the ongoing Yemeni conflict. The eruption of the uprisings offered an unprecedented opportunity for Doha to break the patterns and routinized networks of Saudi control. The Islamist strands of the Islah movement provided a concrete network which Qatar could activate, as a core for a much broader, expansive network of activists—many of whom certainly did not consider themselves Qatari proxies. This type of coalition-building was a key feature of Qatari soft power in the early days of the uprisings. Breaking apart those constituent parts by highlighting sectarianism and hostility towards Islamism became a key dimension of Saudi and Emirati strategy in the following years.

For the first two months, the protests remained broadly nonviolent, even as Saleh's forces escalated their use of violence. The tense standoff broke in mid-March, at almost exactly the same moment when GCC forces invaded Bahrain, NATO forces began bombing Libya, and Syrian protests ignited after the abuses in Deraa. Regime snipers opened fire at protesters at Sanaa University, killing dozens of protestors. The images were horrific, by the standards of the preceding several months. Violence soon reshaped the protest arena. In the chaotic aftermath, General Ali Mohsen defected to the opposition along with several key military units. The unity of the uprising was quickly overtaken by elite infighting and a dangerous standoff between factions of a splintered military. Change Square persevered, but governance and security across the country rapidly deteriorated.

The escalating violence and divided military convinced Riyadh and Washington that Saleh, like Mubarak, could not survive as a viable president. They feared that spreading violence and state collapse could create an opening for al-Qaeda or humanitarian catastrophe. The Saudis now quickly needed to rethink their role in Yemen. Saleh had made many enemies during his thirty years in power, and even his backers in Riyadh and Washington worried about the ability of the aging President to remain in control. Saleh had made himself indispensable to the United States in its war on terror, cooperating with its drone strikes against AQAP, but many critics warned against his double game of manipulating extremists to ensure continued Western support. The American and Saudi interest in sustaining the regime did not necessarily require Saleh himself—a shift of which Saleh was keenly aware, and determined to resist.

There was another way that the regional politics intruded. A template was being drawn on the fly by which regime violence elevated Arab uprising cases to a level of potential international intervention. The expectations of rapid regime change surrounding NATO's Libya intervention, including the GCC's leading role, changed the calculations for many Yemenis. Rather than regime violence signaling the impending end of popular protest, it suddenly seemed like a potential trigger for regional and international intervention against the violator. The sudden defection of General Ali al-Mohsen arguably had less to do with sudden squeamishness about regime violence than with the expectation of an imminent regime change from which he might benefit. His alignment with the coalition challenging the Saudi status quo signaled, perhaps, where he thought events might be leading.

Saudi Arabia took the lead, under the auspices of the GCC and with close American involvement, in brokering a political transition which would preserve its position of influence while satisfying enough of the demands of the protestors to end the instability. The GCC transition plan sought to preserve Saudi interests in the existing power structure, even if that meant sacrificing Saleh. The GCC plan provided for a transfer of power to Saleh's vice president along with a 'National Dialogue' on a new constitution and a promise of amnesty to persuade Saleh to go along.

This was not about any real transition to democracy, of course. Riyadh was as viscerally opposed to any form of democratization or popular participation in Yemen as everywhere else, and sought to work through the military and state officials. Qatar, unwilling to cede Yemen to Saudi Arabia at its peak moment of regional ascendance, challenged the GCC plan indirectly by publicizing critical Yemeni voices and sponsoring competing dialogues. Washington, inclined to support the push for democracy in the headstrong early days of the Arab uprising, also had a strong vested interest in ensuring that whatever government succeeded Saleh would continue his cooperative policies towards AQAP.

The fate of Saleh remained the principal stumbling block in the long months of negotiations which followed. The president clung tenaciously to his grip on power, presenting himself as the only thing standing between Yemen and total anarchy. Dislodging him proved difficult indeed, especially given the weaknesses of the Yemeni state. In April, he was badly wounded in an assassination attempt and airlifted to Riyadh for treatment at a Saudi hospital. But even in this weakened condition, Saleh could not be compelled to step down, a revealing statement of his grasp of Yemeni politics and the limits of Saudi influence.

Ultimately, in November 2011, the GCC gained Saleh's agreement to a transitional plan guaranteeing his personal immunity from prosecution. The key to what came to be called the Yemen model was the negotiated departure of the president and his inner circle, but the maintenance of the state and a carefully stage-managed political transition. Maintaining the state was seen as essential for preserving basic services and avoiding a security vacuum. It also, however, became a vehicle for preserving the networks of corruption and patronage which had been a principal driver of the protest eruption.[14] For many Yemenis, a transition which removed Saleh but kept the existing networks of power, economic privilege, and influence in place "change[d] everything... and changed nothing."[15] Saleh's vice president, Abd Rabbo Mansour al-Hadi, took office, and in February was elected president while running unopposed. This pseudo-election, mostly endured as a fait accompli and a necessary evil by activists and foreign analysts, would have long-term implications as the basis of his claim to legitimacy when the transition later fell apart.

The most controversial part of the GCC plan was the immunity from prosecution granted to Saleh as the price of his departure. Activists whose protests had begun with a primary focus on Saleh's crimes raged against this immunity, warning—presciently—that this impunity would come back to haunt Yemen. For several years after 2011, this model was often suggested as a path forward in other contentious cases, including Syria's. When Saleh played a critical role in pushing Yemen back into civil war following the failed transition, such proposals would lose much of their luster. Saleh's changed regional alliances were notable, however. After decades as a close Saudi and American ally, Saleh would reemerge aligned with the Houthis as a primary Saudi adversary—a shift which is remarkable even for Yemen.

The National Dialogue offered the promise, at least, of meeting some of the core concerns of the various strands of the protest coalition. The focus on issues of political representation and regionalism, which consumed old and new political elites, tended to sideline underlying demands about deeper reform of state institutions, governance, and corruption. The prospect of a revised structure of federalism also created openings for a revitalized southern secessionist movement and frightened Houthis scarred by years of conflict with Saudi Arabia and the central Yemeni government. The intense negotiations over decentralization and federalism would ultimately prove fatal to the transition. Still, well into 2014, the "Yemen Model" of a brokered transition preserving state institutions was widely touted as a road map for Syria and other protracted conflicts.

BAHRAIN'S TRAGEDY

Bahrain attracted an even more direct Saudi intervention. Activists on Internet forums enthusiastically discussed their hopes of emulating Tunisia and Egypt, while regime media insisted that Bahrain was nothing like those two countries. Activists online and offline called for a nonviolent demonstration on February 14, the date of a decade-old national referendum. The call for protests gained support from a wide range of political and civil society organizations. In his February 4 sermon, Sheikh Ali Salman, Secretary-General of the al-Wefaq, declared that Bahrainis shared the Egyptian and Tunisian demands for peaceful change. A week later, Salman and leading Shi'a cleric Sheikh Issa Qassim each repeated the call for protests on February 14. "The winds of change in the Arab world," Qassim reportedly said, "are unstoppable."[16]

The political leadership of the protest movement drew on two major political parties, a well-developed civil society, and young activists.[17] Within weeks, more than half the country's citizens had joined the protests. The protests were initiated by youth activists, but could draw upon more than a decade of civil society development. Many of the protestors were Shi'a, as were the majority of the country's citizens, but slogans focused on democracy and human rights rather than on sectarian concerns. Al-Wefaq and the core activist leadership kept demands limited, calling for reforms rather than the overthrow of the regime. Their moderation did not sit well with other political forces or with the energized youth movements flooding the streets. Al-Wefaq and the activist youth faced challenges from their more radical flanks, which grew stronger as regime repression escalated and the protests stretched on without resolution.

The protest organizers drew heavily on the Egyptian model, starting multiple marches from different locations and converging on the downtown Pearl Roundabout. They attempted to enforce nonviolence despite heavy-handed regime attacks and to keep demands focused on achievable political and human rights concerns. And they emulated the Egyptian Tahrir model by setting up their camp in the Pearl Roundabout. The response to the protest calls far exceeded their expectations, with huge numbers of citizens joining in the marches despite the heavy presence of security forces. The deaths of two protestors stoked popular anger, with funeral processions serving to bring more people into the streets. On February 17, the police moved in to clear the Roundabout encampment by force, removing the nearly twelve thousand protestors who had congregated and restoring the flow of downtown traffic. Police killed several more protestors and injured dozens, as violence between angry citizens and police began a dangerous spiral. On February 20, the opposition called for a general strike, which was honored by more than 80 percent of Bahraini employees.[18] More than a hundred fifty thousand Bahrainis—nearly 30 percent of the entire country's population—joined the February 22 demonstrations.

Bahrain's regime was divided over how to respond to these protests. The crown prince had been meeting from the start with al-Wefaq and other moderate opposition leaders. Such a political deal over constitutional reforms could have put Bahrain on the Jordanian and Moroccan path. This dialogue would continue for the next month, with American support. But Saudi Arabia and the long-serving prime minister viewed the proposed concessions as going much too far towards empowering civil society. As a result, the regime issued contradictory signals about its willingness to offer reforms. Meanwhile, security forces showed little restraint against protestors, and opposition leaders struggled to restrain enraged youth participants. The spiraling violence strengthened hard-liners on both sides of the divide.

Regime media relentlessly insisted that the protests were, in fact, an Iranian-sponsored campaign of subversion. While the opposition leadership firmly rejected the charge, the propaganda campaign made inroads with its intended audiences.[19] Bahraini Sunnis rallied to the regime, while wider Arab audiences began to have their doubts about a movement which had initially been embraced as a part of the collective Arab uprising. Painting Bahraini Shi'a as Iranian proxies was the key move for winning broad-based Sunni support for the crushing of what had been understood as another in the wave of popular uprisings for democracy. Al-Wefaq and other opposition leaders fully understood the regime's sectarian strategy and labored intensely to maintain a nonsectarian and nonviolent front. They struggled to enforce this discipline in the face of mounting regime repression and propaganda along sectarian lines. The regime's violence could not suppress popular demands or force people from the streets, but it proved quite effective at radicalizing the political arena and cutting the legs out from beneath regime and opposition reformists.

The Bahraini security regime was already remarkably transnationalized. The island state hosted three major foreign military bases, including, most crucially, an American naval base. British advisers constructed the state security apparatus, with Col. Ian Henderson serving for decades as the head of the Security and Intelligence Service. In recent years, the monarchy had turned to foreign Sunni communities in an effort both to staff the security services and to reduce the Shi'a demographic majority. Thousands of Jordanians and Pakistanis serve in Bahrain's security forces, and a significant but untold number of Sunnis have been granted citizenship over the years. The Western military presence protected the monarchy from external threats, but in the past had often acted as a check on the more brutal instincts of the security services. In 2011, this restraint would be lost as the regime fought for its survival.

The Bahrain intervention commanded a consensus across the GCC which would not be seen in any other of the uprisings. Few dissenting voices were heard from the Gulf leadership when Saudi troops rolled into Bahrain. Even otherwise pro-uprising Qatar joined the counterrevolutionary

Saudi-Emirati axis on Bahrain, with al-Jazeera either ignoring or covering favorably a Saudi intervention, which, in almost every other circumstance, it would have angrily denounced. The more cautious Kuwaitis and Omanis tacitly approved in the name of GCC solidarity. Bahrain was widely recognized to be a Saudi dependency, and its regime a red line in the long-running Saudi-Iranian cold war. Qatar's support for the intervention undermined its efforts to position itself as the champion of the regional protest wave. America's reputation was hurt even more directly, as its acquiescence to the Saudi intervention directly contradicted the Obama administration's rhetoric towards Egypt and the broader Arab Spring. Still, most observers understood the realpolitik in play, and few could seriously pretend to be surprised at either the Saudi repression, the GCC support, or the American silence.

On March 14, just as a final deal seemed to be in the works, Saudi Arabia led a GCC military force across the causeway at the king's invitation to assist the regime's beleaguered security forces. They quickly cleared the streets, rounding up protestors and ordinary citizens alike and unleashing a wide campaign of repression. The hypocrisy on display was hard for many Arab fans of the uprisings to swallow, even with the sectarian sweetener. But repeated constantly on the Gulf-based media, the sectarian propaganda eventually did seem to reshape popular views on Bahrain, which came to be written out of some of the dominant narratives of the uprisings.

Bahrain's discarded negotiations, extremely violent repression, regime-sponsored sectarianism, and reliance on external support previewed one template for the counterattack against the Arab uprising. Bahrain's place as a GCC member firmly within the Saudi defensive perimeter normalized the intervention. The sectarian narrative highlighting the Shi'a character of the protestors and blaming Iran for fundamentally domestic political problems resonated just enough to break the transnational identification uniting the uprisings across the region. Most GCC-based media, including al-Jazeera, either downplayed the events or actively promoted the regime's sectarian narrative. Saudi diplomatic muscle and the American interest in its naval base shielded Bahrain's regime from the most severe international repercussions.

Advocates of intervention against regimes in Libya, Syria, and for the regime in Bahrain struggled to show how their violence differed. In June, for instance, the leading Saudi editor, Tareq al-Homayed, used his column to denounce those who compared Syria to Bahrain as serving the Asad regime's agenda.[20] But his favorable comparisons of the Bahraini king's outreach to the opposition with Asad's military repression came at a time when thousands of Bahraini activists remained imprisoned and subject to torture, abuse, and sectarian repression. Iran may have been the real motivation for Saudi decisions, but the public discourse at this point emphasized instead the Libyan regime's rapid adoption of extreme violence. The indifference to repression in Bahrain tended to undermine this explanation.

The depth and sectarianism of the clampdown which followed was difficult to keep from public view after the 2012 publication of the Bahrain Independent Commission of Inquiry's painstakingly researched report documenting the abuses. Blocking popular mobilization came at a horrifying cost, one which could alienate a majority of the population for a generation and radically circumscribe the legitimate base of an already shaky regime. The unrepentant repression would place Bahrain's regime beyond the pale of international society for several years. But the monarchy would survive, and within a few short years international celebrities like Kim Kardashian and international conferences filled with policy worthies would return to Manama. Bahrain's monarchy had survived at great cost, at least for the time being.

| 3 |

INTERVENTION AND
MILITARIZATION

The international community reconciled itself rather easily to Bahrain's repression. This contrasts starkly with the remarkable international response to the violence unfolding nearly simultaneously in Libya. The contrast between the two crises is striking. The Arab media ignored the Bahrain crackdown while lavishing sensational coverage on Libya's rapidly escalating violence. Libya's rebellion was placed at the center of the Arab uprising narrative, while sectarianism was used effectively to write Bahrain out of it. The Arab League and the United Nations mobilized rapidly to respond to the Libya crisis while studiously ignoring Bahrain's. NATO intervened to protect the Libyan opposition from violent repression exactly as its Gulf coalition partners intervened to violently repress Bahrain's opposition. This starkly illustrates the difference between the protection offered to those within the Saudi-backed regional order and the intensification of the challenge to those outside of it.

Violence alone was not the difference between Libya and the others. Almost every Arab regime employed violence in some form against its challengers, and none could credibly claim innocence of a long history of repressive violence at home. Neither were any of the protests fully peaceful, even in the paradigmatic cases such as Egypt. It is true, and vitally important, that Egypt's military refrained from opening live fire on protestors. But its riot police struck hard against marchers using tear gas, water cannons, rubber bullets, and truncheons. Protesting crowds did not pick up automatic weapons, but they fought hard against the police, seizing public spaces by force and burning down police stations across the country. Violence marked key moments in Tahrir's eighteen days, most notably when regime-backed thugs injured hundreds of protestors in Tahrir Square on February 2 in the so-called Battle of the Camel.

Still, when Libya's uprising began on the eve of February 17, nonviolence was seen as a core element of the Arab uprising. Protestors in almost every country experiencing demonstrations ostentatiously emphasized their commitment to peaceful resistance ("silmiyya"). This nonviolent posture earned them moral support in the West and raised the costs to regimes of resorting to excessive force. It had been decisive to the outcomes in both Tunisia and Egypt that the military had publicly committed to not responding with deadly force. Many viewed this dual commitment to nonviolence as the key to the successful model of change which had just played out twice, and which many Arab activists and Western observers hoped would soon be replicated.

Libya's use of traditional military forces against peaceful protestors less than a week after Mubarak's departure stood out as the first of its kind. A similarly violent response even a few weeks later might not have attracted nearly as much attention. Qaddafi's rapid turn to violence followed directly and rationally from his reading of the events of the last few weeks. He had no intention of following Ben Ali and Mubarak into prison or exile because of a failure to use the military power at his disposal. At this point, he had little reason to believe he would pay a major price for military reprisals no matter how bloody. Had Qaddafi succeeded in putting down his challengers with indiscriminate force after Mubarak and Ben Ali's restraint had cost them their jobs, it would have offered a clear lesson to other dictators.

Libya received an exceptionally high level of media attention, mostly filtered through the narrative of a broader Arab uprising. Qaddafi's violent response might also not have mattered without this intensifying impact of social media and broadcast media coverage. Al-Jazeera from the start covered Libya's repression intensively, highlighting the brutality of the regime's response and placing it firmly within the narrative frame of an otherwise peaceful Arab uprising. Al-Jazeera's coverage relied heavily on user-generated videos and reporters embedded with rebel fighters. The "Arab uprising" social media ecosystem similarly embraced the Libyan cause. Western media largely adopted this Arab uprising framing of Libya as well.

Today, most of us have become numbed to scenes of intense brutality from the region. But in mid-February 2011, the scenes which unfolded on al-Jazeera and social media were almost unfathomably shocking and appalling. Flush with fresh memories of the deliriously happy crowds in Tunis and Cairo, Arabs and Americans alike struggled to comprehend the war footage which now filled their television screens and Twitter feeds. Many Arab activists argued, and I agreed, that a failure to respond to the state violence at that moment would have been fatal to the hopes for peaceful change in the Arab world. Qaddafi's profiting from his brutality would be a green light for all other despots to unleash their hounds and would likely lead to either the defeat or the militarization of the vibrant protest movements still very much in bloom. As it turned out, that hard lesson would be learned soon enough anyway.

In sharp contrast to Bahrain, Libya had no international patrons to shield it from criticism. Libya had long been an international pariah for its support of terrorism, internal repression, and highly idiosyncratic policies in the Middle East and Africa. In 2003, Qaddafi agreed to surrender his mostly moribund WMD programs and settled a lawsuit over its role in the 1983 Lockerbie bombing. It cooperated effectively with Western intelligence agencies against jihadist groups, while piloting a highly publicized effort to rehabilitate prisoners from the Libyan Islamic Fighting Group (LIFG). The promise of sanctions relief and oil sales opened Libya to foreign investors, delivering new financial resources and diplomatic opportunities to the regime without challenging its control. Qaddafi's son, Saif al-Islam, led an effort to cultivate a more favorable image in the West by reaching out to academics and journalists. In August 2009, Senator John McCain famously tweeted about meeting Qaddafi at his ranch, declaring it an "interesting meeting with an interesting man."[1]

But despite these efforts, Qaddafi's Libya had few real strategic friends. Arab regimes who viscerally opposed the broader uprising rapidly embraced Libya's uprising. Qaddafi had personally alienated both the Qatari emir and Saudi king in recent years with his grandstanding performances at Arab Summit meetings. He had allegedly even supported an attempted assassination attempt against King Abdullah. From the Saudi perspective, if the popular momentum could not be stopped, then there were few better places for its energies to be directed than at Libya.

Many of the activists and participants in the other Arab uprisings embraced the Libyan rebellion as one of their own. Qaddafi commanded little personal admiration, and his regime was generally seen as a particularly brutal version of the dictators being challenged elsewhere. People risking their lives to protest across the region were horrified by Qaddafi's violence, easily imagining themselves facing a similar fate. There was less consensus about the NATO intervention to come, however. While the Arab League and the Gulf media seemed to speak with one voice in favor of intervention, a strong undercurrent of opposition ran through certain sectors of the Arab public. Whatever their feelings about Qaddafi, many leftists and voices associated with the "resistance" trend were immediately suspicious of NATO's motives. Drawing on the potent memories of the invasion of Iraq, they warned of civilian casualties, Western occupation, and a grab for Libyan oil. This critical trend was largely discounted in the Western and Gulf media, which preferred to portray the intervention as responsive to a unanimously popular Arab demand. These divisions previewed the even more intense arguments to come over Syria.

While some activists were uncomfortable with the Libyans taking up arms and calling for intervention, the Gulf regimes were quite pleased to see a peaceful uprising devolve into a violent armed conflict. A peaceful mass mobilization for democratic reforms challenged autocratic regimes in novel and uncomfortable ways. Proxy wars did not. Regimes which struggled to respond to the peaceful demands of their citizens were well-equipped to channel money and guns to favored insurgent groups and to use their media empires to promote rebel causes.

There were other demonstration effects, which would be triggered by the Western intervention, though, and other agendas at play. The Qatar-driven, Arab League-legitimated NATO action in Libya established a precedent for future military interventions wrapped in humanitarian discourse. For the Gulf states, cooperation with the West in a military campaign in Libya helped to deflect any possibility, however slim, of opposition to their simultaneous military moves into Bahrain.[2] The military intervention in Libya opened the door to the proxy wars which would shape the fate of the Arab uprisings. This confluence shaped the expectations and behavior of threatened regimes, regional powers, and protest movements across the region—most notably in Syria, where Libya's model shaped the gradations of violence and diplomacy surrounding intervention.

THE LIBYAN UPRISING

Libya's uprising began very much like the others. Qaddafi's portrayal of his opponents as al-Qaeda inspired Islamists did not match the reality of a broadly based civil uprising. Courageous activists inspired by Tunisia and Egypt began to plan their own nonviolent protests using an already familiar mix of online and offline mobilizational tools. They selected February 17 as their revolutionary moment, and presented themselves as organically part of the broader Arab uprising which fit comfortably in the narrative of a regional revolutionary wave.

These protests changed to war almost immediately, without the long soul-searching and divisive argument which would soon consume the Syrian uprising. The early days of the war offered a bewildering but exhilarating spectacle of "do it yourself" armed rebellion. The Arab media's transition from the cheering crowds dancing in Tahrir Square to the war footage was jarring. Flush with the impossible victories over Ben Ali and

Mubarak, the mobilized Arab public had come to expect the once un-thinkable. Footage of rebels commandeering pickup trucks and carrying out lightning raids against Qaddafi's forces thrilled Libyans and foreign audiences alike. But those images were misleading. Qaddafi's military had an overwhelming power advantage, which it rapidly brought to bear against the rebellious regions. The early gains of the rebels were quickly erased, as Qaddafi's armor steadily advanced. By early March, his forces had pushed to the outskirts of Benghazi.

On February 22, Qaddafi warned that he would mow down protestors with tanks if needed. Such extremely hard-line rhetoric, aimed at a domes-tic audience, badly undermined his prospects abroad. Qaddafi's tone may have been intended to restore the fear and perceived inevitability upon which his regime had for decades depended. But such public commit-ments created their own reality. His forces would almost certainly have carried out at least some massacres had Benghazi fallen, if for no other reason than to punish the challengers and restore the broken barrier of fear. To an international community primed by memories of Rwanda and Srebrenica, and guided by a highly partisan Arab media, his words sig-naled impending doom. His apocalyptic language thus played into the hands of the Libyan opposition and their Arab backers. The extermina-tionist language helped them enormously in their campaign to win Amer-ican and ultimately United Nations and NATO military backing. The Obama administration blanched at the prospect of what one senior official vividly warned could quickly become "Srebrenica on steroids."[3]

The Arab push for intervention in Libya is one of the more remarkable moments in recent regional history. Since the founding of the Arab League, the regional order had been grounded in the principle of state sovereignty.[4] This did not prevent competitive interventions, obviously, as the history of the Arab cold war of the 1950s makes abundantly clear. But direct cross-border invasions or overt military interventions were exceed-ingly rare in Arab politics. Egypt's intervention in Yemen in the 1960s and Syria's very brief incursion into Jordan in 1970 were among the very rare exceptions to this rule prior to Saddam Hussein's shocking invasion of Kuwait in August 1990. His violation of that foundational norm of Arab politics was invoked repeatedly to mobilize Arab support for the coalition to liberate Kuwait and the war which followed. That norm weakened slightly in the following years, particularly with episodic Saudi campaigns against the Houthis in Yemen in the mid-2000s. But in general, the norm held. Indirect subversion remained the coin of the realm, while direct interventions remained infrequent and controversial.

The call for intervention in Libya violated another core norm governing Arab politics: opposition to Western intervention. While many Arab states had supported Operation Desert Storm in order to restore the Kuwaiti royal family to the throne, even this had been broadly unpopular with publics outside the Gulf. Arab hostility to Western military action and to the United States more broadly had spiked over the previous decade. Arabs loudly condemned America's 2003 occupation of Iraq, support for Israel's 2006 war with Lebanon and 2009 war on Gaza, and the War on Terror. The Arab League's invitation to NATO to intervene militarily against one of their own was thus revolutionary. So was the general (though, certainly not universal) Arab public embrace of that war. How could Qatar and the Arab League have gone from decades of near-universal denunciation of American intervention to a resounding public embrace of a NATO air campaign?

The common explanation for the invitation to NATO and the direct Arab military intervention was the extremity of Qaddafi's brutality towards his own people. But, as the Bahrain campaign amply attested, the Arab regimes were hardly in a position to complain of such things given their own fiercely repressive ways. Arab states had shown little concern over Saddam Hussein's late 1980s genocide against the Kurds or Hafez al-Asad's leveling of Hama in 1982. Every Arab regime maintained power through an extensive security apparatus which employed variable degrees of brutality against its own people. To be blunt, refraining from violence against one's own people was not and had never been a widely accepted norm governing Arab political order.

Qatar's voice was the loudest in the mobilization of the Arab League in support of intervention. It took the driving role behind the unusual GCC activism on Libya, framing it as an intervention in support of, rather than against the regional uprising. Al-Jazeera, like Qatar's official diplomatic rhetoric, emphasized its continuity with the other regional protests.[5] This fit well with the generally enthusiastic support for the uprisings from Qatar, uniquely among the Gulf states. More surprising, perhaps, is that the Libya intervention initially became a vehicle for GCC cooperation rather than competition. Qatar, the UAE, and Saudi Arabia were initially on the same side, mobilizing their distinctive resources against Qaddafi and in support of the rebels. This unity did not last. As in Yemen, Egypt, and Tunisia, they were competing with each other from the start for influence with power brokers in the anticipated new Libya. The competition for rebel proxies in Libya helped to ensure that its transition would fail, and it set the stage for even worse to come in Syria.

For most of the external players, the initial choice of proxies was mostly a question of availability and convenience. Both Qatar and the UAE relied heavily on the networks of expatriates who happened to be resident in their countries as political exiles or businessmen from previous years.[6] The Libyan journalist Mahmoud Shammam, who had happened to be involved with al-Jazeera and other Qatari media ventures in previous years, convinced Doha to support a pro-revolution television channel, which started to air almost immediately.[7] Arif Ali Nayid, a Sufi cleric and telecoms magnate, played a similar role in Abu Dhabi, serving as a key contact point for Mahmoud Jibril to develop a network for funding and arms shipments from the UAE to compete with Qatar's.[8] Meanwhile, Turkey worked primarily through the Libyan Muslim Brotherhood but also engaged with more radical figures associated with the Libyan Islamic Fighting Group.[9]

In Libya, as elsewhere in the region, the historical presence of important Brotherhood figures in Qatar created a ready-made network upon which to draw.[10] Muslim Brothers fleeing Nasserist repression in the 1950s and 1960s had played a crucial role in the construction of the Qatari state and educational system. The Muslim Brotherhood's Yusuf al-Qaradawi featured prominently on al-Jazeera's programming. It was not just Muslim Brothers, though. As Qatar rapidly expanded its diplomatic presence in the region during the 1990s and 2000s, it had positioned itself as a bridge between the competing camps and able to facilitate talks with anyone. Al-Jazeera played a useful role here, with invitations to appear on the station providing opportunities for Qatari officials to cultivate relationships with a wide range of political figures, intellectuals and activists. For instance, Ali Sallabi, Qatar's key point of entry into Libya, was an Islamist who had run Saif al-Islam al-Qaddafi's controversial deradicalization program and was friendly with al-Qaradawi.[11] His regular appearances on al-Jazeera made him familiar to Qatari diplomats, while allowing him a privileged place in shaping regional understanding of events in Libya.

Qatar and the Arab League mobilized both publicly and behind the scenes. The public face of the Gulf efforts came at the Arab League and the United Nations, and then the inclusion of its warplanes in the military coalition. On February 21, Ibrahim Dabashi, Libya's deputy ambassador to the UN, resigned to great publicity and accused the Qaddafi regime of planning to carry out genocide. With very little media presence on the ground, his call for a no-fly zone and warnings of impending massacre shaped the international media coverage of unfolding events. Al-Jazeera filled in this gap eagerly, sending its own camera crew (one of whom would be killed in mid-March) and mobilizing an innovative network of citizen journalists to upload videos. An al-Jazeera report based on a supposed eyewitness to helicopter gunships shooting protestors from the air had an especially large impact, though those claims later proved difficult to substantiate.[12]

The Libyan rebels urgently needed a political body to represent them abroad. Qatar again took the lead, sponsoring the creation of the National Transitional Council. The NTC had been formed on the fly in Benghazi on March 5, with Mustafa Abd al-Jalil named its president and the membership made to represent all of Libya's regions. Its leadership was dominated by a small group of Western-educated technocrats and early defectors, many of whom had been affiliated with Saif al-Islam Qaddafi's reform initiatives in the year 2000. Such personalities had earned some measure of trust from Western governments. The NTC was almost immediately recognized by the international community as the legitimate interlocutor for the military campaign and as the recipient of aid via the "Friends of Libya" coalition. Its main role at first was to work with the international community to muster financial and political support and to secure a reliable flow of weapons from abroad.

The speed and novelty of the international moves on Libya were frankly remarkable. The UN Security Council voted on February 26 to refer Libya to the International Criminal Court—only the second time it had ever done so, and the first unanimous referral of its type. The notoriously cautious ICC opened its investigation only five days later, and on May 16 issued arrest warrants for Qaddafi, his son Saif, and intelligence chief Abdullah Senussi for crimes against humanity. France recognized the NTC as the legitimate representative of the Libyan people on March 10, some two weeks after its creation. Qatar followed suit on March 28, with broader acquiescence from the rest of the GCC. The Arab League soon suspended Libya's membership. This shift in international recognition came incredibly rapidly given that Qaddafi's government continued to control more than half of the country.

The international response rapidly moved towards military intervention. On March 12, the Arab League called on the UN to impose a no-fly zone as Qaddafi's forces continued to advance, taking Ajdabia and moving rapidly towards Benghazi. On March 17, Saif al-Islam declared on radio that "in 48 hours, everything will be over." This was followed, fatefully, by Qaddafi's radio address declaring that the next day his forces would "cleanse the city of Benghazi . . . [W]e will track them down, and search for them, alley by alley, road by road." The declaration of genocidal intent could not have been more perfectly timed for the supporters of the rebels feverishly seeking a Security Council vote for intervention.

On March 17, the Security Council voted for Resolution 1973, authorizing "all necessary means" to protect Libyan civilians. Qaddafi halted his advance as he waited to see what precisely this meant, and announced his acceptance of a cease-fire. There is little reason to believe that there was a deal to be had at this point or that a cease-fire would have lasted more than a few days.[13]

On March 19, NATO began bombing. The initial air strikes had a powerful psychological effect on both regime and rebel forces. Benghazi celebrated rapturously, to the delight of Gulf and Western capitals eager for validation of their risky military venture. Many, perhaps, expected a rapid rebel victory to follow from the introduction of NATO forces into the conflict. But Qaddafi, predictably, did not fold. His forces quickly adapted to the threat of air strikes, moving away from easily targeted convoys and massed forces to a more dispersed deployment. This slowed the tempo of the battle, as regime forces sought to avoid NATO air strikes while rebels chafed against restrictive NATO rules of engagement.

Air power could only accomplish so much, beyond stabilizing front lines and supporting the available forces on the ground. The United States had made clear that it would only operate in a support role, and that no ground forces would be forthcoming.[14] The coalition forces rapidly ran low on obvious targets. They also, to Russia's open consternation, quickly expanded their interpretation of the UN mandate from defensive operations to prevent mass slaughter to support for offensive operations and, ultimately, regime change. In Misrata, NATO support involved "precision air power, combined with the presence of foreign ground advisors working alongside the city's defenders."[15] NATO targeting was tightly constrained by the UN mandate to protect civilians, leading to frequent clashes with and complaints from rebels who wanted more active and aggressive support for offensive operations. Obama, for his part, hawkishly watched for any hint of mission creep. But such restraint did not extend to the initial decision to expand the mission from civilian protection in Benghazi to support for the insurgency to topple Qaddafi by force.

Quite early on, Qatari, UAE and NATO special operations forces became actively involved, embedding in rebel units to provide training and to call in air strikes. The presence of British and French Special Forces in Benghazi and Misrata was an open secret, as were the planeloads of Qatari weapons arriving by early April.[16] These small numbers on the ground had an outsized impact. As Frederic Wehrey has explained in a comprehensive survey of the role of air power in the war, "[T]he presence of foreign ground advisors working with Libyan opposition forces had a transformative effect on air power. Libyan interlocutors described how, in the operations rooms of Misrata, Zintan, and Benghazi, these advisors built trust between Western forces and the opposition and—most importantly—coordinated air strikes." The NTC and rebel leaders routinely met with Qatari, UAE, British, French, and American senior military officials to plan strategy, coordinate public messaging, and solicit additional support. These military operations centers and joint operations rooms would become a standard operating procedure to coordinate indirect military support operations in Syria and the other coming limited interventions.

The decentralized and indirect nature of the intervention helped to bring about the proliferation of the militias, which would later come to plague the transition. Many of these militias were actually local defense forces, in cities such as Misrata, which became the primary vehicle for external support. Others came from wider political or ideological trends, whether Islamist, tribal, or ideologically affiliated. Connections to some outside source of weapons and funds was a vital currency for influence in this environment. Islamists affiliated with the Muslim Brotherhood or with the Libyan Islamic Fighting Group had considerable independent sources of funds and weapons from Qatar and elsewhere in the Gulf. Qatari and other Gulf-supplied weapons continued to pour in from Tunisia and through airlifts. Rebels frequently complained about the limitations of NATO bombing, inadequate supplies, and the other usual grievances.

As the NTC began to evolve from a coordinating body for the international community into a proto-government in waiting, the struggle for representation and its relationship with the armed militias took on ever greater significance. The external powers jockeyed to get their people into leadership positions, leading to debilitating internal politicking at a time of urgent military threat. The NTC's decision-making was typically opaque, given the primary focus on engaging international sponsors and the constant sense of crisis surrounding the revolution. The NTC's members, many of whom were honest and competent, commanded little local constituencies or support on the ground. More liberal-minded Libyans wondered about the democratic legitimacy of a self-appointed and Western-backed council, while every faction and region which considered itself underrepresented demanded a greater share of seats. Meanwhile, questions about the true loyalties of defectors and rumors of corruption circulated wildly through the unregulated new media.

Finances were key for the NTC's viability and legitimacy, and international players were central to this dimension. On March 29, with the support of the US and UK, Qatar took the lead in organizing oil sales for the NTC, facilitated a line of credit in order to ensure its solvency, and began direct cash transfers in late June. In June, Turkey stepped in, transferring $100 million in cash and a similar amount of humanitarian aid directly to the NTC. It was followed by cash transfers from Kuwait and Bahrain. Finally, on July 15, the US also recognized the NTC and allowed the release of some $400 million in frozen Libyan assets.

Weapons too were a vital currency. On March 22, in a meeting in Doha, Qatar agreed to supply the Libyans with a shipment of weapons. This commitment was made public on April 13 at the Contact Group meeting in Doha, and the next week shipments directly to Abd al-Fattah al-Younes, rebel military commander, from Doha began to arrive. In April, however, these arms shipments began to flow directly to Tubruq via Sallabi's Islamist networks, bypassing the NTC structures and infuriating Younes.[17] Qatar also worked through local Misrata networks, often flown directly to the front lines and directed towards individuals with Qatari personal connections. Jibril and Nayid, in turn, began to rely more heavily on direct weapons flows from the UAE. The same competition applied with joint operations centers and the coordination of the air war: Qatari forces embedded with key Islamist battalions, while Emirati advisers supported the efforts of General Abd el-Salam al-Hasi and then, later, Mahmud Jibril's faction.[18]

In July, this struggle threatened the survival of the rebellion itself. Younes, the commander of the rebel forces, had defected on February 22 and played a pivotal role in organizing the nascent rebel forces and carving out a physical base for the insurgency. On July 28, he was killed in highly mysterious circumstances, throwing the rebellion into sharp internal disarray. The NTC survived, in part due to the success of the move into Tripoli, but in the interim the entire executive board of the NTC was fired and a transitional road map was adopted setting out the conditions for the NTC to dissolve itself upon liberation.

Even as the war against Qaddafi raged, the militias associated with different external patrons were jockeying for position within the expected post-Qaddafi Libya. Once NATO entered the fray, Qaddafi's eventual defeat was almost universally expected. This reduced the urgency of cooperation among the rebel factions and increased the political stakes over seats on the National Transitional Council and control over access to weapons and other resources. This infighting, along with the resilience of the Qaddafi forces and the limitations on the mandate for NATO intervention, prolonged the conflict dangerously. NATO governments were keenly aware of the propaganda implications of civilian casualties, and by the summer faced growing political pressure either to escalate or end the war. The air war bogged down, and frustration set in. The longer bombing went on, the greater the risk of a spectacular civilian casualty event, which could fatally undermine international support for the mission.[19]

The August 20 move into Tripoli, which unseated the Qaddafi regime, temporarily masked these emergent issues. This operation had been meticulously planned and largely implemented with Qatari, British, and NATO support. Rebels captured the presidential palace to delirious enthusiasm. Photographs of rebels planting the Qatari flag were met with somewhat less acclaim, particularly since the Tripoli operation had preempted a rival plan for liberating Tripoli developed by the UAE and Mahmud Jibril in early July. Both of these competing plans relied upon NATO involvement, each hoped to block the success of the other, and both played out to some degree during the chaotic moment of liberation.[20] This would not be the last time that the Qatari-Emirati competition overshadowed decisive moments in Libya.

In the immediate aftermath of the seizure of Tripoli, the Qatari and UAE-backed networks were locked in an intense showdown over who would take control of Tripoli. Libyan leaders shuttled between Doha, Abu Dhabi, and NATO, while local forces met suspiciously on the ground. By September, tentative steps had been taken to establish state authority over the flows of military and financial aid, and to establish central political control. But external patronage loomed large. As General Khalifa Haftar complained, "If aid comes through the front door, we like Qatar. But if it comes through the window to certain people [and] bypassing official channels, we don't want Qatar."[21]

This would become a constant refrain as politics polarized and militias carved out autonomous roles in post-liberation Libya. The networks, foreign linkages, and channels of influence which had developed during the course of the war continued to shape the course of politics. The celebrations, which greeted the Qatari flag when Tripoli was taken, soon faded as attention turned to post-Qaddafi institutions and power. The distribution of power among the militias and within the ruling councils were an artifact of those linkages, not a naturally occurring reflection of power on the ground. Access to sources of weapons and funds constituted real power in the institutional void which followed Qaddafi's fall, and those with such access had little incentive to surrender it to the nascent state institutions.

The refusal to surrender arms by these forces was not purely a matter of self-interest or ambition. In the violent transitional period, the state was in no position to guarantee their survival or to credibly guarantee against the re-centralization of power or predatory rule. The importance of these wartime networks was compounded by the relatively light hand of international forces in the reconstruction phase. The US had quite wisely ruled out any American peacekeeping force, while allies such as Britain and France, who had been expected to play such a role, failed to do so. Above all, Libya's new leaders consistently rejected any international peacekeeping forces in the country. Their objections forced the United Nations to scale back even its limited August 2011 plan for several hundred armed military observers.[22]

This meant that it fell upon the victorious rebels and the external backers to build a new Libya from the aftermath of decades of Qaddafi and six months of war. The failure of the new transitional government to disarm or integrate the militias is now widely seen as the critical failure dooming the transition. In truth, it is difficult to see how they could have done so given the realities of power on the ground.[23] The revolutionary brigades had played as much of a role in overthrowing Qaddafi as had the new government. They were locally popular and heavily armed. In comparison, the Libyan state had only minimal armed forces and much more limited access to military support from abroad.

Many now argue that these problems might have been avoided had the United States been willing to deploy stabilization forces, either its own or from its coalition partners. Few supporters of the Libya intervention called at the time for such peacekeeping forces, primarily because they knew that it would have been a political kiss of death for the campaign. The retroactive advocacy for such a force often seems to be more a matter of finding an excuse for the intervention's failure which would not compromise future interventions. Even had it been possible, the idea that a stabilization force would have made the difference misses the many ways in which such an international military deployment could have gone wrong, without solving any of the deeper problems. An international force would have confronted the same array of heavily armed militias, forcing it to tread carefully. Its presence could have disincentivized rather than facilitated the creation of national security forces. It could easily have become a target for nationalist mobilization and Islamist attacks. And, once established as a vital guarantor of stability on the ground, it would have been virtually impossible to withdraw.

The limited postwar international presence responded to the political demands of the new Libyan leadership and aligned with the preferences of the Obama administration. As the former White House coordinator emphatically put it, "Libyans had to shape their own future."[24] But there was never a moment when Libyans had the option of shaping their own future free of foreign influence. The regional interventions which had shaped the entire structure of the postwar political arena would continue with devastating effect.

LIBYA'S IMPACT ON THE ARAB TRANSITIONS

Libya's course had direct and indirect effects on the region far beyond those originally anticipated. The intervention likely did, as promised, give a vital jolt of new energy to challengers in other Arab countries and give regimes pause as they considered the use of violence. NATO did get some credit for saving of Benghazi from its fate, although its actions would always be criticized as too little and too late. The positive effects did not last long, given the greater priority of urgent local considerations over calculations of possible international involvement, but they were clearly felt in the early stages.

When the initial expectation of rapid victory for Libya's rebels following the NATO intervention failed to materialize, the war consumed an enormous amount of Western attention through the end of the summer. Coordinating the international alliance, nurturing the nascent Libyan opposition, and running the war left less time for the complex political situations elsewhere in the region. The need to maintain the Gulf component of the Libya alliance bound Western hands when it came to other arenas such as Bahrain and Yemen. The sheer pace and diversity of simultaneous political crises overwhelmed the diplomatic agenda.

The war directly impacted its neighbors. Refugees pouring into Egypt, Algeria and Tunisia affected local economies in both positive and negative ways. The neighbors became key organizational and transit points for the evolving rebellion. Meanwhile, the fighting left Libya awash in weaponry, great quantities of which would ultimately find a way into not only its neighbors but also into more distant conflict zones such as the Sinai and Syria.

Libya was not the only regional playing field emerging over the summer of 2011. The key transitional cases of Tunisia, Egypt, and Yemen all involved significant and growing regional effects and interventions which shaped their transitional path—usually for the worse.

Tunisia

Tunisia, the first and most hopeful of the transitions, enjoyed tremendous international goodwill. The new government was keenly aware that its legitimacy would depend on an improvement in the country's grim economic conditions, and desperately needed economic assistance to consolidate a transition towards democracy. They received generous promises of support from the international community, including significant new flows of foreign aid and expert assistance in constitutional design.

Regional powers rarely put Tunisia at the top of their list of priorities, however. When they did, the aid was rarely neutral. The Gulf states and Turkey invested in building up the capabilities of local allies.[25] Foreign funding became a potent political issue as the transition unfolded. Most attention and public ire was directed towards perceived Qatari and Turkish funding for Ennahda. The leftist and secular forces looked in turn to the United Arab Emirates for support. This external support came with political strings, which would fuel the polarization which brought Tunisia to the brink of failure in 2013.

Tunisia's political drama unfolded in the context of both transnational demonstration effects and the direct involvement of regional rival powers. External players tried to intervene in multiple ways, while regional demonstration effects—especially from Egypt—profoundly affected the pace and nature of change. This polarization had yet to set in when the first post-revolutionary elections were held on October 23, however. Ennahda won a commanding victory, taking 37 percent of the vote and eighty-nine seats in the Constituent Assembly—nearly three times as many as its closest competitor.

Ennahda's success is more surprising than the usual narrative of Islamist advantages would have predicted. For all of its deep local roots, decades of repression had decimated its organizational structure and membership. Those leaders who had escaped prison had lived abroad for many years. Unlike Egypt's massive Islamist social sector upon which Muslim Brothers and Salafis could draw, Ennahda had to begin from scratch. Ennahda had begun to reconstitute itself even as Ben Ali fled the country, but it started from a very thin institutional base. For that, it needed to raise significant funds. Ghannouchi's regional and international renown was a major asset in the efforts to rebuild, but also a source of local controversy. While he jealously guarded Tunisia's independence and retained full autonomy from the broader Muslim Brotherhood movement, Ghannouchi drew upon the resources which that network could offer. He regular appearances on al-Jazeera kept him in close contact with Qatar and magnified his regional profile. He also enjoyed considerable credibility with the West, where his political savvy, inclusiveness, and moderate discourse contrasted favorably with the Muslim Brothers in Egypt.

Ennahda consistently played a long game. Rather than press an advantage such as its initial electoral victory, Ennahda sought to build a broader consensus. It nominated the secular leftist human rights activist Moncef Marzouki as president and governed through a three-party coalition (known as the Troika). This strategy helped to win broader legitimacy for the new government and to avoid the conflicts which would follow other transitional elections. This coalition did little to mollify the partisans of the regional wars, however. Marzouki was no Islamist, but like Ennahda, enjoyed close relations with Qatar. The replacement of the staunchly pro-Saudi Ben Ali with Ennahda and Marzouki was viewed as a regional victory for Qatar.

Nedaa Tounis crystallized in 2012 around an anti-Islamist message, which closely mirrored the UAE's regional campaign against Egypt's Muslim Brotherhood.[26] This anti-Islamist message had deep roots in a country where Ben Ali had presided for decades over an aggressively secularizing state and a comprehensive crackdown on Ennahda. Nedaa Tounis's unwieldy coalition was united only by a fear of Islamists and ample financial resources uniting old regime stalwarts, big business, and frightened secularists.

Tunisia, while far from the center of regional politics, could not escape the new Arab competition. Qatar put its weight behind Ennahda, while Nedaa Tounis enjoyed support from the UAE and Saudi Arabia. The restoration of the old elites favored by Saudi Arabia aligned well with the UAE's anti-Islamist campaign, while both hoped to reverse a Qatari advantage. This competition would manifest in the intense polarization which would soon grip Tunis, inflamed by sensationalist regional media coverage and by widely rumored external support to the rival trends. Tunisian politicians looked to Gulf patrons for support, while those regional powers sought to impose their regional gamesmanship on the unfolding transition.

Egypt

Egypt was as central to the Arab regional order as Tunisia had been marginal. In the latter days of Hosni Mubarak, Egypt may have been a declining, even decrepit, power. It had nonetheless remained a major regional power player and a core member of the Saudi-led regional axis. Israel enjoyed close relations with Mubarak, counting upon Cairo to police the Sinai, maintain the blockade of Gaza, and manage intra-Palestinian politics. Egypt's revolution changed it from a potent contender for regional leadership into a prize in the regional power struggle. This was quite a comedown for a huge, nationalistic country which viewed itself as the center of Arab politics. It would have been difficult before 2011 to imagine Egypt as another Yemen or a Libya, unable to prevent or contest foreign intrusions.

The revolution was not primarily about regional power politics, but it could not escape them. The overthrow of Mubarak and the rise of the Muslim Brotherhood gave Qatar an unprecedented opportunity to incorporate Egypt into its regional coalition at the expense of Saudi Arabia and the UAE. Successfully consolidating such a realignment would fundamentally change the regional balance of power. Qatar positioned itself via al-Jazeera as the champion of not just the Muslim Brotherhood but also of Tahrir itself. It saw potential power flowing through elections or through street protests, either of which could counter the still formidable power of the military and the massive Egyptian state. It cultivated a discourse of democracy and human rights, which appealed to Washington while also standing to benefit its primary ally on the streets, the Muslim Brotherhood.

Saudi Arabia and its allies were shaken by Mubarak's fall not only because they feared the further diffusion of revolutionary sentiment around the region, but also because of the implications of Egypt's realignment towards Qatar. They saw Egypt not only as their "strategic depth" against Iran, but also as an integral part of the regional order. They had powerful local allies in Egypt, even if the revolution had harmed their position temporarily. Mubarak and spy chief Omar Suleiman could be replaced. More worrisome in the longer term was the potential defenestration of their Egyptian networks, whether through corruption prosecutions of wealthy businessmen with intimate Gulf connections or the possibility of a long-term ban on political participation by the "feloul" (the Egyptian term for the remnants of the old regime) in the name of transitional justice. The Muslim Brotherhood's ascendance threatened the primacy of those networks more than it did the creation of an Islamic State.

The revolution rather remarkably did not change the direction of Egypt's foreign policy. Saudi Arabia, the UAE, and Israel could take comfort in the continued leading role of the SCAF and the sheer obstinacy of Egypt's massive state institutions. The SCAF-led transitional process carefully protected the privileges and the power of the military. Indeed, the removal of the neoliberal economic reformers surrounding Gamal Mubarak opened the door for a dramatic increase in the military's share of the economy.[27] The SCAF was the firewall not only against revolution but also against Qatar. It would prove a shaky one, however. Faced with continuing protests, Muslim Brotherhood mobilization, and pressure from the West, the SCAF struggled to restore uncontested military rule or to endlessly defer democratic elections.

The opening bids in the immediate transitional environment focused on defining the new rules of the game. The first big test of the relative power of the post-transitional forces came with the hastily crafted constitutional referendum scheduled for March 19, 2011—a few days after the GCC intervention into Bahrain, and the same day that NATO jets began bombing Libya and the Yemeni army divided. The referendum patched relatively limited, but fundamental, amendments on to the existing constitution. It laid out a road map towards parliamentary and presidential elections and the drafting of a new constitution, while preserving the military's leading role during the transitional period. The road map satisfied the core interests of most of the key players. It kept the SCAF in charge, reassuring Israel, Saudi Arabia, and the UAE. But it also promised public freedoms and relatively rapid elections, which satisfied the Muslim Brotherhood and some Egyptian liberals, along with the United States and Qatar.

Many activists immediately sensed a trap, though, assuming that the military could not be trusted to oversee a transition to meaningful democracy. With Tahrir emptied and the primary demand of the revolution achieved, they found it difficult to either influence mass public opinion or to exercise power over the course of the transition. Activists calling for a boycott or negative vote failed to resonate amidst confusion over the messaging and internal disagreements. The referendum may have been intended to appease the revolutionary impulse while maintaining the core of the status quo, as in Morocco and Jordan. But such partial measures would prove much more difficult in the turbulent Egyptian space, with a political public expecting far more radical change, the old regime in far more disarray and real power still up for grabs.

The referendum passed handily with massive turnout. This established temporary rules of the game. Those rules did not command universal consent, though, which would lead to endless problems in the months to come. Activists continued to challenge the consolidating status quo through street protests. The military worked ever more aggressively to clear the streets and establish a new political order which would guarantee their perpetual domination. The judiciary enforced the laws unevenly, with frequent unpredictable reversals and nakedly politicized verdicts undermining confidence in the courts.[28] The Muslim Brotherhood, famous for its patient long game, now pushed impatiently for rapid elections and scorned the kinds of reassurances being offered by its Tunisian counterparts. This would prove to be a fatal mistake. The revolutionary coalition forged in Tahrir Square fragmented almost completely, producing the deep mutual contempt and mistrust which would consume the coming years.

Street politics took very different forms during the transition compared with the struggle against Mubarak's authoritarian regime. Protests which served to destabilize a dictatorship also complicated efforts to conslidate a new regime. With the SCAF in charge throughout 2011, street protests could keep up pressure against autocratic backsliding and prevent the military from growing too comfortable in power. But not everyone agreed with this continued mobilization. With frequent occupation by groups of activists, Tahrir degenerated from a unifying symbol to a divisive test of strength. Activist demonstrations shrank in size and struggled to maintain a political focus, while security forces exercised ever greater repressive force against them. In late July, Islamists including the Muslim Brothers and

Salafis took to Tahrir Square to signal their own strength and claim their own stake in the symbolic space. Their massive day of demonstrations drove away the activists who had attempted to re-occupy Tahrir and sent a powerful message that Islamists too could mobilize the street.

Protests grew increasingly anarchic and violent. In October, dozens of protestors were killed in an extraordinarily violent attack by security forces and local toughs on Christian protestors outside the Maspero media complex. On the eve of the first round of the parliamentary election, a series of seemingly senseless protests on Mohamed Mahmoud Street off of Tahrir Square turned bitterly violent. Ironically, the clashes mattered far more on the international front than on the domestic. The SCAF felt little reason to make concessions to what it viewed as a ragtag group of protestors who had already been effectively marginalized in the days following Tahrir. The Muslim Brotherhood feared that the protests and violence would offer a pretext for postponing—perhaps indefinitely—the parliamentary elections which they were poised to win.

But Washington cared. Horrified by the excessive violence deployed by the military and police against the protestors, the Obama administration put enormous pressure on the SCAF to accelerate its timeline for a transition of executive power. The scenes of violent unrest in central Cairo unfolded at just the time when Syria was rapidly degenerating into violence, and violence against protestors had justified intervening in Libya.

Scenes of the American-funded Egyptian military viciously attacking crowds of peaceful protestors infuriated the White House. How could the United States credibly push for new regional standards of legitimacy based on nonviolence in Libya or Syria when its chief ally behaved like this with impunity?[29] The SCAF eventually gave in to this international pressure by setting a date for presidential elections and the transfer of power—avoiding what many feared at the time could have easily slid into perpetual military rule and endlessly deferred elections. It is telling that this pressure largely came from the outside, not from domestic forces. The successful efforts to push the SCAF to scale back its violence against protestors, proceed with parliamentary elections, and set a date for presidential elections is one of the few clear victories for American diplomacy in Egypt in the post-Tahrir period.

The timing and nature of elections was a major source of controversy throughout the transition. The United States viewed elections as a critical step towards a real transition to democracy and vital for preventing the reconsolidation of military rule. An electoral delay seemed to many in the West, and to the Muslim Brotherhood, like a recipe for the endless postponement of democracy.

Opponents of early elections offered multiple arguments. Many activists rejected the idea of holding elections at this early stage, viewing it as little more than window dressing for sustaining the authoritarian power structures which January 25 had set out to shatter. They lambasted the Muslim Brotherhood, which eagerly supported the elections, for abandoning the revolution. Many were more worried about their likely defeat in elections than about the principle. Faced with the Muslim Brotherhood's extensive organizational network and considerable financial resources with which to mobilize votes, they argued for postponing elections long enough to give new political forces the time to organize in order to compete with the Brotherhood. Perhaps the best argument came from opposition leader Mohammed el-Baradei, who argued for first drafting a new constitution. It is impossible to know whether such a sequence would have allowed Egypt to avoid the cataclysmic battles over the constitution in late 2012.

The activists associated with Tahrir Square faced a particular quandary. Beset by constant media campaigns accusing them of being American-funded agents, they could ill afford to accept—much less seek—support from Western sources. Their caution would not protect them, as regime-affiliated media personalities would later air provocatively edited snippets of phone conversations insinuating such relationships. For all their ability to occasionally mobilize large numbers of Egyptians into the streets around specific grievances, the activists lacked institutionalized channels for raising money, setting up political offices, or mobilizing voters.

In the end, the elections went on as scheduled. The Muslim Brotherhood won 45 percent of the seats in these parliamentary elections, a stunning victory which cemented their leading position in the political arena and Qatar's rising place in the regional order. The election also introduced a different kind of competition for the Brotherhood: the Salafi party Hizb al-Nour, which won 25 percent of the vote. The remnants of the old National Democratic Party fared extremely poorly. Some non-Islamist parties, such as Naguib Sawiris's Free Egyptian Party, did reasonably well but remained in a precarious minority. Prepared to do battle with the secular opposition, the Brotherhood now needed to triangulate against a new Islamist force—even as real power remained in the hands of the SCAF. Presidential elections slated for the coming summer would be the proving ground for that test of power.

Yemen

Yemen's uprising had resulted in a more carefully managed transition than did Tunisia's or Egypt's. Saudi Arabia and the United States carefully stage-managed the move from Saleh to his vice president, Abd Rabbo Mansour al-Hadi. This was not a transition towards democracy, but rather an attempt to preserve and renew a regime under great pressure. Yemen's state, never strong, weakened precipitously as the protests mounted and external actors naturally moved in to fill the void. Some of their involvement was focused on influencing the composition of the new Yemeni state, while more focused on cultivating clients and influence at the local level with an eye towards a decentralized future.[30]

The Gulf Cooperation Council formally took the lead in managing this transition, though in practice Saudi Arabia closely held the reins. The "Friends of Yemen" grouping, including the US and the UK alongside the Gulf states, was a principal conduit for formal international economic assistance. Originally formed in 2009 as part of a broader initiative to strengthen the Yemeni state against the al-Qaeda threat, its efforts were now intended to stem the collapse of the Yemeni economy and to build the legitimacy of the Hadi government. But there were many other flows of resources coming in to Yemen's largely ungoverned territory.

The "Yemen model" was put forward as a way to respond to popular demands for change without succumbing to the dangers of state failure and anarchy. Less openly spoken, but equally apparent, was that this approach guaranteed political continuity and the ongoing protection of core Saudi and American interests. The Yemeni transition promised some degree of reform and laid out extensive plans for inclusion, but was never in any sense meant to be democratic. Vice President Hadi ran in February 2012 as the only candidate in a presidential referendum, removing any uncertainty from the outcome. Elections served as a marker of "legitimacy" and a box to be checked for the benefit of the international community, but there was no intention of actually putting questions of national power to a real vote.

The potential flaws in this approach were widely noted at the time. The transition plan removed Saleh, albeit with the highly problematic immunity agreement, but failed to address any of the underlying issues which had driven the 2011 revolt. Saleh himself continued to play a political role from the sidelines, just as the activists critical of the GCC agreement had feared. He clung to his position as head of the GPC and maintained an extensive network of connections throughout the bureaucracy, tribes, and the military.[31] His relationship with Saudi Arabia became a pivotal question for the future of the Yemeni transition. While most Yemenis assumed that he continued to be a key Saudi ally, as he had been for nearly thirty years, the Saudi regime appeared to be growing quietly agitated by his refusal to abide by their carefully negotiated agreement for his departure. With Riyadh's prestige very much staked upon the success of Hadi's new government, Saleh's machinations increasingly came to seem a threat. Their break would become a defining problem for Yemen in 2014 when Saleh realigned with the Houthis to try to overthrow the new Saudi favorite.

It took Hadi time to consolidate his authority against the remnants of Saleh's entrenched regime. He only established his control over the military in April 2012, when Saleh's half-brother Mohammed Saleh al-Ahmar finally stepped down after a nearly three-week standoff. In December, he dissolved the Republican Guards, commanded by Saleh's son Ahmed Ali Saleh, and removed Saleh's nephew from his position at the top of the well-funded anti-terrorism forces. Those moves, along with a number of other moves to replace Saleh allies, at least gave Hadi a stronger position within the governing institutions. The long struggle to wrest control over the military leadership from Saleh may have been a dangerous distraction, however. Security across the country became ever more precarious during this time period, with escalating clashes between local actors and the army alongside a pervasive sense of deteriorating public safety and insecurity.

The National Dialogue launched in March 2013 was the primary vehicle for beginning to deal with divisive issues such as federalism, regional differences, corruption, and inequality. Intense negotiations over the list of participants unfolded over the winter of 2012-13, with several high-profile figures dropping out in protest over the agenda. Activists were particularly troubled by the low level of representation for youth and the absence of serious human rights and accountability provisions on the agenda.[32] Revolutionary groups warned that the Dialogue's focus on elite politics would only reinforce the dysfunction which had long marred Yemeni politics—and that rushing towards decisions based on the prevailing discourse of a failing state, impending violence, and national emergency would only succeed in replicating Saleh's centralizing, violent ways.[33]

How to manage the relationship between the central government and the provinces emerged as a central issue in these efforts to craft a new Yemeni political accord. Southern separatism had been a simmering national issue for many years, especially since the 2007 launch of the Hirak movement. Hirak had advocated for a broad range of southern issues, earning fierce military reprisals from Saleh's central government. Its failure to achieve progress on its many distributional and representational grievances, along with the violence suffered at Saleh's hands, drove the Hirak towards overt secessionism. The 2011 uprising and the National Dialogue created unprecedented opportunities to press their case in Sanaa and to carve out greater autonomy in the absence of strong, central authority.

Jihadist Sunni groups also posed an ongoing threat to the Yemeni transition. Al-Qaeda in the Arabian Peninsula enjoyed unique status in the configuration of al-Qaeda affiliates. Unlike most of the traditional franchises, AQAP tried repeatedly to establish effective local governance and to work constructively with local tribes and family structures. It also earned the particular attention of the United States and Saudi Arabia with several high-profile terrorist operations, including the attempted assassination of Saudi counterterrorism chief Prince Mohammed bin Nayef and the failed "underwear bomber" attempt to blow up an American airliner on Christmas. The presence of the popular English-language preacher Anwar al-Awlaki was deemed especially threatening, given his presumed ability to radicalize American Muslims into carrying out terrorist plots. As a result, the US waged a steady campaign of drone strikes against AQAP leadership and other targets, with the opportunistic cooperation of the Saleh government.

In the north, the Ansar Allah movement of the Houthis had been challenging Saleh and the central state for a decade. The Houthis had fought and won a short war with Saudi Arabia in 2009 and fought a nearly continuous armed conflict with Saleh's forces from 2004 until his fall in 2011. Then-President Saleh and the Saudis lost no opportunity to present the Houthis as simple Iranian proxies. Almost all independent Yemen experts and, crucially, the United States Embassy, rejected this description, however. Qatar had taken advantage of this endemic conflict to step in as a "neutral" mediator between the Houthis and Saleh, in one of its emblematic initiatives of its "mediation" decade. The Houthis had always been a regional, not a national, actor, but in 2011 they threw in with the Change Square protests and became an important new player in the politics of the transition.

Finally, there was the Islah movement, the Muslim Brotherhood-aligned Islamist grouping which had been at the center of the Change Square uprising. Islah's place in the regional Islamist networks facilitated regular contact with Qatar, and, as in other arenas, pride of place in al-Jazeera's influential media framing. Islah, like most Yemeni movements, had long maintained decent relations with Saudi Arabia but soon found itself caught up in the regional polarization surrounding the Muslim Brotherhood. Islah was only one of several important Islamist movements across Yemen, including a variety of Salafi trends with varying links to Saudi Arabia and, of course, the dangerously resilient al-Qaeda in the Arabian Peninsula.[34]

By the fall of 2012, a prevailing sense of insecurity and frustration colored the Yemeni transition. Hadi took every opportunity to use the violence as an argument for more international support, warning that his failure would spark a civil war, which could make Yemen worse than Somalia or Afghanistan. But the problems did not reflect especially well on his leadership. Hadi's elevation to power had not created a new Yemeni political consensus, triggered an economic revival, provided security, or allowed refugees and the displaced to come home. A series of armed clashes and terrorist attacks over the course of the year fueled this instability, highlighting Hadi's ineffectiveness and the ongoing pathologies of the state.[35] For months, Hadi was unable to work in his own office because of serious security concerns. The motives behind this violence were never completely clear in Yemen's highly localized and externally penetrated theater. Was a raid on an army checkpoint a sign of local discontent, a gambit in a local gang turf war, a sign of jihadist incursions, or a move by Saleh or some other politician to foment instability in an attempt to undermine confidence in political rivals? State incapacity only invited further interventions by the many external powers with a stake in the outcome, while the youth activists and popular coalitions which had made the initial revolution drifted further from the nascent political order.

THE LAST HOPEFUL DAYS

Despite the new conventional wisdom that the Arab uprisings were always doomed to fail, in fact after the first year most Arab transitional countries were still on track towards reasonably democratic outcomes. Elections for new legislative bodies had been successfully held in Tunisia and Egypt and were soon scheduled for Libya. Yemen, under the GCC transition plan, had a presidential election scheduled. Morocco, too, held parliamentary elections in November and allowed the victorious Islamist Party of Justice and Democracy to form a government.

All of these transitional processes were tenuous and rife with well-documented problems. Nobody had any illlusions that consolidating democracies would be easy. Most analysts obsessively noted the dangers to a democratic transition posed by a security vaccuum, continuing economic frustration, political polarization, and external meddling. One year in, though, it still seemed possible—and even likely—that revolutionary enthusiasm and international support would keep the transitions on track. Neighborhood effects seemed especially promising in North Africa, with mutually reinforcing progress by Egypt, Libya, and Tunisia creating the tantalizing prospect of a mostly democratic North Africa.

From the perspective of regional power struggles, however, it was less important that democracy was surviving than that Qatar was winning. Qatari allies had won every election thus far, winning commanding pluralities in Egypt, Tunisia, and Morocco. Qatari proxies were well represented in the Libyan National Transitional Council and in the recently formed Syrian National Council. For Saudi Arabia and the United Arab Emirates, this could not be allowed to stand.

| 4 |

SYRIA'S UPRISING

Syria's spectacular descent into disaster can make it seem like a completely unique case. But it was in fact fully embedded within the broader Arab uprising, shaped by the same forces and revealing the same regional pathologies. Syria's protestors were inspired by Egypt's and Tunisia's. The course of events was clearly shaped by the Libyan war and by competitive interventions by regional powers. As uniquely horrifying as its civil war has since become, it would make no sense to treat Syria as something uniquely outside the rest of the regional narrative.

Syria occupied a unique place in the Arab order. Prior to the uprising, Syria was Iran's only Arab state ally and the core of the "Resistance Bloc." A serious challenge to Asad would tilt the regional balance of power against Iran more than almost any other conceivable development. Syria's courageous activists would find it difficult to escape the implications of that regional reality. Asad's and Iran's adversaries would use every instrument at their disposal to intensify and accelerate the Syrian uprising. They would fuel its evolution into an insurgency, to disastrous effect. And, in turn, Iran would do everything in its power to ensure that Asad did not fall. As a result, Syria became the uprising most thoroughly consumed by the region's new war.

Syria's relations with the Arab order had ebbed and flowed over the years. Hafez al-Asad had portrayed Syria as a bastion of Arab nationalism and a core of the resistance to Israel. In 1990, Syrian forces had occupied Lebanon as part of a Saudi-brokered initiative to finally end the eight-year-long civil war. But Syria also maintained an enduring alignment with Iran. In 1980, it had been one of the very few Arab states to align with revolutionary Iran against Saddam Hussein's Iraq. It connected Iran with Lebanon's Hezbollah, the most important of Iran's regional allies. As the region polarized along sectarian lines in the 2000s and Iran replaced Israel as the primary concern of the Gulf regimes, Syria's alliance with Iran shifted from an asset to a profound problem.

This shift in the regional order had led to concerted regional moves against Bashar al-Asad. Following the 2005 assassination of former Lebanese Prime Minister Rafik Hariri, Saudi Arabia supported the March 14 coalition, which forced the withdrawal of Syrian troops from Lebanon and pushed for the formation of the Special Tribunal for Lebanon in order to tighten the pressure on the Syrian President. The United States fiercely resented Syria's facilitation of the flow of arms and fighters into the Iraqi Sunni insurgency. In 2007, Israel had quietly bombed an alleged Syrian nuclear weapons program.[1]

Damascus presented itself as the center of Arab resistance to Israel and to American hegemony in the region. This was a popular position at a time of intense popular anti-Americanism and an unsettling one to the many regimes which remained closely aligned with the United States. Syria's regional politics afforded it significant popular sympathy around the region, despite the concerted efforts to isolate and pressure Asad's regime. No single change could have a greater impact on the Iranian-Saudi cold war than breaking the Syrian-Iranian alliance. In the years preceding the Arab uprising, multiple Arab powers had sought to entice Asad away from Iran. Saudi Arabia had rebuilt its relations with Damascus after the intense competition in the middle of the decade. Turkey and Qatar were both investing heavily in the Syrian economy, while both the Qatari emir and the Turkish prime minister cultivated strong personal relationships with Asad. The Obama administration explored avenues of cooperation in Iraq, testing Syria's ability and willingness to clamp down on the Sunni insurgency, while several leading members of Congress met with Asad to discuss relations.

On the eve of the uprising, Syria's entry into the regional order seemed to be very much in play. Within months, however, the same leaders who had been so keen to work with Asad would be leading the international effort to force him from office.

This does not mean that the Syrian uprising was the creation of opportunistic foreign powers, as claimed by Asad and his supporters. Outside powers took advantage of the uprising, supported and magnified its efforts, and drove it towards militarization. But they did not create a very real protest movement driven by precisely the same motivations and aspirations found elsewhere in the region.

Syrians would not have protested without the example of the Arab uprisings. They had suffered political repression, police abuse, and economic stagnation for generations with little organized protest. A decade earlier, a tentative political opening had been easily snuffed out as soon as it seemed to pose a threat to the regime. Little popular mobilization had accompanied the massive pressure on the Asad regime in the years following the 2005 assassination of Rafik Hariri, even as massive protests in nearby Beirut drove occupying Syrian forces from Lebanon after fifteen years. It was the regional example of the Arab uprisings and the Libya intervention, not preexisting conditions, which changed the calculus for many Syrians, who suddenly saw the prospect of success, which had never previously been within the realm of imagination.

THE UPRISING

The initial uprising involved almost unbelievably heroic popular participation in the face of extreme state violence and decades of lessons that protest would bring down certain harsh reprisals. Syrians too watched the unfolding Arab uprisings and dreamed that they could somehow do the same. The early Syrian protestors took unfathomable risks. The early experience of the Syrian protest movement resembles that of many other countries around the region. Inspired by the example of Tunisia and Egypt and replete with manifold local grievances, small numbers of young, cosmopolitan activists attempted to emulate the nascent protest models.[2] They tried to organize flash protests in Damascus and upload footage to YouTube, to coordinate via mosques, and to place Syrian activism into the broader regional wave. The protests had little initial success, however, in large part due to the Syrian regime's extreme repression and pervasive security apparatus.

Initially, few internal or external players believed that Asad would be seriously challenged. As the violence and size of the protests mounted, the calculations began to change. Syria began to seem like a target of opportunity for some, and an impending humanitarian catastrophe to others. Asad clearly believed that his regime's resistance credibility would shield his regime from the Arab uprisings.[3] While Asad projected confidence, his regime clearly recognized the potential threat.[4] Hamas's Khaled Meshal warned an overconfident Asad as early as February 2011 that "Syria won't be spared by the Arab Spring."[5] For all Asad's outward bluster, a regime determined to hold on to power above all else hardly needed to be warned.

Asad's methods did not at first fundamentally differ from those employed by other Arab regimes. Asad adopted a mixed strategy, involving both offers of token political reform and selectively inflicted violence.[6] He did not have the resources to throw money at discontented citizens as in the Gulf states, but he could and did experiment with Jordanian and Moroccan-style preemptive reforms. His political reforms went considerably further than anything offered by Mubarak or Ben Ali, comparing in their substance and timing to the effective divide and rule gambit of Morocco's King Mohammed VI and Jordan's King Abdullah. In the early stages of the uprising, Asad revised the constitution, released political prisoners, and ended the nearly fifty-year-old state of emergency. On February 27, 2012, Asad revised the Syrian constitution, and in May held new parliamentary elections.

Those political reforms were difficult to take seriously, however, when accompanied by a far more brutal exercise of state violence than in the other countries. Syrian state violence included not only attacks on protestors but also an expansion of arrests, torture, surveillance, and personal intimidation.[7] The violence was modulated in line with the lessons of other regional cases. The Egyptian or Tunisian policy of restraint seemed an obvious failure, as did Qaddafi's cavalier use of regular military forces which had invited the intervention. Syrian security forces cracked down hard on any manifestation of protest, infiltrating potential protest sites such as mosques and public squares. The always pervasive surveillance intensified, with suspected activists arrested, beaten, and tortured and potentially subversive gatherings broken up by force. Most other Arab security services were doing the same around this time. Asad's violence was tailored to remain below the international threshold of attention, with deaths in those early days measuring in the tens rather than the thousands. Often, the violence was inflicted by the "shabiha," gangs of plainclothes thugs, who offered plausible deniability for the state.

Protests remained relatively small and scattered compared to other Arab countries for the first two months. This changed in March, at almost exactly the same time as GCC troops rolled into Bahrain, Yemen's protest camps dissolved into armed violence, and NATO jets began bombing Libya. The initial spark was the atrocities committed by a local abusive police chief in Deraa. His treatment of a young child arrested for scrawling anti-Bashar graffiti became an iconic symbol for the uprising to follow. Crowds which gathered to protest were repressed violently. The wanton killing of peaceful protestors had a galvanizing effect. Syrians offer a strikingly consistent narrative about the inspirational power of these early abuses and the indiscriminate nature of the subsequent crackdown.[8]

The regime's violence against mounting protests set in motion a cycle of escalation, which rapidly snowballed to other regions and cities within Syria. Asad's careful calibration began to break down as the protests escalated. The Libyan precedent of international intervention to prevent extreme state violence against protestors clearly affected at least some Syrian opposition calculations.

Online activism and citizen journalism played a crucial role in framing perceptions of this violence. Social media activism took on a very different character than it had in Egypt or Yemen.[9] With very few journalists on the ground to provide independent verification, videos captured on mobile phones were uploaded or physically moved out of the country through networks of activists who actively curated their contents to support the rebellion. These activist campaigns played out across heavily trafficked Facebook, YouTube, and Twitter pages. They were tightly integrated with Arab television networks such as al-Jazeera and al-Arabiya, which regularly aired footage either taken from activist social media accounts or directly uploaded by those activists to dedicated sites. Western media relied heavily for information and sources upon activists they came to trust, thus acting as megaphones for one side of a complex war.

Overlapping networks of activists and state sponsors joined this effort. Muslim Brotherhood activists, riding high from the events in Egypt and enjoying considerable support from Qatar, played a major though little recognized role in generating publicity for these protests.[10] They did this through a growing network of online activists, which connected out into al-Jazeera's network in innovative ways. As early as the end of March 2011, the Doha-based Brotherhood figure Yusuf al-Qaradawi was using his multimedia platforms to condemn Asad's repression.[11] The Brotherhood, which had never recovered inside of Syria from Hafez al-Asad's brutal 1982 repression of Hama, was stronger in the diaspora than on the ground in Syria. This, ironically, positioned them well to take a leading position in the evolving opposition political institutions based outside the country. With Qatari support, the Brotherhood would take a disproportionate role in the Syrian National Council and the international diplomacy of the crisis—a role which in turn provoked intense competition from Turkey and Saudi Arabia to place their own proxies.

Support for Syria's uprising extended beyond the Muslim Brotherhood, however. The Syrian uprising was embraced by most of the activists of the Arab uprising.[12] On March 25, 2011, the leading Egyptian activist Wael Ghonim tweeted, "The Syrian flag has two stars, one for Syria and the other for Egypt." Tweets such as "these leaders in libya, syria and yemen didn't learn the lesson: if your people's blood has flown your end is near!" by Egyptian businessman @naguibsawiris (April 2011, in English); or "Libya, Yemen, Syria . . . all deserve justice and security together . . . and all the Muslim lands" by Saudi media figure @ahmadalshugairi (April 2011, in Arabic) were common. In those early days, few Arab uprising activists drew a distinction between Syria's and their own.

Support for the Syrian uprising also came from multiple, interlocking Gulf Islamist networks beyond the Muslim Brotherhood's. Islamist public figures in Saudi Arabia, Qatar, and Kuwait early on began to prominently feature Syria in their sermons, charitable campaigns, and social media accounts. Personalities such as the Kuwaiti Salafi Islamist Nabil al-Awadhy emerged as key nodes in the campaign to raise awareness of the suffering of the Syrian people and to mobilize action in response. Many of these Islamist figures also strongly and publicly supported Islamists in transitional countries such as Egypt. They thus aligned well with the Qatari and Turkish vision for the Arab uprising, but found themselves increasingly at odds with the Saudi and Emirati camp.

Despite all this, regional support for intervention proceeded more slowly than it had in Libya. Early on, the Gulf states and the Arab League remained conspicuously silent about Syria, while some reports even circulated about a potential bailout package for Asad comparable to those offered to Jordan, Morocco, and the less wealthy GCC states.[13] Turkey and the other Gulf states had many reasons to be cautious about pushing regime change in Syria. There was no obvious immediate consensus on Syria across the Gulf. Businessmen, particularly in Dubai and Qatar, had a wide range of interests in Syria, while others had refrained from investment over political differences. As late as mid-summer 2011, prominent journalists like Khaled Al-Hroub could still demand to know why the Arab regimes had remained silent on Syria while the rest of the world, from the United States and the United Nations to Turkey and Iran, were actively engaged with the crisis.[14]

That would not be the case for long. This reticence changed as the violence escalated and the Asad regime lashed out against Gulf states as the instigators of the uprising. A series of gory massacres by regime forces shocked and horrified Syrians and external observers alike as images and videos flooded social media. Soon, support for the Syrian uprising would became a major shared aspiration binding together otherwise wildly competitive regimes, social movements, and ideological trends. They did not always share the same goals, however. Protecting Syrian civilians from regime repression could, as it had in Libya, easily blur into a push to topple the regime.

Saudi Arabia and Bahrain had little difficulty turning against Asad. Riyadh had long sought to break the Syrian alliance with Iran and quickly saw the opportunity to go even further. Bahrain likely also hoped to find a way back in to the Arab order following its own widely criticized sectarian campaign of repression, but also reflected the hotly polarized and vocal views of a Sunni community newly empowered as part of the campaign against the protest movement. In both, the public rhetoric moved much more quickly to a sectarian reading of the crisis, with angry calls to support Syrian Sunnis against the Alawite (read: Shi'ite) Asad regime.

The turn against Asad was more challenging for Turkey's Prime Minister Erdogan and the emir of Qatar, both of whom had enjoyed very positive personal relationships with Asad. Both countries had invested considerable wealth and political capital in serving as Syria's broker for rehabilitation with the Western alliance. The uprisings changed all this. For Turkey, the key moment came with the June 2011 Syrian attack on Jisr al-Shughur, near the border. As refugees began to pour over the border, Turkey maintained a relatively open border policy, which allowed the opposition to transport goods and people into the areas they controlled—as well as, over time, weapons and jihadists.

Qatar, giddy with its success in driving international action against Libya and the credit it received for the Arab uprising, saw another opportunity to take the lead. Both leaders initially sought to use their ties to Asad to convince him to accept political reforms. When these efforts failed, the two states became among the most fervent supporters of the rebellion. Qatar took a series of steps to replicate the Libyan model by sponsoring the creation of an opposition political body in exile, heavily covering the Syrian rebel cause on al-Jazeera and lobbying the Arab League and the United Nations. Qatar became one of the first states to suspend diplomatic relations and impose economic sanctions on Syria.

Al-Jazeera's coverage of Syria soon actively promoted the rebellion, with the fiery appearances by the Islamist stalwart Yusuf al-Qaradawi and combative segments by Syrian-origin talk show host Faisal al-Qassem attracting particular attention. Al-Jazeera would soon itself divide over Syria in ways which had not been seen in any other uprising, reflecting the tension inherent in the turn against the "Resistance camp" with which the station had long sympathized. Over the first year of the uprising, several star on-air personalities abruptly departed. By the summer, the dynamic but controversial managing director, Wadhah al-Khanfar, would himself depart, as the station came under more heavy-handed and direct control by the Qatari government.

Then came Homs, where large crowds had gathered despite intense regime efforts at intimidation. In early July, some four hundred thousand protestors took to the streets against Asad. US Ambassador Robert Ford and several other Western diplomats traveled to Hama to demonstrate support for the protestors, who received him with delirious cheers.[15] Asad complained bitterly about Ford's visit and soon punished the city with a series of military assaults. Protests continued to grow, nonetheless, until Asad launched a massive military operation at the end of July, which killed hundreds of civilians in what at that point was the bloodiest single day in the uprising's history. The UN Security Council would condemn the atrocities, but could not authorize a response in the face of Russian fears that such a resolution would be used like Libya's as a pretext for military intervention.

The Obama administration was by this point under tremendous domestic and international pressure to take a strong stand against Asad. The Gulf states had come to a rough consensus on support for the uprising against Asad, even if they still competed ferociously behind the scenes over control of the emerging opposition. The massacres in Hama following Ford's visit directly challenged American credibility. The size and power of these popular demonstrations, the converging position of the Gulf states, and growing international outrage over regime violence crystallized a growing sense that Asad would be unable to retain his hold on power. The Syrian opposition, the Arab media, and much of the Western media amplified this narrative at every opportunity.

Crucially, however, there was still no consensus in favor of military intervention—not in Washington, not in the region, and not among Syrians.

The crystallizing sense that something must be done to stop the atrocities did not translate into any clear path to doing so. The primary emphasis remained on diplomacy, as Western and regional powers worked to build international support for ratcheting up pressure on Asad and halting the spiraling violence. These efforts came to fruition in mid-August. The Gulf Cooperation Council issued a démarche demanding that the Syrian regime immediately put an end to the violent crackdown. Saudi Arabia, Bahrain, and Kuwait withdrew their ambassadors.

On August 18, 2011, after coordinating with European and Arab allies, Obama released a statement that "the future of Syria must be determined by its people, but President Bashar al-Asad is standing in their way... for the sake of the Syrian people, the time has come for President Asad to step aside." This American position failed to convince Asad to leave, but did establish a policy benchmark which would determine the future course of the conflict. The Gulf states and the Syrian opposition believed that they had secured an American commitment to action to remove Asad, even if the White House had made no such decision.

THE DEBATE OVER INTERVENTION

Obama's call for Asad to step down accelerated the building expectations of an imminent breakthrough. Few close observers of the Syrian regime had any illusions that it would easily give up, though. Obama's saying the "magic words" that Asad must go did capture attention and embolden the regime's opponents, but predictably did not persuade the Syrian President to step down. Those familiar with Asad's history and the nature of the regime warned that he would likely respond only with ever-escalating violence, and that at some point Syrians would likely be forced to take up arms in self-defense. The prospect of such violence was less inhibiting than it might have been only months earlier, however. NATO had come to the rescue of Libya's protestors, after all, and that month Qaddafi had been driven from Tripoli. Even if Obama himself tried to discourage any expectation of American intervention, many believed that he would ultimately have no choice. His administration was divided, moreover, with many officials sympathizing with the interventionist instincts of the policy community. Actors on all sides thus received mixed messages about the possibility of an American intervention.

The push for intervention often masked the reality that there was no Arab consensus on Syria. Even more than with Libya, Syria produced an exceptionally bitter, intense public argument over its place within the broader Arab uprisings. Those steeped for years in the "resistance" narrative were well-primed to view the uprising as a proxy war against the Asad regime. The broad networks of pan-Arabists, leftists, and the broader "Resistance" bloc which had constituted one pole in the previous decade's divided regional politics had every reason to be suspicious. The role of the Gulf states and the Muslim Brotherhood in promoting the uprising raised concerns. So did the pro-uprising stance of the United States and the European powers, as well as the vocal support of pro-Israeli voices in Washington. The "resistance" media pounded away on the theme of the uprising's dependence on external sponsors.

Nor was there even a Syrian consensus. That's why there was a civil war. Asad retained considerable support among wide sectors of the Syrian citizenry, including not only minority communities but also much of the urban Sunni elites who had benefitted from his rule and feared change. Official media, later supplemented by television stations such as the Lebanon-based al-Akhbar newspaper and al-Mayadeen TV, expertly crafted a narrative of foreign subversion, armed gangs, and exaggerated propaganda about protests and repression. Partisans of the two narratives would clash furiously, as information warfare became a central front of the rapidly evolving conflict.

The international and American demand for Asad's departure triggered increasingly intense debates across the region and within the Syrian opposition over the desirability and possibility of an external role. Where supporting rebels had seemed risky when Asad showed little sign of being seriously challenged, now support for rebel groups seemed to align with an inevitable post-Asad future. As Azmi Bishara put it for al-Jazeera, "[T]he Syrian regime can not continue as it is. Either it will change, or the Syrian people will change it."[16]

The calculus of violence was tricky. Many supporters of the Syrian uprising recognized that their best hope for success was to persuade the still divided Sunni community, religious and ethnic minorities, and the business community in cities like Aleppo to switch sides. Their theory of victory involved maintaining the moral high ground and convincing the Syrian majority to abandon Asad. This required reassuring Alawis and Christians and Sunnis who had thrived under the regime that their interests, and even their survival, would be protected in a post-Asad Syria. The more that protestors took up arms, the greater the fear which the regime could manufacture among its supporters. The turn to armed insurrection, which its advocates argued would be the best way to pressure the regime, instead played directly into Asad's hands by undermining the narrative of peaceful protest and scaring his constituency back into the fold.

The idea of Western intervention was even more controversial than taking up arms within the ranks of the Syrian opposition. For all the relentless lobbying of Western capitals by the exiled opposition for military action, the idea did not command any sort of consensus even among the ranks of the Syrian opposition. The rejection of intervention followed from well-entrenched Syrian and broader Arab norms. Syria's foreign policy and national identity were built around the concept of resistance and a confrontational approach towards Israel and the United States. Those stances seemed to be broadly popular inside of Syria, and with the majority of Arab public opinion. For the opposition, it represented a real challenge: How could those calling to bring down Asad appeal to an enormously unpopular Western alliance for support without burning all credibility with the Syrian public?

A significant portion of even pro-uprising Syrians remained deeply suspicion of American intentions, feared the consequences of military escalation, and preferred to remain an exclusively Syrian and nonviolent movement. Syrians on the inside working with the Local Coordination Committees tended to be far less open to American-led intervention than the politicians and activists in exile who had staked their claims to leadership on their ability to generate international support. While most Syrians fervently hoped for any form of protection from regime military assaults, others quickly foresaw the likely ramifications of a full-scale proxy war on their homeland. They tried, futilely, to adhere to nonviolence and nonintervention.

Their skepticism about armed rebellion and international limited intervention was informed by their precarious situation on the ground. They knew full well how badly they were outgunned, and how little they could trust the armed groups beginning to emerge. They knew all too well the atrocities of which the Syrian regime was capable if threatened. Many doubted the real intentions of the external actors egging them on towards armed confrontation. As the Palestinian-Jordanian columnist Oraib al-Rentawi prophetically concluded, "[M]ilitarization can be justified by many things, including the monstrosity of the regime, but it is nothing but a road to destruction which paves the road to destructive external intervention."[17]

The Syrian regime's brutal crackdown provoked a sharp, difficult debate about the very concept of "resistance." How could Arab popular forces balance between a popular stance of resistance to Israel and fierce repression of a popular uprising? Did Syria's or Hezbollah's confrontations with Israel give them a free pass to murder their own people with impunity? But, on the other side, would backing the protests simply serve Israel's interests by weakening its primary adversaries? Hamas would ultimately vacate its Damascus offices and break with Iran to avoid being dragged in to the polarizing rhetorical war.[18] Hezbollah, by contrast, allowed itself to be dragged ever more deeply into the fighting. The complexities of this debate, mostly in Arabic, were often lost on a Western discourse framed around a simpler story of a united Syrian people against a reviled dictator.

The rejection of violence came from both moral and strategic concerns, with many activists recognizing that the resort to weapons would immeasurably strengthen regime propaganda, cost foreign sympathy, and frighten away fence-sitting Syrians unsure about the potential costs of revolution. Their fears of the costs of turning to violence were well-grounded in the academic literature, though few Syrians were in the mood to listen to lectures on comparative insurgency.[19] The Crisis Group analysts Peter Harling and Sarah Birke captured the logic by which taking up arms could harm the uprising extremely well: "By pushing frustrated protesters to take up arms and the international community to offer them support, it is succeeding in disfiguring what it saw as the greatest threat to its rule, namely the grassroots and mostly peaceful protest movement that demanded profound change."[20]

Syrian National Council leader Burhan Ghalioun continued to insist that the uprising was a "peaceful and civil revolution" with the goal of creating a democratic state.[21] But the turn to arms seemed increasingly like an inevitability. As early as October 2, 2011, the leading Saudi columnist and confidante of its leadership Abd al-Rahman al-Rashed declared that "the armed revolution in Syria has begun."[22] What, as the Syrian intellectual Yasin al-Haj Saleh observed, did the opponents of militarization propose to do about the already existing armed factions fighting Asad?[23] What were Syrians to do when subject to the unending killing and depredations of Asad's military machine?

As 2011 ground on, both violence and intervention became objects of ever more urgent disagreement. As the Washington-based academic Bassam Haddad observed in early 2012, "[P]rivately, most Syrian dissidents recognize that such tactics do not serve the 'revolution.' Publicly, they are far more preoccupied with fighting or escaping repression."[24] Their private concerns were easily lost amidst the din of the Arab media's mobilization for militarization and the loud campaigns by social media activists. For many Syrians on the ground suffering from ever more extreme regime depredations, the ability to deliver international protection came to be the only indicator which mattered of the SNC's value.

The failure of diplomacy is what finally triggered the Syrian opposition's turn to insurgency. The West and its regional partners continued to focus on securing a United Nations Security Council resolution to put pressure on Asad and to legitimate whatever action might be taken. In November 2011, Qatar's Foreign Minister Hamed bin Jassem announced Syria's suspension from the Arab League, an important and unusual diplomatic initiative. In January, he sought to parlay Arab League support for intervention into a UN Security Council mandate. He presented the Arab case in a high-stakes session of the Security Council.

The Security Council debate over Syria at the end of January 2012 proved to be a more decisive turning point than it had perhaps appeared. Many in the Obama administration thought such a resolution was a real possibility. But it failed in the face of a joint Russian-Chinese veto. Russia explained its veto primarily in terms of the lessons it had drawn from Libya, where it claimed NATO had wantonly exceeded the terms of the mandate and turned a limited authorization for humanitarian protection into an open-ended license to pursue regime change. Qatar's representatives left deeply frustrated with the United Nations and determined to find some other vehicle for intervention against Asad.

The failure at the United Nations led many Syrians and their regional supporters alike to abandon hope in diplomatic options and turn instead to force. The debate at the Security Council had not stemmed the growing violence on the ground. February 2012 brought an important escalation moment in the civil war's cycle of violence. The devastation of the Bab Amr neighborhood of Homs unfolded in the midst of active Security Council deliberations, in full view of the international media (which was momentarily galvanized by the death of well-known war correspondent Marie Colvin). The massive assault on a major Syrian city with heavy weaponry and massive civilian casualties marked a point of no return in the militarization of the conflict. It exposed both how far Asad's forces would go and the limits of Syria's armed opposition.[25] From this point, the debate would shift from whether to take up arms to the best way to do so.

ORGANIZING THE INSURGENCY

As it became clear that the Syrian uprising would not end quickly, developing political and functional institutions became essential. Building such opposition institutions required resources, however, which put the new Syrian organizations in a position of dependence upon the incessant internal rivalries and competing agendas of external powers. Four major organizational developments shaped the next stage of the Syrian crisis: the emergence of Local Coordination Councils and the creation of the

National Coordination Committee in June, the announcement of the Free Syrian Army on July 29, and the creation of the Syrian National Council on August 23. These four aspects of the rebellion often disagreed over strategy and priorities.

By June, as violence escalated and life grew difficult, Syrians began organizing themselves at the local level for security and sustenance into Local Coordination Councils. These LCCs were linked together through loose, informal networks which would, over time, evolve into channels for humanitarian relief and political representation. They became key points of contact for international organizations and the media, providing detailed information at the local level about battles and conditions. They also represented the political views and tactical priorities of Syrians on the ground, challenging the claims to representation by nascent, exile-based political organizations. The LCCs in many ways represented the heart of the uprising, the manifestation of the original impulse towards civil resistance and the creation of a better Syria. They had fundamentally different priorities and needs than did the politicians in exile and were far more skeptical of taking up arms and foreign intervention. They would struggle to retain a voice as the insurgency militarized and the political organizations abroad took the diplomatic lead.

In July, seven Syrian military defectors led by Riyadh al-Asa'ad declared the creation of the Free Syrian Army. While it barely existed on the ground, the FSA would become a central front for the debate over the future of the Syrian revolution. It aspired to provide an organizational framework for the many local armed groups, a central location to receive weapons and training, and a magnet for an anticipated wave of Syrian army defectors. The efforts of the Free Syrian Army were portrayed at this point as a response to regime violence, aimed at protecting the protestors and civilians of what was still fundamentally a peaceful revolution.[26] Syrians committed to a nonviolent strategy bitterly opposed the concept of the Free Syrian Army and all it represented. Others Syrians suffering from escalating regime attacks saw the urgent need for an effective military option for protection. These deeply divisive debates over the militarization of the revolution would continue for months.

It took time to figure out how to integrate the Free Syrian Army, however tenuously, with internationally-backed political institutions of the Syrian National Council. The SNC was hopelessly fragmented internally, penetrated by regional power struggles, overly focused on attracting Western military intervention, and disconnected from the realities on the ground. Each of the regional powers working the Syrian arena agreed on the hope of dragging Washington into the fray to topple Asad, but each hoped that the intervention would come on behalf of its own preferred proxies. The Syrian National Council was not only fragmented because of the personalities of its members, or even because of the complexities of the Syrian internal debate; the regional power struggles deeply shaped the fragmentation and thus the impotence of the SNC.

The Free Syrian Army seemed to be a way to overcome these problems, by creating a proxy military force with real weight on the ground which could be a collectively acceptable recipient of international support. The FSA was still something of a myth, with a media presence far outstripping its actual organizational capacity. Its many constituent parts represented a diverse array of local defense forces, ideological trends, and self-interested warlords. It exercised little real command and control, and had little ability to formulate or implement a coherent military strategy. By November, the FSA had attracted attention as a potentially viable vehicle for an externally supported insurgency.[27] Money and arms began to flow to the rebels in spring 2012 through the FSA, which had positioned itself as the most viable conduit for receiving such external military support.[28]

The Syrian National Council, created in Istanbul in late August, was explicitly modeled after the Libyan NTC as a vehicle to receive international support and recognition. The Libyan metaphor was reflected in the suggestion that the SNC could establish itself as an alternative government in a "liberated" part of Syria comparable to Benghazi, which could then receive international recognition. From the start, it was one of the most visible locations of the regional political struggles. Each regional power sought to translate its money, media, and political assets into placing its allies on the Council. The Syrian Muslim Brothers, backed by Qatari money and on home turf thanks to Turkey, emerged with a disproportionate role in the emergent body. This would soon be contested by the Saudis and others.

The National Coordination Committee, formed in June in Damascus, presented a formidable political challenge to the SNC. Fronted by the Paris-based dissident, Haytham al-Manaa, the NCC brought together most of Syria's major secular and leftist movements along with three Kurdish political parties. Problematically for the external opposition bent on armed struggle and intervention, the NCC favored more gradualist solutions, remaining open to a political settlement and dialogue with Asad and rejecting both violence and intervention.

In December 2011, talks between the SNC and NCC broke down over these core strategic questions, as the latter continued to engage in talks with the Asad regime and refused to support the Free Syrian Army or armed resistance. SNC supporters accused the NCC of being too close to Asad, questioning whether they were really even an opposition, while NCC supporters accused the SNC of serving foreign interests rather than Syrian. Such conflicts over political strategy would be a perennial feature of Syrian opposition politics.

Diplomats repeatedly emerged scarred by their experience dealing with the hopelessly factionalized Syrian opposition. This dysfunction was not simply a product of Syrian political culture or of especially demanding personalities. Its disarray was a key obstacle in preventing its recognition or expanded support.[29] The SNC's only real power was its ability to attract and distribute resources from the international community, leaving it highly dependent. This dependence made it fully a creature of competitive intervention and proxy warfare. What looked like indecision was as often the result of intense Turkish, Saudi, and Qatari pressure on the Council members. Had the "Friends of Syria" been a unified grouping pursuing a collectively shared interest, then the SNC might have evolved into an effective and legitimate body. But instead, it became an arena within which its backers could fight their battles.

A Syrian opposition conference in Cairo in December 2011 divided hopelessly on the questions of foreign intervention and militarization. The SNC had launched with the articulation of "three nos: to sectarianism, violence, and international intervention." Over time, however, the center of gravity in the Council, as in its regional backers, had moved in favor of at least the latter two. On December 28, the NCC put out a statement announcing its agreement with the SNC which included a "rejection of foreign intervention."[30] This announcement triggered a revolt against SNC President Burhan Ghalioun, led by those who were advocating relentlessly for just such an intervention. Those internal arguments, along with more venal struggles over power, money, and status, would continue to hobble the SNC.

It was at this point that the failure of the Security Council to reach agreement shifted the emphasis to the militarization of the uprising. Building connections between the political and the armed opposition was one of the highest priorities. On March 1, the SNC announced the formation of a military bureau incorporating the FSA. This new institution had little actual power over the emergent armed groups but signaled an irrevocable shift towards the incorporation of arms into the previously, at least formally, nonviolent struggle. As Burhan Ghalioun explained at a press conference announcing the move, the Syrian uprising may have begun as nonviolent but now had no choice but to "shoulder its responsibilities in light of this new reality."[31] Qatar backed the faction pushing for militarization.

The move, intensely controversial within the SNC, predictably triggered pushback from Free Syrian Army leaders such as Riad al-Asa'ad, who had no intention of subordinating themselves to the political control of the SNC. It also provoked resistance from the other direction, with critics such as Abd al-Bari Atwan warning that "it is obvious that resolving the Syria crisis with the military option is impossible... the regime's security solution has failed and the opposition's hope for military intervention is not on the table and arming the opposition only makes things more deadly."[32]

With the United Nations route blocked and Obama resisting being dragged into the war, Qatar and other interventionist Gulf states sought to energize the Arab League's role. But despite the earlier agreement on suspending Syrian membership, the Arab League proved to be far more divided than the Gulf's interventionist rhetoric would suggest. The Arab

League's monitoring mission, which had begun arriving at the invitation of the Syrian government on December 26, 2011, was plagued by internal divisions and an impossible mandate and limped to inevitable failure.

In February 2012, Qatar's Hamed Bin Jassem became the first Arab leader to publicly call for armed intervention in Syria. But, tellingly, he could not mobilize an Arab consensus in support of such an escalation. Even if all the major players agreed on the need to act against Asad, each worried almost as much about rival powers taking the credit for doing so.

Regional and Syrian differences continued to be on sharp display in the February 2012 Friends of Syria meeting in Tunis. In his invitation, Tunisian Foreign Minister Rafik Abdessalam expected that neither Arabs nor the West would support a military intervention in Syria: "We don't want an Iraqi scenario . . . We have to preserve the integrity of Syria."[33] But since military action was not on the US-shaped agenda, Saudi Arabia ostentatiously withdrew, with Foreign Minister Saud al-Faisal describing arming the opposition as "an excellent idea."[34] As host, Tunisia's president, Moncef Marzouki, endorsed the Qatari proposal of "an Arab intervention in the framework of the League, an Arab force to keep peace and security, to accompany diplomatic efforts to convince Bashar to leave."

Nor did the Arab League unite around an intervention. When the Arab League convened in Baghdad in March, Iraqi Prime Minister Nuri al-Maliki firmly opposed such intervention. His objections were not simply sectarian or dictated by his dependence on Iran, as his critics complained. Baghdad was replete with lessons for Arabs contemplating American military-led intervention, regardless of their sect or ethnicity. Many others, who remembered well the horrors of Western intervention in Iraq, quietly supported Maliki.

Supporters of the rebellion now focused instead on finding ways to build up the capacity of the Syrian opposition. Libya by this point was already proving the dangerous implications of the weakness of post-transition institutions. Indeed, one of the arguments for military intervention would soon become the need to create a safe zone inside Syria where an opposition-led government could establish itself. On April 1, the Friends of Syria meeting in Istanbul pledged major financial contributions to support the rebels. This cash went not only to administrative support and humanitarian relief. The core idea was to ensure that all international resources—including military aid—be channeled through these developing institutions.

This was the right way to proceed. It was also doomed, for reasons that Libyans could easily have predicted. The competing Gulf regimes and Turkey had other interests in play, and little incentive to follow the American organizational lead. Significant amounts of Arab money reportedly went as well towards efforts to supply the Free Syrian Army and to entice defections by Syrian officers and officials. There was no way to prevent the Syrian opposition from using international funds to buy weapons, and much to gain in the regional struggle for influence by arming Syrian proxies.

The US reportedly put heavy pressure on the Gulf states to hold off on implementing their plans for a large-scale covert arming of the rebels, but by this point the momentum towards such operations was already well underway. As the UAE-based analyst Mustafa Alani told the *Guardian*, "The decision to arm the rebels has been taken in principle, but it has not yet been implemented."[35] It soon would be.

Still, the voices most heard in the West were the backers of armed insurgency and Western intervention among the exiled political groupings. Lobbying Washington to change its stance on Syria came to dominate much of the Syrian political agenda in the coming years, time spent at international conferences and luxury hotels which might otherwise have been spent building alternative political institutions on the ground. By November 2011, these debates had tipped in favor of taking up arms, but those pushing for Western intervention had failed to win support for a no-fly zone or other direct military moves.

In this context of failed diplomacy and regional support for arming an insurgency, the concerns over the militarization of the uprising now seemed obsolete. Washington's debates over intervention came into sharp focus at this point, with a strong interventionist policy community pushing hard for American military involvement despite widespread public opposition to any such actions. A wide range of options for international intervention would be floated publicly: no-fly zones, safe havens, air strikes, arming the rebels, "no-kill zones," and more.[36]

These debates relied heavily on the Libya precedent, despite the vast differences between the two cases. Syria looked nothing like Libya's physical terrain. It did not feature military convoys moving across open roads in the desert, a long coastline for naval support, few effective air defenses, or an easy east-west territorial divide. Nor was Libya located in the heart of the Levant, situated between multiple regional powers and some of the most militarized and tightly contested airspace in the world. The intervention in Libya had commanded both Arab League and United Nations Security Council consent, neither of which was forthcoming on the far more controversial question of Syria.

None of these proposals offered any real chance of success on their own. As one senior administration official scathingly put it to me, Washington was full of ideas to get the military in to Syria, but not how to get them out. No-fly zones, safe areas, or no-kill zones would need to be enforced, requiring escalation when the regime violated them as happened to such horrifying effect in Bosnia. Few of the proposals took seriously the likelihood that Asad's backers would escalate in response, restoring a hurting stalemate. Obama administration officials clearly understood that the proposals for limited intervention would only put America on a slippery slope towards direct intervention. In a rare moment of candor in June 2013, one vocal proponent of intervention acknowledged that "'mission creep' provides the hope of a successful outcome rather than a terrifying threat to a major foreign policy initiative."[37] At least this was honest.

MILITARY ESCALATION

The Asad regime responded to this growing military challenge with ever-escalating violence, both by regular forces and through the shadowy plainclothes gangs known as "shabiha."[38] On May 25, 2012, regime forces carried out a particularly horrifying mass slaughter in Houla, northeast of Homs. Images of more than a hundred butchered Syrian civilians circulated widely through social media and reached a broad regional and international audience. The Houla massacre inspired a unanimous Security

Council resolution condemning the Asad regime, a scathing report by the UN Human Rights Council, and a steady series of meticulously researched reports by international NGOs detailing the Syrian regime's crimes against humanity.[39] These international rebukes had little effect. Nor did the international outrage over the late July siege of Hama or the later slaughter of hundreds more civilians by regime forces in the Damascus suburb of Darayya.

The war of narratives surrounding these massacres was equally intense. International media and analysts horrified by the violence and sympathetic to the uprising consistently failed to appreciate the potency of Syrian regime propaganda, which they found laughable. The Syrian government blamed the deaths on rebel forces or dismissed them as routine skirmishes exaggerated by opposition activists and a biased international media. While such claims sounded ludicrous to Western observers, the narrative resonated with the regime's own core constituencies, terrified of advances by groups portrayed by regime propaganda as violent jihadists. Enthusiasts for armed insurgency failed, at great cost, to appreciate how the arming of the opposition strengthened this insular, internally coherent narrative and consolidated rather than undermined Asad's support.

As conditions deteriorated, large-scale massacres by regime forces became increasingly common and the uprising tilted irreversibly towards armed insurgency. By the spring of 2012, Syria had reached the point of a full-scale civil war fueled by growing external patronage which would be difficult to derail through either negotiations or limited intervention. With each escalation, the strategic situation moved another notch up the ladder to a new, more violent and destructive stalemate.

THE ANNAN PLAN

Asad's scorched earth tactics and mass killings destroyed any opening for peaceful protest, and in the eyes of most Syrians opposed to the regime, left little choice other than taking up arms in self-defense. Syria's strategic importance guaranteed that regional players would get ever more involved, particularly since they paid few real costs of their own. As the Syrian al-Jazeera personality Faisal al-Qassem noted in May 2012, "Syria is no longer an internal battle which can be resolved by a deal between the regime and the opposition. It is now in the hands of the powers which support each side and resolving the Syria crisis will require an agreement between the rival powers."[40]

That insight was the guiding principle behind UN Special Envoy Kofi Annan's mission. This diplomatic gambit to convene the major powers to find a pathway towards a political transition represented the last serious opportunity to stop Syria's descent into hell. It failed, despite Annan's best efforts, because neither side wanted such a solution. The rebels and their backers wanted to overthrow Asad by force, felt morally outraged by his atrocities, and did not believe that he could be trusted to abide by any diplomatic agreement. Asad and his backers believed they could win, did not believe the fragmented rebels could deliver on a deal, and expected defeat to mean death or war crimes prosecution. By the summer of 2012, Syria's descent into full-scale proxy war was virtually irreversible. Both sides enthusiastically cheered Annan's failure while steering off the cliff.

The predictably disastrous outcome of the Syrian opposition's decision to take up arms remains one of the greatest unresolved and probably unresolvable questions of the Syrian war. I was among the minority of analysts who vocally opposed the militarization of the opposition, because I feared precisely the disaster which would soon unfold. The turn to armed insurgency struck me then, and now, as a fatally flawed choice which should be discouraged rather than supported. The strongest rebuttal from supporters of militarization was not that armed insurgency could work, or that taking up arms was strategically viable or morally imperative. It was that taking up arms was, in fact, no choice at all. A population facing Asad's brutality had no choice but to find some way, any way, to protect itself and to fight back. Many observers desperately wanted to do something, anything, to protect Syrians from the atrocities being inflicted upon them by the regime. For all the horrors which followed that fateful choice, we should never lose sight of the core reality that it was Asad's obstinate brutality which forced Syria into war and invited the carnage to come.

On April 10, 2012, the deadline arrived after long months of diplomacy led by United Nations Special Envoy Kofi Annan.[41] His peace plan called for an immediate cease-fire and negotiations towards a political transition. Failure to seize this opportunity for a negotiated end to the war, he warned, would result in a catastrophe for Syria and for the region. His plan presented the most plausible and realistic possible solution for a country on the brink of uncontrollable civil war. Of course, critics from every side dismissed his efforts as hopeless. The rapid escalation of violence and the already unbelievable scale of death and destruction left few willing to contemplate co-existence with those they blamed for the horrors. The February 2012 devastation of Homs and the revelation of a series of brutal massacres had indelibly scarred those in the opposition who might have once contemplated a negotiated path. The March 2012 series of bombings of regime targets in Damascus punctured the bubble of security for regime supporters, and emboldened advocates of armed insurgency in the opposition ranks.

Both Annan and his critics were right. A negotiated end to the war was indeed the last and only hope for Syria to avoid descent into hell—and it was impossible to achieve, for Annan or anyone else. The regime still believed that it would win, and that concessions would only weaken rather than strengthen its prospects for survival. The inability of Libya's well-armed revolutionaries to win against a much weaker and isolated Qaddafi for nearly six months, even with direct NATO intervention, may have reassured once-nervous officials.[42] At any rate, regime officials did not believe that its internal and external enemies would be satisfied with compromise when they had so publicly committed themselves to regime change. Insurgents, flush with the first shipments of weapons from external sponsors, dreamed of total victory. With the images of massacred civilians fresh in their memories and renewed on a daily basis, few believed for a moment that the regime could be trusted to adhere to any promises of reconciliation anyway. Everyone was spoiling for a fight and nobody saw the value of compromise. They would have been far better served heeding Annan's council. With Annan's failure, Syria missed its last, best chance for a negotiated alternative to full-scale war.

ARMING AN INSURGENCY

By the late spring of 2012, Syria's uprising had been consumed by the early stages of the grim logic of competitive proxy war. In such situations, every escalation in favor of one side tends to trigger a response from the backers of another—never enough to win, always enough to keep the war going. The political science literature on such wars offered a clear guide on what to expect. The external arming of rebel groups tended to prolong civil wars, making them bloodier and harder to resolve. These problems are typically magnified dramatically when funding to rebel groups comes from multiple, competing powers rather than from a single unified source.[43] They were even worse when the other side could also draw on external patrons for support.

That's exactly what happened in Syria. As rebel groups began to take up arms in response to the Asad regime's brutality, they found ample sources of funds and weapons from abroad to support their insurgency. When they began to demonstrate too much success, Asad's backers ramped up their own support to the regime. Financial assistance on each side gave way to the direct provision of weapons. Indirect assistance gave way to direct intervention by Hezbollah and Iran. After the emergence of ISIS, the US and its allies began a major air campaign against the Islamic State and occasionally against other jihadist groups in the fractious rebel alliance. Then Russia introduced its own troops and air power into the campaign on Asad's side. Each move invited a countermove. The international balance of power superseded the local balance of power, ensuring an ongoing and increasingly destructive stalemate. All of this was easily foreseen in early 2012.[44]

Many backers of arming Syria's rebels acknowledged that such support could not bring about a military victory over Asad. They argued instead that it would improve their bargaining position. Asad would only bargain, this logic went, if he felt mortally threatened. This logic, unfortunately, never made any sense. As Stanford political scientist James Fearon quickly saw, it was virtually inconceivable that a balance of power in favor of a negotiated outcome could be constructed.[45] "Neither side could completely crush the other," he observed, "due to the fact that this has also become a proxy war in which the international parties will adjust their support to prevent complete military elimination of their clients." But nor could negotiations work. Each time one side's relative power increased, so did its objectives. Nor did either side have any faith that the other would adhere to a deal. When Asad was strong, he saw no need to compromise, but when he was weak he felt too threatened to strike a deal. When rebel groups were strong, they wanted to go all the way to overthrow the hated Asad, but when they were weak they did not dare put down their arms.

The fragmentation of the rebel forces was one of the greatest barriers to either victory or a negotiated settlement. The high level of fragmentation in the Syrian rebellion contributed to its problems.[46] The Free Syrian Army had always been a useful fiction rather than an effective hierarchical military organization. Hundreds of fighting groups occupied the scene at any given time, grouped in temporary coalitions typically based more on local demands than on ideological concerns. Most of the groups had only a local presence, so that impressive-seeming numbers of troops did not translate well into the ability to project power. The Syrian National Council could not command the allegiance of the hundreds of rebel factions fighting on the ground, which made it difficult for it to negotiate, or to be able to credibly guarantee that it could enforce any agreement reached. And then, of course, the jihadist groups would continue to fight no matter the status of negotiations between Asad and the Western-backed rebels. As the University of Maryland political scientist David Cunningham has observed, "Civil wars last longer, and are more resistant to negotiated agreement, when they contain more actors who can block settlement."[47]

The uncoordinated, large-scale flows of support to the rebels, which began in earnest in early to mid-2012, ensured that this debilitating fragmentation would continue. The primacy of Islamist-minded Gulf networks in the provision of funds inevitably skewed the character of the insurgency to those who shared (or could be enticed to profess) similar views. If growing a beard were the price of opening the tap of foreign support, there were many prepared to stop shaving. That does not mean that they would easily shave off the beards if American money were offered, though. The longer the fighting continued, the more that fighters internalized the ideas for which they fought and the more the center of gravity shifted to the extremes. Long-running violent insurgencies were no place for moderates.

As the conflict internationalized, external stakeholders proliferated, each pursuing its own sense of vital interests and cultivating its own proxies. No stable outcome could be reached which did not bring all the players to the table, including not just the Syrian factions, but also Saudi Arabia, Qatar, Turkey, Iran, and Russia. Meanwhile, the uncoordinated arming of rebel groups meant that every group had an incentive to protect its access to that source of power, and to align itself to the degree required with its patron's ideology or objectives. The transfer of weapons predictably accelerated the destructiveness and intensity of the war, with each phase of the conflict moving up another notch on the escalatory ladder. Syria became a stalemate, but a dynamic stalemate which grew ever more deadly and destructive rather than settling in to relatively stable front lines.[48]

A succession of UN Envoys followed Kofi Annan, including Lakhdar Brahimi and Steffen de Mistura. Each attempted to build an inclusive diplomatic process, secure local cease-fires, and leverage the armed might of the insurgency. They failed to gain much traction, however, because few if any of these external actors had any real interest in finding a negotiated solution. They paid few significant costs from supporting their proxies in the war and saw little reason to accept a negotiated agreement which fell short of their objectives. The role of Bashar al-Asad became a vital symbolic sticking point, far beyond his actual significance: Gulf states simply would not accept any plan which included his remaining in power, while Iran and Russia would not accept his departure as a precondition. And thus diplomacy spun its wheels for years on end.

Obama was constantly lambasted for failing to arm the Syrian rebels, even as arms poured into those very groups. This has always been misleading. The United States remained publicly cautious about arming the insurgents, but rapidly developed a covert program to arm and support vetted rebel groups. Special forces from Qatar and Saudi Arabia cooperated closely in training camps for rebels in Jordan and Turkey. Qatar, Turkey, and Saudi Arabia each lavished support on their preferred clients, as did non-state Islamist networks and groups of Syrians living abroad. Tens of thousands of rebel fighters reportedly received training in these camps over the years.

Rebel groups actively sought out sources of such support, playing the field looking for the best deal. As in Libya, their choice of proxies was only partly driven by ideology. Availability and convenience played almost as big a role in the scramble for local assets. Both supply and demand for weapons boomed in this period, making it difficult for external backers to exercise any real control over the groups they funded or the weapons they supplied.

There was close to a consensus inside the Beltway for arming the Syrian rebels, despite all the logistical and strategic problems this entailed. Some of the best American Middle East hands pushed for what they called a "managed militarization."[49] In their view, with a full-scale external proxy intervention well underway, the best Washington could hope for was to join the game in sufficient weight to tip the insurgency in a more moderate direction and retain American influence over its course. This approach had little hope of success, though, in an environment where rebel groups had a bonanza of potential funding sources, and with Gulf funds coming faster and with fewer strings attached. Managed militarization made sense to US officials concerned about losing their role and desperately seeking policy instruments of value in the new Syrian war. But in reality, it would only speed up the destructive path of militarization without buying significant control over the spiraling insurgency. Syrian fighting groups had little interest in being managed, and there were plenty of other managers on offer.

While the largest share of the funds came from state sponsors, large-scale public campaigns to raise funds for Syrian rebel groups also played an important role in the radicalization of the insurgency. Islamists across the Gulf held massive pledge drives and public charitable events. Syrian expatriates also mobilized to organize such support. While most of these campaigns initially focused on humanitarian assistance, over time they shifted palpably in the direction of support for armed groups. Kuwait became an epicenter for these efforts, particularly as a worried Saudi Arabia began to crack down on fundraising and recruitment within its own borders. Islamist figures hosted iftars, coordinated charity drives, and spoke out frequently about the Syrian tragedy.

Syria soon became the central cause of an increasingly sectarian and extremist Islamist popular movement. The massive flows of aid into the rebel groups were fatally uncoordinated, which systematically and fatally encouraged fragmentation rather than consolidation of the insurgency. What is more, the need to demonstrate efficacy to foreign sponsors put a premium on dramatic military acts and ideological performances. Videos of military acts and rhetoric attuned to the proclivities of potential state and private sector sponsors were uploaded to YouTube in part as advertisements. Where the US looked for evidence of moderation, most of these Gulf sponsors put a higher premium on Islamic authenticity and demonstrable military success.

The principal-agent problem familiar to political scientists was endemic to the Syrian proxy war. The external powers needed local proxies as much or more than the local clients needed their patrons, and their interests were only imperfectly aligned. Qataris, Turks and Saudis were not especially picky about who they armed, as long as they fought well. Where the US, for instance, might want its proxy forces to articulate a democratic platform and refrain from human rights abuses, the forces themselves might have a greater interest in killing regime opponents and consolidating their local power base. Tight supervision might be possible on clearly defined issues, such as the transfer of advanced weaponry to jihadist groups, since that could be closely monitored with a credible threat to cut off rebel groups who broke the agreement. But such control was far less viable with regard to the core identity and interests and local behavior of the fighting groups.

The US was more deeply involved in the training, arming, and coordinating of the insurgency than the American political debate reflects. Its role was never sufficient, though—and probably never could have been. The US tried to exercise maximal control over its agents, particularly with regard to access to advanced weaponry and their broad strategic orientation, leaving the recipients frustrated and constantly lobbying publicly and privately for more independence and—always—more weapons. Qatar, Turkey, and Saudi Arabia gave a much freer hand to their proxies, which won them greater influence on the ground at the cost of having less control over rebel activities or ideologies. American fears that such a loose approach to insurgent proxies would lead to rampaging extremism and uncoordinated violence would prove amply justified in the months and years to come.

This continuous, ongoing negotiation between patrons and clients played out predictably in the media. Every few months, stories would flood the American media featuring the Syrian rebel commander du jour accusing the Obama administration of failing to support their cause. Op-eds pleading the case of Salim Idriss or Zahran Alloush or the newest savior appeared in the American press with dispiriting regularity. These transparent bids in the patron-client bargaining game were typically taken at face value by a credulous policy community keen to find ways to bash the administration or to flash insider credentials, amplified by backers of the rebel commander in question hoping to parlay publicity into material support.

THE DRIVE TOWARDS DAMASCUS

At first, the arming of the opposition appeared to be paying dividends. The FSA seemed to be showing dramatic progress in the late spring and summer of 2012. All the signals seemed to indicate the rapid deterioration of the Asad regime's position. A growing flood of high-level Syrian officials were defecting publicly, and even more were quietly moving their assets out of the country and seeking safe passage. FSA forces were advancing south towards Damascus. In July 2012, a mysterious explosion in Damascus killed a number of top regime security officials. Many observers believed that the Syrian conflict was approaching its climax.

The Saudi and Qatari media filled with triumphalist rhetoric. Al-Sharq al-Awsat editor Tariq al-Homayed crowed that "Iran[,which] had thought that the Arab Spring was its great victory and that it was a great Islamic Awakening, now sees it only as a conspiracy as its greatest ally is close to the end, and soon Syria and the whole region will be freed of its worst regime."[50] His colleague, Abd al-Rahman al-Rashed, saw "everyone jockeying as signs of Asad['s] collapse mount."[51] The end, claimed Lebanese columnist Hussein al-Haydar, on July 19, is near.[52] The international media too embraced this expectation of an impending endgame.

But Asad did not fall. The Damascus offensive stalled, the regime reconstituted itself, and Syria fell into an even more violent stalemate. What happened? The regime's survival was actually not especially surprising, given that it still enjoyed an overwhelming military advantage and the support of both external powers and a significant portion of the Syrian population. The media commentary of the summer might be best understood as a psychological campaign in support of the Free Syrian Army offensive, aimed at convincing Syrian regime supporters that the time had come to defect, and Syrian oppositionists skeptical of the armed insurgency to overcome their reservations and commit. It also aimed at forcing the Obama administration's hand by convincing a cautious White House that the right side of history had arrived. The Obama administration came under withering attack for failing to understand the realities of what was unfolding in Damascus. Obama was also, of course, right.

As the insurgency settled in for a long war, regional powers fought as much to establish their control of rebel institutions as they did to unseat Asad. Qatar, Turkey, and Saudi Arabia schemed to empower their local proxies within every new institution, polluting each effort to unify the opposition with the same toxic dynamics.[53] In November 2012, Qatar sponsored the creation of the National Coalition for Syrian Revolutionary and Opposition Forces. The Coalition was initially fronted by the Syrian moderate Islamist Moaz al-Khatib. As the Coalition became the central political organization for the Syrian opposition, Saudi Arabia pushed to dilute Qatari control by placing their own clients in leadership positions. Khatib resigned as president in April, and in July was replaced by the Saudi-backed Ahmed Jarba.

The armed opposition was also struggling towards political organization and inclusion within these opposition institutions. In December 2012, a broad array of insurgent factions came together in Antakiya, Turkey to select an official leadership for the Free Syrian Army. The Supreme Military Council, headed by General Salim Idriss, was designed to connect the military and the political wings of the insurgency. All of these efforts were meant to provide a single channel through which external arms and funds might flow, under the effective control of an accountable political leadership. In late May 2013, representatives of the Free Syrian Army would join the Syrian National Coalition for the first time.

Civil society organizations and NGOs worked hard at this time to insert questions of human rights, transitional justice, and post-Asad governance into an agenda dominated by urgent military challenges and bitter political rivalries. With Asad's regime looking shaky but not facing imminent collapse, some organizations used the time to address the vital question of what would follow his regime. Indeed, some came to believe that Asad falling too soon would be as damaging as his surviving indefinitely. Working groups assembled regionally and globally to tackle prospective questions of transitional justice, the provision of security, the creation of representative institutions, and the preservation of essential state services. These were admirable efforts, but they consistently struggled to gain purchase amid the escalating violence and political bickering.

The Obama administration continued to be cautious and divided in the absence of any good options. Some members of the administration, such as CIA Director David Petraeus and (more passively) Secretary of State Hillary Clinton, advocated joining the Gulf's insurgency strategy by covertly arming and training rebels. A significant number of American officials working on Syria, especially in the State Department, agreed. Obama himself, along with key White House advisors and many in the Pentagon, had long been wary of the insurgency strategy, which they correctly anticipated would lead not to easy victory but to a long and bloody stalemate. They foresaw that Syria's allies would increase their support to the regime at each point it faced increased pressure. They also worried intensely about the security vacuum which could follow a sudden regime collapse, which could lead to reprisal massacres, the disintegration of the country, or the incubation of an Iraqi-style jihadist insurgency. At the same time, Obama maintained a rhetorical posture that Asad must go. This public agreement on objectives meant that even though there were real and important disagreements about the desired endpoint, the intra-alliance (and public political) battles were primarily about means, not ends.

American caution infuriated the Gulf states and Turkey, which had hoped to be able to harness American power in support of their own objectives. They began to publicly advocate going it alone, a rhetorical posture which paradoxically seemed largely meant as an intra-alliance threat aimed at pressuring Obama to get with their program. "Don't wait for America," implored Lebanese columnist Hassan al-Haydar.[54] Relying on the United Nations had never solved any Arab problem, grumbled another Saudi columnist.[55] Restraining or at least coordinating these regional covert arms flows to the rebels would come to consume the attention of American diplomats in the coming months. Their efforts would fail.

| 5 |

DEMOCRACY'S CHANCE

Syria's plunge into the abyss came at a point when there was still hope elsewhere in the region. Tunisia's 2011 Constitutive Assembly elections had produced a remarkable coalition government which seemed determined to complete a transition to democracy. Egypt's Parliamentary elections had gone ahead, producing a freely elected body dominated by Islamists. Yemen's carefully managed transition from President Ali Abdullah Saleh frustrated many activists, but the February 2012 election of Abd Rabbo al-Mansour al-Hadi and the establishment of a National Dialogue kept the process moving forward. Morocco's king allowed the appointment of a government led by the moderate Islamist PJD following its victory in November 2011 elections.

Libya, too, remained hopeful. The NTC seemed overwhelmed by the challenge of state building and repeatedly deferred major decisions such as the distribution of oil wealth, the nature of federalism, and the disarmament of militias. Still, it moved in fits and starts towards a foundational election which could begin a meaningful transition. Non-Islamists did well in the July 7, 2012 election, but all major parties won representation. Most of the major parties were willing to give democratic institutions a chance, even as they hedged their bets by retaining their guns and their sources of external patronage. Libya's election reassured the Gulf regimes that Islamists would not always win elections, following the victories of the Muslim Brotherhood in Egypt, Ennahda in Tunisia, and the PJD. Now, raved one Saudi commentator not normally known for his love of democracy, July 7 would henceforth be known as "the day when the idea, not just the body, of Qaddafi truly died."[1]

The most electrifying moment came on June 26, 2012, as a riveted world watched an Egyptian judge grimly announce the election of the Muslim Brotherhood's Mohammed Morsi as president. Up until the announcement, many observers had expected that Mubarak's former prime minister, Ahmed Shafik, would be declared the winner, regardless of the actual voting. Morsi's 52-48 percent victory became one of the only elections in the history of the Arab world in which an opposition figure of any ideological description had won a position of real power through an election.

Before the Arab uprisings, the idea of a Muslim Brother winning a free, fair presidential election was literally unthinkable. The closest analogue was when Algerian Islamists had come close in 1991 to winning a super-majority in Parliament. The military had responded with a military coup, which set the stage for half a decade of bloody civil war.

It is important to remember that there was nothing novel about elections themselves. Parliamentary votes had been held routinely in most Arab countries outside the Gulf for decades. These elections served many purposes, including shuffling the spoils of rule among elite factions, letting off public steam, co-opting parts of the political opposition, and placating foreign observers. The peaceful rotation of power was not one of them. Elections might be confined to legislative institutions with little real power, or the rules carefully rigged to ensure the victory of regime supporters. The Egyptian election offered something tantalizingly different: the peaceful rotation of power through elections, the inclusion of Islamists in the democratic process, and the realization of democratic change through popular protest.

At that moment, anything seemed possible.

Americans often view democracy as important in its own right, both a normatively good system of government and the best guarantee of stability. Most Arab players took a wholly instrumental view of democracy: a fine thing if their own candidates won, unacceptable if their adversaries won. Even the fiercely anti-democratic rulers of the Gulf were fine with electoral systems which helped to keep their people in power, and quite comfortable playing the game of supporting friendly political parties and politicians. Saudi Arabia would have been quite content to tout democratic legitimacy had their candidate Ayad Allawi won the 2010 Iraqi election, but dismissed the actual winner, Nuri al-Maliki, as a Shi'ite Iranian proxy. Yemen's Abd Rabbo Mansour al-Hadi was viewed as legitimate for winning the (uncontested) 2012 election, but Morsi was not. This is a critical distinction: most saw little sense in supporting "democracy" in the abstract, rather than supporting one's own allies.

Egypt remained the centerpiece of the Arab uprising and the greatest strategic prize for the regional contenders for power. If Islamists won elections to Tunisian or Libyan Assemblies, it barely mattered for the broader regional balance of power. The Egyptian election tilted the regional balance of power towards Qatar's Islamist and activist networks. Shafik's victory would have kept post-revolutionary Egypt comfortably within the Saudi-led regional order. Morsi's victory signaled Cairo's potential shift into the Qatari coalition. Few realized at the time that they were witnessing the high-water mark for Qatari power.

The year following Morsi's inauguration featured virtually nonstop political warfare, polarization, and institutional combat. The Muslim Brotherhood, Qatar, and democracy all lost—with tremendous ramifications for the entire course of the Arab uprising. On July 3, 2013, four days after a large popular protest, General Abdel Fattah el-Sisi announced Morsi's removal as president, the suspension of the constitution, and the imposition of martial law. The coup received enthusiastic support and massive financial assistance from Saudi Arabia, the UAE, and Kuwait. Morsi's democratic legitimacy offered little protection. Six weeks later, the army attacked two Islamist protest encampments in central Cairo, killing almost a thousand people in broad daylight. The campaign of repression against the Muslim Brotherhood and secular activists alike ushered in a dark new phase in the Arab uprisings with effects far beyond Egypt's borders.

The road from the exuberance of Tahrir Square to the horrific public massacres in Rabaa circle reveals both the potential and the failure of the uprisings. As with everyplace else, domestic factors were the primary driver of events, but the battles between those domestic forces were deeply shaped by regional and external factors. It is striking how little reference is made to the external role of Egypt's politics in the thousands of analytical essays published over the course of the transition—except for denunciations of Qatar for its alleged sponsorship of the Muslim Brotherhood. But the activists of Tahrir in January 2011 had been deeply embedded within the broader Arab uprising and clearly understood themselves to be part of a regional wave. The Muslim Brotherhood and the Salafis who dominated the electoral politics of the transition drew on broad and deep transnational networks. The putschists of July 2013 were funded and encouraged by the United Arab Emirates and Saudi Arabia, which helped them to mobilize effective campaigns and to generate genuine popular support through months of hotly polarizing political conflict.

FROM PARLIAMENTARY ELECTIONS TO THE PRESIDENCY

Egypt's political arena heading into elections was shaped by the aftermath of November's violent clashes and the results of the 2011 parliamentary election. Under US pressure following the chaotic battles at Mohamed Mahmoud Street, the SCAF had firmly committed to presidential elections and the transfer of power by June. The parliamentary elections had demoralized activists and the feloul, while empowering Islamists. Qatar was naturally thrilled, and the UAE horrified. While the Saudis were likely pleased by the performance of the Salafis, who had long enjoyed their patronage, the overall political situation did not favor their efforts to restore the status quo.

The election's losers put their weight behind efforts to delegitimize the new Parliament and to ensure that it could not effectively operate. The state sought ways in which to limit the powers of Parliament and prevent the Muslim Brotherhood from translating its electoral legitimacy into real power. They were aided in these efforts by the constitutional vacuum created by the absence of a president, their close relations with the still-ruling SCAF, and the resistance to any meaningful change by the majority of the judiciary, the security services, and the rest of the state. Few doubted the political motivations behind these judicial decrees, especially after the powerful head of the Judges Club, Ahmed el-Zeki, delivered an inflammatory public denunciation of the Parliament, which clearly targeted the newly elected Islamists. Zeki left little to the imagination: "From this day forward, judges will have a say in determining the future of this country and its fate. We will not leave it to you to do with it what you want."[2]

The Brotherhood's new parliamentary bloc played into their hands by alienating potential allies with its heavy-handed efforts to shape the new legislative body and its pursuit of action on highly symbolic issues. The Parliament was unable to actually do much on practical issues because of the institutional gridlock in the transitional political structure, but the Brotherhood did itself no favors with its legislative behavior.

This manifested most fully in the intense battles over the composition and functions of the constitutional drafting assembly. Critics of the Muslim Brotherhood accused them of seeking to pack the Assembly with Islamists in order to draft what would surely be an Islamist document. Their withdrawals and boycotts helped to create a self-fulfilling prophecy. It is not clear that any process could have worked at this point, but the failure to prioritize inclusivity and a broad consensus in this first major attempt at constitutional drafting ranks as one of the biggest missed opportunities in the Egyptian transition. Its failure left the subsequent phase unmoored from clearly defined institutional commitments or rules and kept the most potent existential questions about the country's identity open at the expense of more pragmatic issues of institutional design and effective governance.

The existential uncertainty bedeviling the transition was not helped by the judiciary's repeated interventions in the transitional process.[3] Their most inopportune interventions came in the runup to the presidential election. They disqualified several leading candidates on flimsy grounds, including the Salafi favorite Hazem Abu Ismail, Muslim Brotherhood heavyweight Khairat al-Shater, and Mubarak's old intelligence chief Omar Suleiman. While few really mourned the exclusion of any of these problematic candidates, the judiciary's arbitrary and politicized decisions set a dangerous precedent of its unchecked power. This became even more apparent when the Supreme Constitutional Court dissolved the Parliament only two weeks before the presidential election. This did not speak well for the neutrality of state institutions—and posed an unmistakable threat to the Brotherhood as they contemplated their place within the emergent political system.

Public opinion surveys and the elite consensus had settled on two front-runners: the former Arab League Secretary-General Amr Moussa and the former Muslim Brotherhood reformist Abd al-Munim Abu al-Futuh. While most external powers maintained public neutrality, the Gulf and the United States likely preferred Moussa, a longtime diplomat with whom they were deeply familiar (and who was too old to have ambitions of becoming another president for life). Qatar, Turkey, and parts of the revolutionary coalition inclined towards Abu al-Futuh. Some revolutionaries preferred the Nasserist Hamdeen Sabahi or the socialist lawyer Khaled al-Ali. The most potentially troublesome candidates, including Shater, Suleiman, and Abu Ismail, had been disqualified.

Neither of the front runners survived the first round of the elections, however. Moussa, Abu al-Futuh and Sabbahi split the revolutionary vote, dividing an outright majority of the vote among themselves. Instead, Morsi faced off with Mubarak's final prime minister, Ahmed Shafik, in a runoff despite neither candidate winning more than 25 percent of the vote. Activists, liberals, and much of the international community were horrified. Mubarak's old warning that the choice to rule Egypt was either him or the Muslim Brotherhood had somehow staggered back to life.

The Morsi-Shafik runoff was the worst possible outcome for the hopes of consolidating a democratic transition. The matchup highlighted the most polarized and intransigent political trends, while sidelining the vast middle ground of revolutionaries, liberals, activists, and unaffiliated citizens who had been drawn in to the new politics. At the regional level, it also transformed the Egyptian election into a fairly straightforward showdown between the Qatari and the UAE regional networks. Qatar's support for the Muslim Brotherhood and for the revolutionary coalition was well-established. The UAE support for the Ahmed Shafik campaign was a very thinly veiled secret. Shafik, who actually lived in the Emirates, seemed to have inexhaustible financial resources and exceptionally favorable coverage from the Gulf-based media.

Their showdown forced the activists and the more passive supporters of the January 25 revolution to choose between what they saw as two evils: a return of the regime they had sacrificed so much to remove, or a handoff of power to an Islamist party they mistrusted and feared. In the end, just enough tilted towards a leap of faith on the Brotherhood to elect Morsi. Less than two years after millions had taken to the streets demanding the overthrow of Hosni Mubarak, some 48 percent of the Egyptian public had voted for a representative of his fallen regime. Still, the election represented a final gasp of Tahrir's revolutionary coalition. Just enough of the activists and those hoping for change were still willing to give the Muslim Brotherhood a chance to provide a narrow majority. That would not last long.

PRESIDENT MORSI

Egypt's presidential election of 2012 represented both the high point of its attempted democratic transition and the fiercest challenge to the revolution. The election results revealed a highly polarized country, and one which had not been kind to the Tahrir coalition. The Egyptian deep state gritted its teeth and agreed to ratify Morsi's election by a 52-48 margin, but it never accommodated itself to the reality of an Islamist president. The foot-dragging resistance and active subversion of governance by the Egyptian bureaucracy was an important part of the declining public confidence in his rule. Before he could take office, the Supreme Constitutional

Court dissolved the Islamist-dominated Parliament and the SCAF issued constitutional revisions which limited presidential power. By late July, Morsi seemed to have become a political joke, unable to deliver on his promises or to impose his authority.

Many of Morsi's problems were primarily domestic and of his own making. But not all. After the coup, many thoughtful observers would put full blame for Egypt's failure on Morsi.[4] There is no question that he ruled in a divisive and insular way, but it is also clear that significant parts of the Egyptian political class—with the support of similarly skeptical Gulf states—refused from the outset to be involved in any constructive way. Goodwill and a commitment to sustaining a transition were in remarkably short supply. Their boycott of Morsi's invitations to dialogue or to participate in the government may have been justified by his insincerity, but they were also a conscious political strategy. The non-cooperation by the state bureaucracy and the newly limited powers of the presidency seemed to leave him with little more than a megaphone at his disposal—and a chorus of opponents determined to drown out whatever he might have to say. Morsi's lack of inclusiveness was not simply a feature of his personality or an outgrowth of the Muslim Brotherhood's insular organizational culture. It was an outcome of the political process itself.

The Obama administration, while anxious about what to expect from a Muslim Brotherhood presidency and concerned for core interests such as the peace treaty with Israel, nonetheless welcomed the results of the election as a step towards consolidating Egyptian democracy. It signaled clearly its willingness to work with Morsi as the elected president of Egypt. This public American posture complicated matters for the Gulf states, which felt somewhat constrained in acting upon their clear disdain for an elected Islamist in the presidential palace. This was not because Obama had any illusions about Morsi. The American posture was grounded in the determination to facilitate meaningful political democratization, and to cement the participation of mainstream Islamism in democratic politics.

There was also a counterterrorism component. In Obama's conception of the war of ideas against al-Qaeda, as articulated in his 2009 Cairo speech to the Muslims of the world, bringing mainstream Islamists into formal politics was absolutely crucial. Accepting Morsi's victory could also combat the well-earned belief among most Muslims in the region that the United States would only support democracies which produced pro-American outcomes. The administration clearly recognized that no political system which excluded a group the size of the Muslim Brotherhood could ever be truly democratic. Obama was prepared to pay the short-term costs of an unsympathetic Egyptian president in order to achieve a long-term consolidation of Egyptian democracy.

Morsi's enemies were not. For the Muslim Brotherhood's adversaries, Morsi's election was an unalloyed disaster. Some in the Gulf counseled prudence, calling for efforts to work with the new Egyptian government and ensure its continued alignment with the prevailing regional order. But most looked to block the Brotherhood's rise to power and Cairo's tilt towards Qatar, even at the cost of Egyptian stability. Saudi Arabia and the United Arab Emirates refused to contribute financially, while many Egyptian businessmen withdrew investments. Qatar stepped in to fill this void, extending some $5 billion in economic assistance to Egypt. The other Gulf states muttered grimly about the dependence created by the fact that injections of Qatari and Turkish cash were the only thing keeping Egypt's economy afloat. Following the July 2013 coup, Egypt would return more than half of this money to Doha.

Morsi tried to position his presidency as a vindication of the Egyptian revolution, not as a triumph for Islamism. He clearly understood the importance of maintaining a working relationship with the United States, Israel, and the Gulf states. Key Brotherhood officials like Khairat al-Shater consistently assured visitors that their highest priority had to be economic development. His efforts to establish his authority triggered the fears of his opponents. So did the role of unelected Brotherhood figures such as Shater and Supreme Guide Mohammed el-Badi'e in the formulation of government policy. Reforming state institutions, from the media to the Interior Ministry, had been a principal demand of the revolution. Now they were portrayed as a sinister plot to "Islamize" the state by purging secular bastions and installing Muslim Brotherhood sympathizers across the bureaucracy.

Morsi made his move in early August. In a sweeping set of changes, Morsi removed the heads of General Intelligence and the Military Police, along with the two most senior members of the SCAF. General Abd el-Fattah el-Sisi, elevated to the leadership of the SCAF, endorsed this leadership shuffle, leading to rampant speculation about his possible Islamist sympathies. Egypt's polarization was already so well advanced by this point that this removal of widely detested military leaders was seen not as the fulfillment of the revolutionary demand to establish civilian control over the military, but as an Islamist threat to capture the state.[5] Morsi's move against the intelligence heads and the SCAF leadership suddenly and dramatically changed public perceptions of his presidency, from an ineffectual joke to being regarded as a real player in Egypt's treacherous political gamesmanship. This alarmed the Gulf regimes, for whom the senior intelligence and military leaderships had long been a primary point of connection.

It soon got worse for Riyadh and Abu Dhabi, particularly in terms of the wider regional war. On September 1, Morsi visited Tehran for a meeting of the Non-Aligned Conference, the first visit by an Egyptian president in some 30 years. Saudis feared that a key pillar in the anti-Iranian regional bloc was now following Qatar into a neutral, if not pro-Iranian, stance. As Saudi columnist Jamal Khashoggi observed, "the Muslim Brotherhood's stance will go a long way to determining whether Iran will remain locked in to its current isolation."[6] Morsi's appearance in Tehran offered mixed lessons. While he showed few signs of aligning with Iran, Morsi's presence signaled a relaxing of Tehran's regional isolation. The notion of the new Egypt serving as an honest broker between the region's competing factions reflected the influence of the Qatari approach to regional affairs. Nothing could be more alarming to Riyadh.

Morsi's stance on Syria was more pleasing to the Gulf states. Nobody had known quite what to expect from Egypt under Morsi on such policy issues. If his visit to Tehran had infuriated the Saudis, he proved more reliable on Syria.[7] Whether because of his Muslim Brotherhood network, his Qatari backing, or his identification with the Arab revolutions, Morsi took a strong stand against the Asad regime and in favor of the Syrian uprising. Even this was not always sufficiently robust for some Gulf tastes. In July 2012, the journalist Mishari al-Zaydi acidly advised ignoring the Egyptian-led Arab League, "which is clearly subordinated to the official Egyptian discourse in the age of the Brotherhood, which only expresses sympathy for the Syrian people but opposes any intervention to save them...why did the Muslim Brotherhood leaders welcome NATO jets in Libya but not in Syria?"[8]

Morsi's Syria stance continued to evolve. In May 2013, he hosted a controversial conference in Cairo featuring Yusuf al-Qaradawi which called for a jihad in Syria. This was a delicate moment. The call for jihad, framed in blatantly sectarian terms, was portrayed by many critics as evidence of Morsi's previously concealed extremism and a hard turn towards jihadism. But all was not as it seemed. The rhetoric of jihad was perhaps new for Cairo, but had by this point become completely standard fare in the Gulf. Similar language could be heard routinely in the mosques and the fund-raising events in Kuwait, Bahrain, Saudi Arabia, and Qatar. Morsi's endorsement of the Syrian jihad was less a revelation of his true religious beliefs than a cynical bid to align himself with the Gulf states on Syria at a time of deep contention on other issues.

The September attack on the US Embassy during the *Innocence of Muslims* protests offered Morsi another chance to prove his intentions. He could side with the protestors and please an Islamist base, or he could crack down on them and protect the embassies to prove that he could govern responsibly. He chose the latter. This choice was not uncontroversial among many of Morsi's supporters, for whom the United States remained a prime enemy and who could hardly believe that an Islamist president would protect it from their protests. But pragmatic political calculations governed Morsi's behavior, allowing him to turn a potential diplomatic disaster into a signal to the West that he could be trusted with state power.

Morsi was very quickly tested again by a flare-up of violence between Israel and Hamas in Gaza. Once again, Morsi was torn between the enthusiasm of his base for confrontation with Israel and the pragmatic dictates of the national interest in preserving relations with the West. For

Israel, this was the first test of how an Egypt under new management would deal with Gaza. Mubarak had been a close partner to the Israeli security forces, a fierce enemy of Hamas, and a primary architect and enforcer of the siege of Gaza. Morsi, friendly with Hamas and hostile to Israel, once again proved more responsible and diplomatically effective than most had expected. Morsi's administration brokered a truce after four days, which ended the violence and promised (though did little to later deliver) humanitarian relief for Gaza. While the military may have remained in charge of the Israel file through this crisis, Morsi did not attempt to overrule their mediation or resort to inflammatory rhetoric.

Morsi's behavior through these crises looked like a powerful validation of the idea that domestic politics would end at the border and that any leader would rationally follow the dictates of the national interest. By mid-November 2012, Morsi's international diplomacy had bought him considerable, if grudging, regional and international acceptance. Isarel and the Gulf states remained deeply suspicious, but their worst fears had not materialized. The United States had been impressed with his effective Gaza diplomacy and willingness to control the mobs attacking the embassy. Morsi was beginning to look more like a president than like the floundering neophyte of July. His foreign policy successes resonated at home, as his growing diplomatic acceptance forced the security state to take more seriously a figure whom they believed they had effectively neutered.

But then, he pushed too far, too fast. On November 22, Morsi took an extraordinary measure to push through a controversial constitutional draft. With an eye on the frequent interventions of the Supreme Constitutional Court, he declared ultimate presidential authority without judicial review. Morsi presented his move as a temporary measure to ensure the passage of the constitution, and as a necessary response to the judiciary's obvious politicization. But the optics were terrible and the potential implications alarming. In Egypt's intensely polarized environment, his move was immediately seen as an exceedingly dangerous power grab designed to impose unimpeded Islamist rule on the nation. Ultimately, Morsi's constitution would pass by referendum on December 15, with 57 percent voting in favor based on a very low turnout of approximately 30 percent. On December 26, it came into effect.

The new constitution did nothing to settle down the political crisis or to establish consensus rules of the game. The process was widely seen as fatally flawed, and the environment tainted by nasty clashes between protestors and Brotherhood supporters. A violent attack on protestors outside of the presidential palace in Ittihadiya in mid-December became a defining moment in a narrative of Islamist perfidy, and a rallying point for the campaign against Morsi. Prominent liberals such as Mohammed el-Baradei issued apocalyptic warnings of impending disaster. To combat Morsi, they formed the National Salvation Front, encompassing some three dozen political groups and many prominent personalities. The National Salvation Front would spend the next six months working to unseat the president—and would find powerful allies in their quest, including many of the same institutional forces that the revolution had once sought to overthrow.

THINGS FALL APART

The National Salvation Front facilitated a reconciliation between the political opposition and the military, leaving the Muslim Brotherhood without allies. Breaking the temporary coalition between secular activists and the Brotherhood had been a key ambition of the Brotherhood's opponents since Tahrir Square itself. In Egypt as elsewhere, the key to defeating the Islamists was to strip away their coalition partners and leave them exposed in a bipolar political environment in which regime forces were the only viable alternative. Hostility between the activists and Brothers had mounted throughout the post-Tahrir period. For much of the transitional period, the activists accused the Brotherhood of aligning with the military in its quest for power. Now, they would do the same.

Following Morsi's power grab, polarization entrenched itself. Anti-Islamist themes flooded the media, most of which either remained state-owned or were owned by wealthy businessmen with ties to the old regime and to the Gulf.[9] This propaganda emphasized the radicalism and exoticism of the Islamists: stripping away their humanity by denigrating them as robotic sheep following the commands of their supreme leader; questioning their nationalism by highlighting their transnational and international networks; shaping attitudes by endlessly repeating and exaggerating every dubious incident or statement. Islamist media reciprocated by denouncing their critics as secularists or atheists, or as servants of America, Israel, and the United Arab Emirates. Al-Jazeera Direct Egypt became a virtual mouthpiece for the Brotherhood, while Saudi-backed media like al-Arabiya amplified every anti-Brotherhood message. Every event or political gambit would be filtered through dozens of highly partisan new media outlets, creating two virtually irreconcilable narratives about Egyptian politics.

Events on the ground gave these dueling media narratives plenty of ammunition. Following the passage of the Constitution, Morsi pushed to hold parliamentary elections, which would finally end the institutional void at the heart of the Egyptian political system. This made good sense, and could have been seized upon by the opposition as an opportunity. Morsi's power was magnified by the absence of any competing institution with democratic legitimacy. If the Muslim Brotherhood were as unpopular as its critics claimed, then its weakness would be exposed by the elections. Such an outcome would have created an institutional balance of power and a system of checks and balances for the first time in modern Egyptian history. An electoral setback would also likely have forced Morsi to recalibrate his approach and seek compromise. But the opposition rejected the calls for elections, largely for instrumental reasons. They believed they would lose.

Meanwhile, violence on the streets spiraled, as protestors began attacking Muslim Brotherhood party offices, buildings, and buses. Violent clashes became increasingly common, with the police nowhere to be seen, creating an impression (eagerly encouraged by the media) of a country in free fall. The growing sense of insecurity was compounded by unprecedented and inexplicable energy shortages and power cuts. The *New York Times*, noting the "apparently miraculous end to the crippling energy shortages, and the re-emergence of the police" following the July 3 coup, would later quite plausibly attribute the sense of impending doom to the efforts by the state to undermine Morsi's government.[10] Whatever the truth of the case for state complicity, the combination of political polarization and insecurity helped to drive the narrative that Morsi had lost control of the country and could no longer govern. This would justify the military coup.

The United States struggled valiantly to convince both sides to remain committed to the democratic process. Its public rhetoric infuriated the anti-Islamist coalition, which hoped instead to subvert that democratic process to bring down the president. On February 10, 2013, Ambassador Anne Patterson told an assembly of civil society leaders in Alexandria that "the people who will build Egypt's future are the ones who are best at finding reasonable compromises and building national consensus."[11] The Tamarod movement, a high-profile national campaign collecting millions of signatures against Morsi, called for a mass protest on June 30. This became the focal point for the anti-Morsi campaign. On June 18, with the Tamarod protests less than two weeks away, Patterson outraged activists who sensed impending victory by warning that "some say that street action will produce better results than elections. To be honest, my government and I are deeply skeptical. Egypt needs stability to get its economic house in order, and more violence on the streets will do little more than add new names to the lists of martyrs."[12]

But by this point, Morsi's opponents at home and abroad had no interest in finding common ground. The National Salvation Front had spent the last six months in full-scale confrontation mode, focusing its efforts on hounding Morsi out of office. Morsi, for his part, clearly believed that the Tamarod protest would fizzle, or at least be manageable as part of the ongoing political negotiations.

Delirious media coverage on June 30 made outrageous but widely repeated claims of thirty million participants, supposedly making it the largest protest event in human history.[13] While those claims were wildly exaggerated, the protests were unquestionably huge. Some speculated that this surge was due to the active support of the United Arab Emirates and the security services, but there were also plenty of Egyptians who had become deeply frustrated with the political stalemate and felt deeply hostile towards the Brotherhood.[14] Indeed, the seemingly widescale turn against the Brotherhood, undoing its decades of careful cultivation of popular support seemingly overnight, has yet to be convincingly explained. Had the June 30 protest fizzled, the military likely would have stayed its hand, and Morsi would probably have contained the crisis.

Instead, following the huge turnout on June 30, events unfolded quickly. Morsi rejected demands that he immediately step down, ignoring a deadline set by the military leadership. The military then removed him. While Egyptians and Gulf media would spend months furiously claiming that this should be seen as a second popular revolution rather than as a military coup, this is nonsense. General Abdel Fatteh el-Sisi's seizure of power was as close to a textbook case of a military coup as it is possible to be. Like countless military men before him, Sisi seized the political opportunity created by mass mobilization to remove and imprison an elected leader along with much of his political party, suspend the constitution, and declare martial law. That he managed to generate considerable popular support for his coup makes it a distinctive kind of coup, but no less a coup for that.

It is now common to hear that Egyptian democracy could never have succeeded, and that the military had no choice but to step in to prevent state collapse. This is not convincing. Right up until the moment of the coup, there were possible outcomes that would have saved the transition to democracy. Morsi could have agreed to early Presidential elections, even if this would set a dangerous precedent for future administrations. The opposition could have taken up Morsi's offer of new Parliamentary elections. If it had used its increased leverage to bargain for an equitable election law, it would have had a fighting chance to exploit the Muslim Brotherhood's failures to take a majority of the new legislature. This would have created the first government divided between political groups commanding electoral legitimacy in Egypt's modern history. The National Salvation Front's support for the military coup represented an historic abandonment of democratic possibility.

Why did Morsi not see the coup coming? Perhaps because he had read the balance of forces a bit too accurately. He simply did not take the

National Salvation Front or the activist community seriously, given their unpopularity and their history of infighting and empty posturing. He seemed to believe that the protest called for June 30 was part of politics as usual, just another of the failed mass protests called by the opposition over the previous two years. Morsi likely felt that he was secure as long as the military stayed onboard, and believed the assurances that General Sisi presumably had given him to that effect. He also likely overestimated American power, trusting that Washington's frequent private and public messages of commitment to the democratic process would protect him and deter his enemies.

On this, more than anything else, he misread not only the depth of popular dissatisfaction and Sisi's real stance, but also the rapidly changing regional order. The Saudis and Emiratis were not going to miss this opportunity to reverse Qatar's greatest strategic advance and regain control over the region. Nor were they in a mood to be coerced by Washington to stay their hands. The Egyptian crisis came to a head in the late spring and summer of 2013, when the Gulf states had broken with the United States over Syria and were deeply alarmed by its diplomacy with Iran. Washington's waning influence over Riyadh and Abu Dhabi was a variable that Morsi, steeped in generations of belief in America's total power in the region, had failed to appreciate.

General Abdel Fattah el-Sisi's July 3, 2013 coup against Morsi marked a new phase not only for Egypt but also for the region. The primary positive American project following the Arab uprisings, the transition to a democratic Egypt, had been decisively ended at the hand of some of America's closest regional allies. The success of the anti-Morsi coalition emboldened its backers to consider similarly aggressive policy initiatives in other stalemated conflict zones such as Libya, Yemen, and Syria. The Muslim Brotherhood, so recently in ascendance, was suddenly thrown into existential crisis and forced to rapidly evolve new survival mechanisms and political narratives. The coup reshaped the domestic politics of countries as different as transitional Tunisia and monarchical Kuwait.

The new military government did include several well-known liberal figures, including the human rights defender Ziad Bahaa al-Din and the opposition icon Mohammed el-Baradei. These liberals, like many of the enthusiasts for the June 30 protest, presumably believed that the coup represented a second chance for democratic transition after the Brotherhood's failure. They counseled restraint, warning of the domestic and international repercussions of a violent response. Better to entice the Brotherhood back into the political game after a brief pause, they argued, and to focus on putting Egypt back on to a democratic path. American and European Union officials worked quietly with them to find a path towards reconciliation with the Brotherhood.

They found little appetite for compromise on either side. The Muslim Brotherhood had not easily accepted the removal of Morsi and arrest of much of its senior leadership. They mounted daily marches against the new regime and established the Rabaa protest site in a central Cairo roundabout as a focal point for sustained pressure for the reversal of the coup and the restoration of the legitimately elected president.

The Egyptian regime was divided over whether to pursue reconciliation or a hard line. Inside the government, the eradicators and their external backers advocating an iron fist policy against the Brotherhood decisively won the argument. On August 6, the military moved against Rabaa, killing approximately a thousand protestors in a single day. This was one of the single largest body counts of any single day in the Middle East—greater even than all but the worst days in Syria. With this spasm of violence, the die was cast. Baradei resigned his position as vice president, and Egypt's military regime consolidated as a new autocracy. The media devolved into state-controlled regime propaganda, whipping up toxic new forms of nationalism and xenophobia alongside a personality cult for the new president. Activists were arrested under a draconian new protest law.

These heavy-handed policies predictably failed to restore stability. Sisi's regime soon faced a spiraling insurgency. The Sinai began to spiral out of control. Shadowy groups of previously unknown jihadists took advantage of the chaos and some members of the shattered Brotherhood began to carry out acts of sabotage. Policemen were shot and official buildings and vehicles attacked. The economy continued to struggle, particularly the moribund tourism sector. Only frequent infusions of cash from the Gulf states kept the economy afloat—a temporary solution that only highlighted Cairo's dependence on its external backers.

The primary drivers of Egypt's failure were Egyptian, not foreign. The UAE and Saudi Arabia alone could not have decided the fate of Egypt's democratic transition. Morsi made ample mistakes of his own, which alienated wide swaths of the Egyptian political public. Their grievances against Morsi were very real. Egyptian state institutions and most of the old elite were dead set against him for their own reasons. Desperate Egyptians yearned for a return to stability and hoped for some economic relief. The external backers of the anti-Morsi movement worked with very real grievances. Their role was arguably greater at the international level, where the Saudi, Emirati, and Kuwaiti willingness to offset any cuts to American aid neutralized the few policy instruments to prevent or reverse a coup at Washington's disposal.

THE REGIONAL POLITICS OF THE EGYPTIAN COUP

The regional coalition backing the coup was hardly a secret. Sisi's new regime immediately received massive financial support from the anti-Iran bloc in the Gulf. Saudi Arabia, the UAE, and Kuwait contributed more than $20 billion to keep Egyptian finances afloat, while providing essential political protection from American pressure for reconciliation. Egypt's intense anti-Brotherhood campaign following the coup soon became a regional one, as Saudi Arabia joined the UAE in declaring the Muslim Brotherhood a terrorist organization and pushed (with limited success) for a broader international campaign against the Islamist organization.

These Gulf states would soon find, however, that Egypt was not an easy client state. Even when almost completely dependent on their financial backing, Egypt would break with the Saudi position on Syria, demur on full participation in the war in Yemen, and fail to undertake desperately needed economic reforms.

The anti-Islamism at the core of the Sisi coalition often lay beneath these problems. While this aligned comfortably with the UAE's political posture, it caused conflict with the more complex Saudi stance. On Syria, Sisi inclined more towards Asad's militarized war than towards an insurgency it viewed as Islamist to the core. Where the Gulf regimes had long since devoted themselves to the armed overthrow of Bashar al-Asad and had lavished support on factions of the Syrian insurgency, an Egyptian regime that came to power over the dead bodies of the Muslim Brotherhood identified more closely with the Syrian dictator fighting a bloody war against jihadists. This conflict became even more acute in 2015, when the new King Salman eased Saudi hostility towards Turkey and the Muslim Brotherhood. While the Gulf states sharply objected when Russia began bombing in late September 2015, Egypt welcomed the Russians as a useful addition to the struggle against terrorism.[15] As the Jordanian journalist and al-Jazeera director Yasir Abu Hilala marveled, "as soon as the coup happened, Egypt's military hastened to reverse Morsi's Syria policy 180 degrees... and apparently have a deep alliance with the Bashar regime... what is strange is that the first supporter of the coup was Saudi Arabia, which has led the political and military campaign against Bashar. Why has there not been pressure on Sisi to join the coalition against the Syrian regime?"[16]

The violent crackdown on the Brotherhood aligned nicely with both the extreme anti-Brotherhood preferences of its principal financial backer, United Arab Emirates, and with the Saudi determination to reverse Qatari gains. The coup represented a major reversal in the balance of power between competing Gulf networks, with Qatar's ascendance abruptly overturned in favor of those aligned with the UAE-Saudi coalition. But those two different priorities would not always align so well.

The Saudi and Emirati victory over Qatar in Egypt was accompanied by a stunning change in Doha itself. On June 25, the emir of Qatar abdicated in favor of his son, Tamim. Qataris insist that the timing of the emir's departure was a coincidence, with the succession long planned and driven by health concerns, and that regional policy would not change. Perhaps. But the new emir quickly moved to repair relations with Saudi Arabia. Most dramatically, he stripped the architect of Qatar's Arab Spring policies, Hamed bin Jassem, of his positions as prime minister and foreign minister and removed him as the director of the Qatar Investment Authority. Qatar continued to support its allies and push its policies in Syria and Libya, but it had been chastened by defeats.

The legitimation of these interventions required some careful juggling acts. In Egypt, the Muslim Brotherhood seized upon the concept of "legitimacy" in its defense of the overthrown President Morsi. Gulf backers of the coup dismissed these arguments, echoing Egyptian arguments that his failure to govern as an inclusive president and the massive size of the June 30 protest constituted a popular impeachment. But even as they dismissed electoral legitimacy in Egypt, they explained their support for the Libyan House of Representatives and ousted Yemeni President Hadi in terms of electoral legitimacy. Saudi voices furiously denounced Russian or Iranian interventions in Syria as illegitimate violations of state sovereignty but happily endorsed their own bombing campaigns in Libya and Yemen. Intellectual consistency was not a major coin of this realm.

The decision by the Gulf states to crack down on the Muslim Brotherhood was one of the most remarkable, and polarizing, decisions of this period. The grueling events of summer 2013 badly disrupted the Brotherhood's comfortable place in the regional constellation. Egypt's military coup triggered a regionwide crackdown on the Muslim Brotherhood and its affiliates. While the UAE was the driving force behind this anti-Brotherhood campaign, Saudi Arabia threw its considerable weight behind it. The abdication of Qatari's emir in favor of the young and less experienced Shaykh Tamim left all Brotherhood affiliates uncertain about their future during the pivotal year between the conclusion of the National Dialogue and the Houthi coup.

The Brotherhood had enjoyed a privileged status in most Gulf states for years. Well-established Brotherhood organizations and political parties operated in Kuwait and Bahrain. In Saudi Arabia, the Brotherhood did not formally exist as an independent organization but thrived within the Sahwa Islamist networks that had driven Saudi politics in the 1990s.[17] In Qatar, the Brotherhood had formally dissolved itself in the late 1990s but retained a powerful presence in state institutions and the religious sphere best symbolized by the exceptionally influential Yusuf al-Qaradawi. Only in the United Arab Emirates was the Brotherhood viewed as anathema, where the generic Emirati distaste for any form of political opposition was exacerbated by the personal anti-Islamist attitude of Abu Dhabi's Mohammad Bin Zayed.

The UAE's ability to rally a mostly Islamist-friendly Gulf to its extreme anti-Brotherhood cause is therefore remarkable. It is especially so given that the Gulf Islamists were simultaneously extremely active in mobilizing support for the Syrian insurgency. The Islamist successes following the Arab uprisings triggered deep anxieties among the Gulf's rulers, who suddenly began to worry about the potential threat the Brothers might pose to their own rule. Their regional ascendancy and perceived tightness with Qatar triggered Saudi concerns about the Brotherhood, even after Morsi made a point of making Saudi Arabia his first foreign visit after his election. Saudi official concerns also revolved around the role played by Brotherhood-aligned Sahwa Islamists such as Salman Odah in pushing Saudi political reforms.[18] In March 2013, Odah had issued a widely discussed open letter to King Abdullah warning of the potentially disastrous consequences of failing to begin serious reforms. This constellation of concerns helps to explain why the UAE's eliminationist approach to the Brotherhood suddenly surged to the fore—and why it faded almost as quickly following Abdullah's death and the coronation of King Salman.

Gulf Islamists were almost universally outraged over the Egyptian coup. Yellow four-fingered Rabaa Twitter avatars spread like wildfire through these networks. Initially, there were some remarkably bold challenges.[19] A popular hashtag quickly appeared on Twitter: "King Abdullah's Speech Does Not Represent Me." The popular Kuwait-based preacher Tareq Suwaidan was curtly dismissed from his position at the television station al-Risalah by Saudi Prince Waleed bin Talal with a series of tweets that "there is no place for any member of the Muslim Brotherhood in our group," and explaining that Suwaidan had "confessed to his membership in the terrorist Brotherhood movement." Suwaidan was vocal indeed in his criticism of the crackdown, but he was hardly alone.

The condemnation of Egypt's crackdown and of the official Gulf support extended across multiple Islamist networks and prominent personalities.

The popular Kuwaiti Islamist personality Nabil al-Awadhy (one of the top supporters of the campaign to support Syrian rebels) raged that "the blood of innocents is flowing in Egypt...the murderers unleash their bullets without mercy and lay siege to mosques and burn them...and they want you Muslims to watch in silence!" When the Saudi Abd al-Aziz Tarefe tweeted that "what is happening in Egypt is a war against Islam," he received 1584 re-tweets in twenty-four minutes. Saudi Islamist Salman al-Awda tweeted in English on August 15: "Whoever helps a murderer—whether by word, deed, financial support, or even a gesture of approval—is an accomplice. Whoever remains silent in the face of murder to safeguard his personal interests is an accessory to the crime." And a group of fifty-six Islamists, including a number known to be close to the Saudi Muslim Brotherhood networks, issued an open letter: "We express our opposition and surprise at the path taken by some countries who have given recognition to the coup...thereby taking part in committing a sin and an aggression forbidden by the laws of Islam—and there will be negative consequences for everyone if Egypt enters a state of chaos and civil war."[20]

For an insecure Saudi regime, this public rallying to the Brotherhood's cause against regime policy crossed a red line. The shifting political environment empowered members of the Saudi regime who had long viewed the Brotherhood skeptically. Former Crown Prince Nayef had in previous years blamed the Brotherhood for al-Qaeda and the spread of global terrorism, and sympathetic Saudi officials and pundits had frequently peddled anti-Brotherhood propaganda to credulous Westerners.[21] The evident public sympathy with their criticisms of the coup, and not just Emirati pressure, may have helped tip the king to crack down on the Brotherhood. The subsequent crackdown on the Brotherhood played out in multiple channels. The Saudi-owned media filled with opinion essays criticizing the Brotherhood's politicization of religion, rigid ways, and duplicity. In February 2014, Saudi Arabia and several other states joined Egypt in declaring the Brotherhood a terrorist organization, putting severe pressure on its regional operations, finances, and public presence. The Gulf states even pressured the British government into opening a half-hearted inquiry into the Brotherhood's alleged terrorist ties.

Saudi Arabia could not sustain an open-ended war with the Brotherhood, however, given its deep networks and the broad sympathies felt by much of its population. The abdication of the emir of Qatar and the ascension of his more pliable son relieved some of the intensity of that dimension of regional competition, and reduced the salience of the Brotherhood in the battle of Gulf networks. Almost as soon as Salman replaced Abdullah, Saudi policy backed away from its year-and-a-half-long crackdown on the Brotherhood. The Yemen war offered the opportunity to restore these frayed relations. Al-Islah was a useful proxy on the ground for Saudi Arabia as it looked for ways to counter the Houthi surge into Sanaa. A shared focus on the Shi'ite threat was always a useful way to gloss over intra-Sunni competition. The enthusiastic support for the GCC military intervention in Yemen thus provided cover for an otherwise contentious relationship.

Egypt's coup offered a significant opening to the Islamic State of Syria and Iraq (ISIS) and to al-Qaeda. The destruction of the Muslim Brotherhood removed the most powerful mainstream competitor to the jihadist trends. The coup utterly discredited the Brotherhood's strategy of peaceful democratic participation, proving to everyone that Islamists could not actually achieve their goals through such peaceful means. The coup severely damaged the Brotherhood's organization and its social services infrastructure. Hundreds of its leaders and tens of thousands of its members were imprisoned, hundreds of clinics and businesses appropriated by the state, and intense pressure brought to bear on its public and private functions.

The coup also internationalized the Brotherhood, after years of its intense focus on domestic political battles. Most of the leaders who escaped Morsi's repression ended up in Qatar or Turkey, where they set out to rebuild the organization from afar. Exile left them far more dependent on these sponsoring states, and cut them off from developments on the ground. The organization struggled to maintain message discipline and control. Incitement from Turkey-based social media might have a different set of motivations and try to portray a very different image from Cairo-based Brotherhood social media. Disillusioned former leaders of the

Brotherhood encouraged a restructuring that they for the most part did not believe was possible.[22] Social media became, in this context, an essential skeleton for the rebuilding of the shattered organization.[23] Key social media administrators working from exile in Europe formulated strategy through online interaction and observation, in the absence of easy direct communications across the organization.[24]

This left thousands of Muslim Brotherhood members alone and bereft, furious over their treatment and eager for revenge. This would make them prime recruiting ground for new jihadist groups popping up in Egypt. In this environment, the Brotherhood's angry young cadres increasingly inclined towards violence.[25] It is difficult for many of these youth to see a peaceful strategy as anything other than collective suicide.[26] The precise membership and identity of the many small groups comprising Egypt's new insurgency remains murky, but it seems likely that at least some percentage of them are made up of former Brotherhood cells.[27]

Egypt's successful revolution had driven the Arab uprising to every corner of the region. Its transitional failure would similarly have ramifications far beyond its borders. It is to those effects in Libya and Tunisia that I now turn.

| 6 |

AUTOCRATS ON OFFENSE

In early September 2012, Arab public attention was gripped by reports of an appalling film appearing on YouTube. Entitled *The Innocence of Muslims*, this noxious (if little-seen) clip portrayed the Prophet Mohammed as a homosexual pedophile and mocked the tenets of the faith. As with the 2006 frenzy over Danish cartoons insulting the Prophet, politicians and Islamist movements across the region seized the opportunity to compete over who could most angrily denounce a film that few would otherwise have ever noticed.

In the age of the Arab uprisings, however, such mobilization carried far greater potential for escalation into broader political challenges. On September 10, major protests erupted in Cairo and several other Arab cities. In Cairo, protestors scaled the walls of the American Embassy complex to hang the black flag then associated with al-Qaeda—posing a major challenge to President Morsi, forcing him to navigate between his vital relationship with Washington and the Islamist sensibilities of his electoral base. Those dramatic events in Egypt would soon be overshadowed by the events the next day in Libya, when Ambassador Chris Stevens and two other US officials were killed in Benghazi.[1]

While the American political public would soon fixate on the events in Benghazi as a political scandal for the Obama administration, the events of that dreadful day had far greater meaning for the trajectory of the Arab uprisings.

The period between the fall of 2012 and first half of 2013 was a tipping point. This is when the Arab uprisings decisively shifted on to the track to damnation. The arming of the Syrian insurgency escalated, at just the moment when its composition shifted decisively towards Salafi jihadist groups. The Egyptian democratic transition went off the rails. Libya's wobbling transition collapsed into open struggle between armed militias. Iraqi Sunni protests spiraled into violent confrontation with the Maliki government. Israel attacked Gaza, causing enormous human suffering. Even Tunisia's transition seemed destined to collapse, though it would ultimately pull back from the brink. Israel came close to launching a unilateral military strike on Iran, and the U.S. sought to begin serious, secret negotiations with Iran over its nuclear program.

Egypt's July 3, 2013 military coup, discussed in the previous chapter, was a seismic event in regional politics, the effects of which spread quickly across multiple arenas. Its most immediate impact points were in the fellow transitional country of Tunisia and Libya. Sisi's military coup and the massacre of Islamists at Rabaa six weeks later frightened both sides of the polarized Tunisian political sphere, strengthening the push by civil society organizations to find a consensus on the way forward and likely encouraging the ruling Ennahda Party to make deep concessions in order to avoid a similar transitional failure. In Libya, the coup emboldened General Khalifa Haftar to launch a military campaign to defeat the rival Islamist coalition; the Egyptian coup and its external backers helped to accelerate Libya's collapse into civil war. The spiraling confict in Libya soon attracted UAE and Egyptian air strikes.

And then, in August, the revelation of the use of chemical weapons by the Asad regime against civilians in East Ghouta led the United States to mobilize towards war. For weeks, the Obama administration patiently built domestic, regional, and international support for air strikes against Damascus—only to call them off when Asad suddenly agreed to a Russian proposal to surrender his chemical weapons arsenal under international supervision. Gulf rage over Obama's last-minute reversal led them to even more recklessly pour weapons indiscriminately into Syria, and into increasingly direct military interventions of their own in Libya and Yemen.

No one thing caused this regional death spiral. It was fueled by a conjunction of drivers at the local, regional, and international levels. But failure was also not inevitable, as many have since concluded. Different choices, and even a little luck, could have pushed the region down a different path. But the same integration of the regional political arena that had proven so empowering for the early Arab uprisings now worked in the other direction. Failure in one country bred crisis in the next, while the impact of civil wars were felt through both the torrent of horrifying imagery and the all-too-real flood of refugees into neighboring countries.

As things turned grim, the same forces that had once served as accelerants to protest mobilization now began to act as a brake. Images of peaceful protests celebrating impossible victories had been inspirational, but images of Arab countries collapsing into violence and polarization frightened those who might once have wanted change. Jordanians, for all their continuing unhappiness with the economy and the government, frequently admitted their fear of following in Syrian footsteps. This regional atmosphere allowed Kuwait's *al-Rai* newspaper to frame protests in June 2013 not as a trigger for reform but as a potential precursor to civil war: "In Tunisia and Egypt and Libya and Yemen events escalated quickly...and then Syria."[2] Such sentiments had once been dismissed out of hand by eagerly impatient young Arabs. Now they began to resonate.

THE DIPLOMATIC OPENING TOWARDS IRAN

The reelection of Barack Obama in November 2012 also likely accelerated events. As with every presidential election, the outcome ended a protracted waiting period as regional actors put their aspirations on hold while waiting to see who would be steering American policy over the next four years. Obama's return to the White House encouraged the leadership of Iran, which had been impatiently waiting to see whether nuclear diplomacy had a chance of proceeding. It deeply frustrated Israeli Prime Minister Benjamin Netanyahu, who had campaigned hard to unseat the president and now had to face the consequences. It also disappointed many leaders in the Gulf, who had hoped that an inexperienced but hawkish new president would prove more open to joining their aggressive campaign in Syria and abandoning the drive for talks with Iran. While some had speculated that Obama would abandon his foreign policy once the election had passed, it quickly became clear that the broad contours would not change. This established a global context for at least the next few years in which Israel, Saudi Arabia, the UAE, and others would be in a confrontational mode with Washington over what they viewed as existential issues.

The intense diplomacy with Iran and the intricate intra-alliance politics with Israel and the Gulf states represents a crucial backstory to the unfolding Arab wars. The Iran talks likely informed the Obama administration's thinking about the possibility of a diplomatic breakthrough on Syria that few others thought likely. It may have helped stay an already cautious administration's hand on more direct military actions in Syria as well. It almost certainly lay beneath the private agitation and public sparring with the administration by Israeli and Gulf leaders. While the nuclear diplomacy is not the master key unlocking the administration's Middle East policy, it did represent a primary foreign policy initiative that everyone understood would define the administration's legacy, bring to a climax a decade of high-stakes regional bargaining, and ultimately reshape the regional map.[3]

The Obama administration had from the start identified the Iranian nuclear program as a top priority on its Middle East agenda. Obama, in close alignment with the public posture of Israel over many years, identified Iran's pursuit of a nuclear weapon as one of the greatest threats to American and regional security. Early diplomacy had gone nowhere, however. The turmoil in Iran following the controversial re-election of President Mahmoud Ahmadinejad in 2009 had disrupted the first Obama administration's intentions of diplomatic engagement. Widespread international condemnation and the manifest insecurity of the Iranian regime at home had made for an unpropitious time to commence serious nuclear discussions. Instead, the United States had fallen back on a "two-track" policy of escalated sanctions combined with the offer of diplomacy—a policy that most of its advocates likely believed was really just a thinly veiled policy of semipermanent containment. But Obama sought to make the best of the sanctions-driven approach by keeping the diplomatic prospect open.

The early Arab uprisings further delayed any serious diplomacy with Iran. The intense uncertainty about the future made it difficult for either side to make long-term commitments or to assess the future balance of power. What is more, the spread and complexity of the uprisings consumed an enormous amount of bandwidth in Washington. Managing Egypt, Libya, Syria, Yemen, and the rest of the region's turbulence left little time for harried administration officials to think strategically about Iran. Still, the growing signs of Israeli plans to launch an attack on Iranian nuclear facilities forced the issue on to the crowded American agenda.

The first secret meeting between Iranian and American officials was held in July 2012, almost immediately in the aftermath of the Syrian rebel assault on Damascus. These meetings came amidst a flurry of speculation about Asad's imminent fall and at the peak of the internal administration debate about arming Syrian rebels. Secret talks in Oman continued over the course of 2013, along with less promising public talks. Exploratory talks continued as the Yemeni transition sputtered, Israel launched yet another controversial war on Gaza, the Benghazi attacks turned Libya radioactive in Washington, and Egypt's military coup shattered hopes for democratic transitions. With few targets of opportunity presenting themselves, Obama's team decided to focus on talks with Iran as the one major goal that could actually be done to try and manage a region going dangerously wrong.

TUNISIA'S TURBULENT TRANSITION

Tunisia's transition nearly collapsed in 2013 under the weight of its own problems and the Egyptian example. It pulled back from the brink, in large part due to Ennahda's willingness to compromise rather than to fight to the death.

The polarization that gripped Tunisian politics in the years following its revolution eerily mirrored Egypt's. The similarities are particularly compelling because of the vast differences between the two countries. Tunisia had a much stronger secular left than did Egypt, a better educated population, a relatively homogenous population, a history of state-led secularization, a stronger economy, a weaker military, and a more robust women's movement. Compared with the Muslim Brotherhood, Ennahda had a far weaker social base and less developed social sector, and the more cosmopolitan and politically savvy leadership of Rachid Ghannouchi. Egypt was far more central to Arab politics than Tunisia.

Tunisian politicians also chose very different political strategies. Ennahda did well in the 2011 parliamentary elections, but showed self-restraint by not exploiting its power to its full extent in order not to appear to be seeking domination. Rather than installing an Ennahda member as president, it chose the leftist human rights activist Moncef Marzouki. Rather than ruling alone, it formed a coalition government with three parties, which came to be known as the Troika. Rather than forcing through a controversial constitution, it followed the agreed-upon road map through a Constitutive Assembly, making notable concessions along the way.

With all those differences, one might have thought that Tunisia could have avoided Egypt's polarization trajectory completely. It did not. Tunisian politics soon polarized along the same lines as Egypt's, between Islamists and their adversaries. The continuing economic problems created a palpable atmosphere of frustration among disappointed Tunisians who had believed the revolution would deliver a better life. The Troika struggled to deliver on the promise of its new democracy, in part because the economic situation remained grim. International aid helped marginally, but could do little to address the crushing unemployment burden and struggling industries. The tourism industry was devastated by the effects of multiple terrorist attacks. The lives of Tunisians on the margins who had sparked the revolution had not improved. Political polarization and media sensationalism fueled a pervasive sense of insecurity, political stalemate, and revolutionary failure. Opposition media increasingly blamed Ennahda for tolerating jihadists, failing to provide security, seeking to impose Islamization, and bringing Libya's problems on to Tunisia.

The regional battles over Islamism therefore shaped Tunisian discourse in highly unproductive ways. Ennahda found itself the target of massive media campaigns, intense suspicion, and growing anti-Islamist mobilization. It is striking how closely the critique of Ennahda mirrors the bill of complaints against the Muslim Brotherhood in Egypt. Critics of Ennahda focused on its inherently alien qualities, attaching a distinctly Tunisian form of leftist secularism to the broader anti-Islamist critique. The complaint that Ennahda sought to Islamize the state, using its transient electoral power to fundamentally reshape state institutions by appointing its own people and changing core educational texts, exactly mirrored Egyptian complaints about the Muslim Brotherhood.

Tunisian politics attracted less regional intervention than in Egypt, but the regional networks in conflict were essentially the same. Qatar and Turkey were the primary allies of Ennahda, while the UAE and Saudi Arabia backed Ennahda's adversaries. Qatar became a focal point for secularist Tunisian outrage, while many on the other side would agree with the Ennahda Parliamentarian who complained to me that the UAE was playing a uniquely "dirty" role in the country's affairs. Having lost Ben Ali and then the subsequent March 2011 battle to retain the core of his government, the UAE-Saudi network focused on undermining Ennahda's legitimacy and promoting the reformation of a viable anti-Islamist bloc. This coalition would take the form of Nedaa Tounis, headed by the aged politician Beji Caid Essebsi. Nedaa Tounis brought together an unwieldy group spanning the far left to the extreme right, united only by their common disdain for Ennahda and Islamists. Because this was the only thing holding the coalition together, Nedaa had every incentive to heighten the contradictions with the Islamists to win votes rather than to offer distinctive economic policies or to promise specific political reforms.

Ennahda struggled with competing Islamist trends which frightened Tunisians but which it could not control. The emergent Salafi movement with which Ennahda had long had a bitter rivalry, and extremists of un-known identity, were behind the most dramatic events driving Tunisian polarization. In January 2012, Salafi students at the University of Ma-nouba demanding the right to wear the niqab held a sit-in and occupied the office of Dean Habib Kazdaghli. His trial over accusations that he slapped a female student lasted for more than a year, becoming a focal point for secularist concerns over the Islamization of the country.[4]

Those clashes over religion and identity manifested in darker ways as the year wore on. Tunisian protestors joining the regional wave of demon-strations against *The Innocence of Muslims* on September 12, 2012 attacked the US Embassy, leading to several deaths. While those events paled next to the horrifying events in Benghazi the previous day, the protests seemed to show a mobilized Islamist constituency pushing boundaries and a gov-ernment unable or unwilling to maintain public order.

Those concerns grew even worse on February 6, 2013, with the shock-ing assassination of the leftist activist Chokri Belaid. Belaid had been vo-cally critical of the Ennahda government, and shortly before the murder had publicly warned that "all those who oppose Ennahda become targets of violence."[5] Massive protests broke out, leading President Marzouki to cut short a foreign trip. Egyptian liberal leader Amr Hamzawy drew a direct connection between Belaid's assassination and the growing tensions in Egypt, noting that "confronting violence, radicalism, and the forces of darkness is the main priority for societies if they want freedom and de-mocracy. Assassinating Chokri Belaid is a warning bell in Tunisia, and in Egypt too."[6] In contrast with Egyptian President Morsi's firm line against his critics, Ennahda condemned the killing and Tunisia's Ennahda Prime Minister Hamadi Jebali tendered his resignation. This did not stop the polarization or violence. On July 25, Belaid's colleague Mohammed Brahmi was murdered in a very similar attack outside his home. Protestors again rallied against the Ennahda government.

These shocking murders, so deeply at odds with Tunisia's political his-tory, fed a sense of popular panic already being fanned by media sensa-tionalism and images of escalating warfare in neighboring Libya and Syria. This would grow even more intense in later years, as the Islamic State seized a North African foothold and carried out a series of devastating terrorist attacks in Tunisia. Tunisian state television remained firmly in the hands of the holdovers from the Ben Ali regime, while new privately-owned television stations and radio stations shared the anti-Islamist agenda. The security services fed these stations and websites a steady stream of damning leaks hinting at Islamist perfidy. Ennahda defended itself with reference to its electoral legitimacy, the inflexibility of its opponents, and its own claims to revolutionary credibility.

By the end of July, Tunisia's polarized politics seemed set to go down the same path as Egypt's. Belaid's murder had led to protests that brought down the Jebali government, and the protests over Brahmi's murder might have aimed higher. Egypt's military coup against the Brotherhood inspired many of Ennahda's opponents. Many Tunisian anti-Islamists were openly enthusiastic about emulating this part of the Egyptian model. Nedaa Tounis planned a massive rally for August 6, 2013, which they likely hoped could trigger their own coup against Ennahda. That demonstration would have occurred at exactly the same time as the Egyptian military's final deadly assault on the Rabaa encampment—a sobering reminder to even hard-line Tunisians of where the confrontational path could lead. Ennahda again opted for compromise, agreeing to replace their prime minister with a neutral technocrat and plan for new elections. The competition would remain within political institutions.[7]

Would they have done this without the Egyptian precedent? The American scholar Monica Marks has argued that the impulse to compromise in order to avoid conflict escalation is deeply ingrained in the Ennahda political ethos, and that Ghannouchi would likely have steered away from disaster even without the coup. The civil society forces represented by the Nobel Peace Prize–winning Quartet, a coalition of labor and other organizations that worked to push for political compromise, would still have sought to mediate the conflict.[8] Tunisians were watching Egypt very closely, though. Had that coup actually produced a rapid return to liberal democratic progress, it might have continued to inspire Tunisian imitators. The consolidation of military rule and the violence at Rabaa did not.

When I asked an exhausted Ghannouchi about it in November 2014, he insisted that Ennahda wanted a national unity government and that its first priority was to protect the democratic transition. By stepping down from the prime minister position and not fielding a presidential candidate, Ennahda "had lost the government but won democracy." He also candidly noted the regional dimension: Tunisia avoided the fate of Egypt and the rest of the shattered transitions in part because, compared with Egypt, Syria, or Libya, it "doesn't have to suffer under [the] weight of international attention." Tunisia just didn't matter enough to the regional powers for them to ruin.

Tunisians would not waste this reprieve. On January 26, Tunisia's Constitutional Assembly passed a new constitution after more than a month of intense debate. Unlike Morsi's unfortunate power grab, the Tunisian drafters managed to maintain consensus and produce a document that commanded widespread approval. The Assembly discussed each article at length, with all sides making important concessions along the way. The constitution was passed with an overwhelming majority.

With the constitution drafted, Tunisia went back to the polls. This time, Nidaa Tounis won a parliamentary majority while Ennahda lost half a million votes compared with the previous round of elections. Ennahda then declined to field a presidential candidate, though it was widely known to back the incumbent Marzouki. Essebsi won the presidential election. Some viewed his victory as a license to repress the defeated Islamists and restore the old order. Essebsi, like Ghannouchi, proved to be a shrewder and more principled politician, opting instead for a more inclusive approach.

In the end, the UAE's network had again defeated Qatar's. But this was neither an absolute victory nor a clear restoration of the old regime. Ennahda remained an active, full player in the political realm. Nedaa Tounis did not seek to dominate and would soon begin to fracture under the weight of governing. A wave of terrorist attacks in 2015 would test these commitments, as Essebsi struggled to find the right balance between security and freedoms. Tunisia's settled institutions, balanced parliament, broad international and regional goodwill, and broad political consensus positioned it well to survive the challenge.

LIBYA FRACTURES

Libya did not fare nearly so well. In contrast to Tunisia, which needed to escape the heavy hand of a near-totalitarian state and find a balance between two powerful coalitions, Libya needed to build a state largely from scratch. It had to build this state without enjoying actual sovereignty on the ground. Its entrenched militias and political movements could draw upon well-lubricated flows of weapons, media, and cash not available to the would-be state.

Libya started well. The unusual decision by the National Transitional Council to foreswear ambitions to remain in power indefinitely was nothing if not admirable in a region where leaders preferred to fight to the death before giving up power. Many would have understood if these unelected leaders had chosen to ride their revolutionary legitimacy into a longer-term position at the top of the nascent state. Instead, they opted to stand down and rapidly transition to democracy. The transitional road map adopted in November laid out a very fast series of elections, given the absence of settled institutions.

The first of these elections, in July 2012, established the General National Congress. Qatari networks were shocked by the poor performance of the Islamists in these elections, so noticeably out of step with developments elsewhere in the region. The Islamist defeat seemed even more shocking given the magnitude of Qatari investment in the uprising and transition. In the immediate days following Qaddafi's fall, Qatari flags had flown across Libya and it seemed exceptionally well-positioned to take the lead in the unfolding transition. Saudi-backed and Western media, for their part, reveled in the victory of ostensible moderates.

How had Qatar's stock fallen so far in only a few short months? Partly, simply due to nativist resentment of a too-public foreign role. Partly due to dissatisfaction over the perceived rampaging of the militias, viewed as an unfortunate legacy of the revolution by a growing portion of the population. And partly, to be sure, because of resentment and concern about the real intentions of Islamists, particularly given the unfolding contentious reception of elected Islamists in both Egypt to the east and Tunisia to the west. A final factor, far less often remarked, is the effective pushback by the Libyan clients of the UAE and the efforts of the Saudi-backed media to discredit and demonize their Qatari rivals. This included efforts to delegitimatize the nascent Libyan state that would come back to bite them when power changed hands in their favor.

The General National Congress soon began to face its limits, however. The Islamists who had failed in elections remained a potent constituency, and ultimately constituted a majority of the Assembly despite the first wave of election results. No militias were ready to surrender their weapons, preventing the consolidation of meaningful state sovereignty. Those problems would soon be pushed to the brink by continued political stalemate, state incompetence, foreign competition, and—fatally—Ansar al-Sharia's September 11 attack on the American consulate in Benghazi.

The near-absence of a preexisting state after decades of Qaddafi's novel statecraft created both opportunities and challenges. Indeed, many at the time saw the weakness of Libyan state institutions as a major positive difference compared with other Arab transitional countries. The absence of the dead hand of bloated, corrupt state bureaucracies encouraged many to see the chance for the rapid building of a modern, democratic state. Libya, the argument went, enjoyed oil wealth and a relatively small and homogenous population which might avoid the pathologies of the sectarian Levant.

The absence of a state to enforce legitimate order rendered discussions of the new political elite somewhat fantastical, with their carefully negotiated agreements proceeding on an altogether different track from the balance of power among the hard men with guns.[9] While the old elite was not esconced in bureaucratic fortresses that survived the decapitation of the regime, as in Egypt or Tunisia, it remained potent nonetheless. Beyond Qaddafi's inner circle, this elite—as in virtually every other Arab transition—remained largely protected from transitional justice and free to mobilize resources to seek new positions of power.[10]

In the months following Qaddafi's fall, an estimated 125,000 Libyans were members of dozens of official armed militias, handily outgunning the nascent official security forces.[11] This would soon grow, as financial incentives attracted new members to sign on with the armed groups. The General National Congress (GNC), like the NTC before it, allowed for the consolidation of the Revolutionary Brigades in order to give them a stake in the emergent order. Without the support of such militias, the nascent Libyan state would have been simply incapable of establishing order at all.

Those militias had their own quite reasonable concerns, as well, which were exacerbated by the impunity granted to Qaddafi-era officials and by the hotly polarized media rhetoric that surrounded them. State officials, including then-Prime Minister Ali Zeidan, publicly described the militias as the primary source of violence and instability in Libya and a problem that needed to be resolved. Following a series of highly publicized attacks by militias across the country, including some targeting police, courts, jails, and other public offices, many Libyans agreed.

Such rhetoric, however justified by the fears of local citizens or the concerns of a would-be state lacking a monopoly on legitimate violence, inevitably triggered the worst fears of the militias. Scarred by decades of Qaddafi's erratic violence and lawlessness, how could groups that had just fought so hard for their liberation now be expected to put their trust in another set of distant and inscrutable rulers? Most of the militias viewed themselves as carriers of revolutionary legitimacy, and bristled at now being labeled enemies of the state by those they had helped to install in power. How could they now surrender their weapons under conditions of profound institutional uncertainty, with absolutely no guarantees that a neutral state would protect them from future reprisals? Their legitimate fears helped to drive what the International Crisis Group accurately described as a vicious cycle: as they took law and order into their own hands, acting outside any legal accountability and often in defiance of the commands of the new state, they invited efforts to establish control, which triggered new clashes and heightened mistrust.

Once again, the local and the regional interacted in highly complex ways. Politics and power were highly localized and fragmented, but external powers deeply shaped those local balances of power and exploited them in pursuit of interests that extended far beyond Libya. The immediate post-Qaddafi days were still Qatar's time. There was enormous gratitude for the Qatari role in supporting the rebellion, and initial welcome for its presence. But, as is so often the case, that initial bubble soon began to deflate as ambitious Libyans chafed at a domineering foreign presence and began to fear the implications of Qatari selective patronage. Local players cultivated rivalry between Qatar and other Arab states, trying to play them against each other in order to extract valuable resources while maintaining their own autonomy. The ability to solicit and sustain a consistent source of external funding was key to being a player in post-Qaddafi Libya. The competition between Gulf states and transnational networks ensured that power would remain fragmented. As long as factions could draw on Qatari or Emirati support, they had little reason to limit their demands to what their domestic resources would allow. They had little incentive to make domestic compromises, to acknowledge the sovereignty of a weak and ineffective state, or to unify—especially if the price of unification would be to sacrifice their independent sources of funding.

The Benghazi attack of September 11, 2012, which resulted in the death of Ambassador Christopher Stephens, has taken on a mythical status in American politics. Seven different congressional panels have launched inquiries, there has been a virtual cottage industry of books, and even feature films have developed around exposes devoted to the topic. On October 22, 2015, Hillary Clinton sat for an epic eleven-hour hearing of the Benghazi Select Committee. It would be pointless to review here the endless arguments over altered talking points, inadequate security details, or Clinton's personal email account. But the absurdity of American partisan politics should not distract from the real importance for Libya of this tragic day.

The significance and even reality of the protests against *The Innocence of Muslims* has become the most hotly politicized question surrounding Benghazi. This is not a very interesting question. Major protests, many violent, had already occurred in Cairo, and would hit American embassies in the coming days in Tunis, Kuwait City, Sanaa, Amman, and nearly twenty other countries. There was no reason to believe that Libya would be immune to a regional crisis unfolding in real time. Obviously, this shaped the American intelligence and diplomatic reporting of what was unfolding.

The domestic, regional, and international costs of Benghazi can hardly be exaggerated. In Washington, the crisis made Libya politically radioactive. It drove the United States and most of its Western partners away from deep engagement with the new Libya, leaving the field open to destructive agendas and players. In March 2014, former Prime Minister Ali Zeidan complained that the West should have put more troops on the ground to maintain security following Qaddafi's ouster.[12] But if that had ever been in the cards, Benghazi put an end to such concepts.

Ansar al-Sharia's brazen attack on the consulate had an entirely different message for Libyans than the one received by Americans in the thick of a heated election campaign. For Libyans, the Benghazi attack exposed the failure of the new state to establish effective sovereignty. The militias who had once been seen as revolutionary heroes had come to be seen as a dangerous element capable of disrupting security at any time. That a jihadist militia could rampage through the streets of the revolutionary capital and overwhelm the American consulate was a damning indictment of the state.

For Libya, the Benghazi attack helped to push its delicate transitional process into a death spiral. The assault followed on a summer of escalating militia violence, including a series of assassinations of former Qaddafi officials, Salafi attacks on Sufi shrines, and unchecked tribal feuds.[13] By revealing the unchecked power of jihadist groups, it undermined confidence in the new Libyan state, heightened fears of all militias, not only the jihadists, and terrified many anti-Islamists into searching for new options to protect themselves in an anarchic environment. The Benghazi assault triggered popular protests from Benghazi to Tripoli against Ansar al-Sharia, and forced the shaky and outgunned Libyan government to begin a futile effort to rein in the militias.

On February 15, 2013, less than ten days after anti-Islamist protests over the murder of Chokri Belaid had forced Tunisian Prime Minister Hamadi Jabali from office, opponents of the GNC called for a massive demonstration in Benghazi. They likely hoped to trigger the downfall of the transitional government. This effort fizzled, but nonetheless revealed the ongoing potential for popular mobilization to disrupt the activities of an already weak government. Even more profoundly, it showed the implications of the absence of any sort of competent state able to provide security or authoritative rule of law.[14] In May 2013, the weakness of the state would be painfully revealed by an armed protest against the Political Isolation Law, designed to block the political participation of former Qaddafi regime members, when disgruntled militias encircled the GNC and briefly detained the prime minister until their demands were met.

Libya's transition was already well along the road to failure by the summer of 2013. The Benghazi rampage had seriously undermined the legitimacy of the state and exacerbated tensions between official institutions and the powerful militias. Bombings by unknown perpetrators, presumed to be Qaddafi loyalists, repeatedly struck Libyan cities. In May, militias closed down the Justice and Finance Ministries for nearly two weeks. In October, Prime Minister Ali Zeidan himself was briefly kidnapped by militias, symbolizing the existential deficiencies of the Libyan state. Public security simply collapsed as militias, tribes, and insurgent groups ran amok. On several occasions, militias surrounded official institutions to enforce their preferences, and in November they stormed a major oil production facility. It seemed that Libya was gripped in a classic state failure spiral: no agreed upon institutional rules of the game, no effective state institutions, a collapsing economy, rampant insecurity, easily available weaponry, and escalating social and political polarization.

The triggering issue for the May 2013 militia protests was the perceived neutering of the Political Isolation Law. Both the substance and the process provoked controversy: the lustration law reached far beyond Qaddafi's inner circle to ban technocratic or politically moderate officials, and it was forced through at gunpoint by militias surrounding the Parliament complex. A second polarizing issue, just as in Egypt, was the process by which the constitutional drafting body would be selected. The stakes were high. Core constitutional issues remained deeply divisive, particularly the nature of federalism and the prerogatives of local authorities.[15] The place of Islam in the constitution was divisive as well, particularly with the feedback effects of the crises surrounding Islamist governments to both its east and west. After long negotiations over selection criteria, the GNC decided to create the constitutional drafting body via elections.

Lurking behind these political issues were the deeper structural problems of state failure and regional gamesmanship. Since Benghazi, at the latest, the Libyan government's inability to exercise effective sovereignty ate away at its political legitimacy. The militias did not simply exist outside of this situation, however. The GNC increasingly turned to selected militias to provide it with the muscle it could not get from the official security services, while other militias increasingly openly sided with the GNC's opponents.[16]

Those militias, in turn, were embedded in networks of foreign sponsorship cultivated during the revolution. Both the GNC and Misrata's powerful and well-armed militias continued to draw on Qatari support for weapons, favorable media coverage, political support, and cash. Other tribes and cities turned to the UAE for similar types of support. The external sponsorship meant that local militias had little incentive to resolve their differences, since that would only mean the drying up of their revenue streams. It also meant that the central state had little hope of imposing its authority over them. As the veteran Egyptian columnist Fahmy Howeydi observed, "There is no hope of resolving the Libya problem without our Arab brothers ending their interventions there."[17] They did not.

The deterioration of the Libyan state also reflected the shifting priorities of the competing regional blocs. The Qatari-Emirati competition at the foundational moment of the revolution had created enduring divides within the new political institutions. The pushback on Qatar had begun shortly after the liberation of Tripoli, with even key nodes in Doha's network such as Mahmoud Shammam beginning to publicly and privately warn it to keep its distance. The wide-open Libyan arena created too many opportunities for outside powers to ignore, in terms of finding local clients to advance their interests. It was not only the Qataris and Emiratis seeking a foothold in the new Libya. Turkey, at least initially, hoped to benefit from its sponsorship of Muslim Brotherhood networks. Saudi Arabia remained in the background for the most part, since there was no Iranian presence to counter, but still had an interest in Libya as part of its broader regional hegemonic designs.

Libya's neighbors were the most directly affected by its turmoil, though, which forced them to take an active role. Algeria, Tunisia, and Egypt all had a stake in Libya's future, as did Libya's southern African neighbors. Its collapse into civil war put all of them at risk.

Tunisians initially had great sympathy for the Libyan uprising. During the war, Tunisia had served as a base for the supply and support for Libya's rebels, and offered sanctuary to countless Libyan fighters, refugees, and expectant diaspora. The Ennahda government aligned with the broader Qatari and Muslim Brotherhood networks to strongly support Qaddafi's overthrow and to advocate a democratic post-Qaddafi system. During my visits to Tunisia, in 2011, it was easy to find Libyan flags and T-shirts for sale along the streets, and to hear positive, excited commentary identifying Tunisia's revolution with the unfolding Libyan struggle for freedom. As post-Qaddafi Libya began to go south, however, Tunisia began to directly feel the costs of its failure. As in many other refugee-hosting countries, Tunisians began to openly resent the Libyan diaspora, blaming them—unfairly, for the most part—for economic and security problems. Tunisians also blamed Libya for spawning the new jihadist groups such as Ansar al-Sharia, which carried out a growing number of attacks and provocations. Tunisian armed forces made multiple incursions into Libya to interdict smugglers, pursue criminals and jihadists, and try to control the flow of weapons into the country.

The Algerian regime had little love for Qaddafi, but Algeria's view of Libya was embedded within the overarching trauma of the failed democratic experiment and brutal civil war during the 1990s, both of which haunted Algerian political culture. The Arab uprisings in general had triggered fears of a replay of the 1988-91 experience with democracy which had ended in a bloody military coup. Algerians looking at Egypt or Tunisia shuddered at the obvious symmetry between their history and the unfolding story of democratic opening, Islamist advances, and—in Egypt, at least—military coup. It should not be surprising that Algeria was at first officially neutral towards the Libyan uprising, and generally leaned towards Qaddafi rather than the rebels.

After Qaddafi's fall, Algerians worried about the potential impact on their own stability, but seemed largely at a loss as to how to deal with the chaotic new situation. The rise of jihadist militias was of particular concern, especially after the January 16, 2013 attack on Algerian oil facilities and killing of dozens of hostages by a jihadist group headed by Mokhtar Belmokhtar brought to the surface the painful memories of the Black Decade of the 1990s, when hundreds of thousands were killed in a horrifying civil war.

Algeria emerged in July 2014 as a key supporter of the United Nations mission tasked with mediating the aftermath of the failed transition and spiraling civil war.[18] In contrast to the endlessly competing Gulf states, Algeria emphasized consensus-building in its mediation, using its good offices to host representatives of both the GNC and its rival, the recently elected House of Representatives, even as they were actively warring on the ground. Its mediation had multiple motivations. Algerian officials were naturally worried about the direct fallout from the Libyan wars, including refugees and the spread of jihadist groups. Beyond these defensive motivations, Algerians surely saw the importance of having cards in the unfolding Libyan game, and quietly cultivated potential allies.

It is telling that Algeria emerged as one of the leading obstacles to a unified Arab League policy towards Syria, as well as Libya. Its recalcitrance towards Saudi and Qatari initiatives to unify Arab ranks against Asad was only partly about Asad or about its limited interests in Syria. Algerian leaders were likely more concerned about the precedent of abandoning long-standing Arab norms governing state sovereignty. And they were even more concerned about the growing Gulf adventurism and its domination of regional institutions. Algeria's return to the regional stage after a long period of relative isolation, at least partly to contest the local intrusions of the distant Gulf states into North African affairs. As a senior Algerian diplomat told the Crisis Group report's author, "I wonder how countries of the Gulf Cooperation Council would react if we intervened in Yemen. I understand the concerns of our neighbors, but not those of others [further afield]."[19]

The greatest interventions would come from Sisi's Egypt. Egypt had long-standing interests in the stability and security of its western neighbor. Following Mubarak's ouster, the SCAF changed little about Egypt's approach to Libya. A regime that now claimed its legitimacy through popular uprising could hardly fail to identify with the Libyan rebels, and Egypt's did support them. The unchanged military leadership and security services ensured considerable continuity in actual policies, however.

Under Morsi, Egypt's policy towards Libya resembled Tunisia's and shifted palpably in the direction of enthusiastic support for Libyan democratization. Egypt's leadership at this time was embedded within the Qatari network, and reflected the views common in Muslim Brotherhood circles regionwide. This would change completely with the July 2013 military coup, however, as Egypt moved firmly into the UAE network and expanded its efforts in Libya dramatically, acting as the muscle behind the UAE campaign.

The Egyptian military coup had a galvanizing effect on Libya, as in so many other areas across the Arab world. Haftar seemed to be emulating General el-Sisi's coup in Egypt, certainly through indirect inspiration and possibly at the direct urging of his external backers. Egypt's military coup rapidly became what Fred Wehrey called the "inflection point in Libya's post-revolutionary narrative." Egypt's lesson was that a regionally backed coup could work. As Wehrey put it: "Without meaning to intervene, at least initially, the Egyptian strongman cast a long and ultimately polarizing shadow over Libya's unsettled politics."[20] Egyptian journalist Hilmi Nimnim recounted meeting with two top Libyan political leaders who "said that what happened in Egypt June 30 gave many outside of Egypt hope that they could rehabilitate the Arab Spring which had turned into an MB or fundamentalist spring."[21] On al-Jazeera, Hisham al-Shalwi identified moves to dissolve the GNC as originating with figures from the old regime who had been inspired by Sisi's coup to overturn the new political system and "return it to square one." The "coup against legitimacy in Egypt," he argued, "would thus move on to Tunisia and Libya and even before that abort it in Yemen."[22] For Libya's Islamists and the GNC, Egypt's coup gave a painful lesson in the futility of democratic participation, and helped convince them of the need to be able to protect themselves with military force rather than to trust a neutral state.

Political stalemate coincided with a frightening escalation of terrorist attacks, local-level violence, and challenges to public order. Late 2013 and early 2014 saw dramatically escalating violence, including assassinations and attacks on government facilities. The pervasive violence and insecurity created a growing popular appetite for the restoration of order at almost any cost. The growing movement against the militias included popular protests, political maneuverings, and ultimately Haftar's Operation Dignity.[23] On February 7, 2014, a peaceful protest demanded the dissolution of the GNC at the expiration of its mandate.

Tension came to a head with a phantom coup attempt by former General Khalifa Haftar on February 14, 2014.[24] Haftar positioned himself in post-2011 Libyan politics as a stalwart against Islamist groups, which earned him support from the Emirates and Egypt and others in the anti-Islamist networks. It naturally provoked equally intense hostility from the wide range of Islamists in Libya, including Qatar, Turkey, and the region's still potent Islamist networks. Haftar found no takers for his call from the military or the public, and the Zeidan government brushed his gambit aside. But the mounting challenge to the transitional government could not be ignored.

Haftar launched his controversial "Operation Dignity" offensive against Islamist militias on May 16, 2014 with strong support from Egypt and the UAE. Haftar quickly became one of the most polarizing and controversial figures in Libyan politics.[25] Haftar, who lived in Virginia for decades, had widely publicized connections to the CIA. But in this case, he did not seem to be acting at the behest of the United States, which instead supported a UN-facilitated National Dialogue.

His initial move to clean out the militias from Benghazi rapidly expanded into Tripoli. Haftar demanded the dissolution of the GNC, which, after the last year's turmoil, was now dominated by a coalition of Islamists and backed by the forces of the Misrata militias. The GNC rejected his call, leading to a tense standoff.

On June 25, new parliamentary elections went forward under intensely polarized, violent, and unstable conditions. The resulting parliament, known as the House of Representatives, was dominated by anti-Islamist forces loosely affiliated with Haftar. The election of a House of Representatives failed to resolve any of the underlying issues. Turnout was low, with entire regions boycotting the proceedings. Still, the HOR gained rapid recognition by an international community eager to see progress towards democratically legitimate institutions. This recognition proved to be a precious source of legitimacy for an otherwise beleaguered body representing only one faction in a complex and rapidly shifting arena. The GNC refused to recognize the transition and continued to present itself as the legitimate government of Libya. In July, Operation Dawn (Fajr) was launched to retake Tripoli and push back on Haftar's military gains. The Dawn coalition was an awkward one, bringing together both mainstream Islamists committed to the democratic process and violent Islamists such as the notorious Ansar al-Sharia Libya.

In early November 2014, Libya's Supreme Court invalidated the HOR's election as unconstitutional, a ruling that the HOR opted to ignore. This judicial intervention produced just the sort of uncertainty so fatefully introduced by Egypt's judicial rulings the previous year, in a far less stable environment. In contrast to Egypt, where the Supreme Constitutional Court's rulings were honored no matter how politicized, in Libya the ruling was simply ignored because, as the HOR's spokesman, Farraj Hassan, explained, "the ruling was made under the threat of guns." [26]

By the summer of 2015, the battle between the HOR and GNC had come to be routinely described as one between two governments. The HOR's international legitimacy and Gulf support could balance but not eliminate the military power on the ground commanded by the GNC.[27] Neither could really claim effective sovereignty over a fractured and divided country as Dawn and Dignity waged a ferocious war across the country.[28]

This war invited new forms of direct regional intervention beyond the already prevalent indirect funding and media campaigns. Two broad camps emerged. One, led by Qatar and Turkey, with general support from Algeria and Morocco, and aligned with the GNC, pushed for a regional diplomatic solution. The other, led by the UAE, and Egypt, and aligned with the HOR, preferred to see a military victory by Haftar. Both the local battles and the political negotiations were thoroughly penetrated by these external coalitions.[29]

Egypt's first direct intervention predated both Haftar's offensive and the declaration of an Islamic State affiliate in Libya. In August 2013, only a few months after Sisi consolidated his power, Egypt launched its first Libya air strikes, in a failed effort coordinated with the UAE to block Operation Dawn's seizure of the Tripoli Airport. It carried out another round of air strikes in November, again to little evident effect. In February 2015, Egypt struck again, this time following the release of a horrific video of Egyptian Copts murdered in Libya by a group claiming the title of the Islamic State. The Egyptian role in Libya was shrouded in confusion but was hardly covert. In August, the columnist Hisham Allam raved that "Sisi is doing with Haftar what Nasser did in 1969 with [the] Libyan revolution," using covert and public aid to protect vital national interests.[30] Egypt's intervention was closely coordinated with the UAE, which also carried out air strikes of its own.

Egypt's interventions were in many respects overdetermined.[31] Egypt had deep, long-standing interests in Libya, and had deep concerns with the failed state and rising jihadist insurgency next door. No Egyptian government could have failed to respond to the videotaped atrocities against its citizens. The most obvious driver, though, was Cairo's deep financial and political dependence on the UAE, which had invested heavily in both the Egyptian coup and in Operation Dignity. Sisi had few higher priorities than the need to sustain the continued financial support of his Gulf backers on which Egypt's floundering economy now depended.[32] Fortunately for Sisi, Libya's polarization between Islamists and their adversaries offered a perfect symmetry with Sisi's own political identity. Sisi seems to have seen Libya at least partly in terms of Egypt's political wars over Islamism, equating General Khalifa Haftar's anti-Islamist campaign with his own regime's struggle with the Brotherhood.

Still, there were limits. On February 22, Sisi took the lead in proposing a joint Arab intervention force for Libya but backed away when no support for the idea materialized.[33] Nonetheless, in the absence of strong international backing, Sisi reportedly declined a request by Abdullah al-Thini, the prime minister of one of Libya's two rival governments, for Egyptian ground forces to enter the fray.[34]

In August 2014, the UAE directly bombed Libyan targets, a rare unilateral intervention beyond the Arabian peninsula. The veteran Egyptian columnist Fahmy Howeydi wrote that in the long history of Arab proxy wars, "the UAE strike in Libya must be read as something else entirely because it represents a shift from indirect intervention to direct military intervention, and it is not to help a friendly state but to support one faction against another faction."[35] In the all too typical fashion of these wars, neither the Emirati nor the Egyptian air strikes had any palpable positive effects on Libya's civil war. Instead, the regional interventions helped to deepen and further entrench the divide between the two competing Libyan governments.

In September 2014, the UN stepped in to attempt to mediate this standoff, with the veteran diplomat Bernadino Leon appointed to lead a year-long national dialogue. Both the HOR and the GNC agreed to join the talks, along with a civil society leaders and other political forces. Such civil society and local actors would complain of being relatively ignored during this process. Multiple rounds of talks were held inside and outside of Libya over more than a year, until Leon finally announced a draft agreement just ahead of the September 2015 deadline. His efforts flew in the face of the momentum of Libyan polarization, state collapse, and regional meddling. Each side resisted compromise that they feared would empower the other. On the brink of the ratification of the agreement, Leon accepted an extremely lucrative job with the United Arab Emirates, an alignment with one highly polarizing party in the contentious process that cast doubt on all of his previous efforts.

Those external interventions would have little constructive effect. With militia violence spiraling, and the government incapable of taking or enforcing meaningful decisions, Libya rapidly spiraled towards the open military confrontation that so many had feared...but had failed to prevent.

| 7 |

SYRIA IN HELL

By the fall of 2012, the American public debate over arming Syrian rebels or direct intervention had faded from the media. Mitt Romney, reading the polls showing the American public overwhelmingly opposed to intervention, declined to take up the call for intervention in Syria as a wedge issue against Obama. Without a presidential politics angle, the issue largely fell out of an election-driven media agenda. Benghazi, Israel, and the Iranian nuclear program instead became the focal points for Republican criticism.

But while the American public focus drifted, the period between fall 2012 and spring 2013 were fateful months for the course of the Syrian insurgency. This is the period when the balance within the insurgency tipped decisively towards the jihadist groups, when the foundations were laid for the emergence of ISIS, and the war's effects decisively changed Iraq. It was also a time when the refugee crisis began to escalate dramatically, as the war moved into Aleppo and desperate Syrians fled the violence. It was the time when a virulent new sectarianism swept the region, fueled by nothing more than the Syrian conflict. More than anything other than Egypt's coup, the regional encouragement of the escalation of the armed Syrian insurgency destroyed the Arab uprisings.

ARMING THE REBELS

With Syria locked in a strategic stalemate, huge volumes of arms and assistance flooded into all sides of the conflict. Iran and Hezbollah moved to prop up the Asad regime both directly and indirectly, with Shi'ite militiamen and Iranian forces entering the fray at decisive moments. Turkey, Qatar and Saudi Arabia poured weaponry into their preferred local clients, while private networks of Gulf donors flooded cash into Islamist factions. The Free Syrian Army and the official political institutions of the Syrian opposition struggled to compete with the lavishly funded and armed jihadists seizing the battlefield initiative. Hopes of avoiding the catastrophic consequences of a militarized opposition were by this point a distant memory.

Washington became much more active in directly supporting the military efforts of the insurgency during this period even as it tried to restrain its worst excesses. The U.S., while deeply concerned about the militarization of the rebellion, was soon actively involved in the arming and training of the insurgency. The Americans saw clearly that the armed insurgency was rapidly devolving into a jihadist field of struggle, and that its regional allies were enabling the worst trends. They also understood that the insurgency was unlikely to overthrow Asad on its own. Obama's secret spring 2013 authorization of arming and training the rebels primarily aimed at counterbalancing the attractions of the jihad by strengthening reasonably moderate groups. It hoped to retain some influence over a radicalizing opposition and to increase the military pressure on Asad in order to eventually bring both sides to the negotiating table.

Obama's widely reported summer rejection of the plan formulated by CIA Director David Petraeus to arm Syrian rebels failed to put the brakes on a program building support inside the bureaucracy and strongly supported by regional allies. In mid-2012, Obama authorized a program of nonlethal assistance and support for the rebels, a determination which was first publicly reported in early August.[1] Supporters of the rebels began covertly shipping arms in early 2012, with the US significantly expanding its contributions in early 2013. Beginning no later than November 2012, the US, joined by British and French soldiers, actively trained rebels at secret bases in Jordan and Turkey, while providing significant material assistance to the Syrian Military Command.[2]

The first publicly reported shipments of arms involved Qatari aircraft via Turkey. The *New York Times* reported that "through the fall, the Qatari Air Force cargo fleet became even more busy, running flights almost every other day in October. But the rebels were clamoring for even more weapons, continuing to assert that they lacked the firepower to fight a military armed with tanks, artillery, multiple rocket launchers, and aircraft."[3] By early 2013, the program had included "more than 160 military cargo flights by Jordanian, Saudi, and Qatari military-style cargo planes landing at Esenboga Airport near Ankara, and, to a lesser degree, at other Turkish and Jordanian airports."

In May, another of the US covert programs to arm Syrian rebels reportedly got underway.[4] The covert program was coordinated with the Europeans and Arab partners to arm rebel groups in the south under the command of General Selim Idriss in coordination with Jordan in order to facilitate a push against Damascus. The US tried to keep close watch on the rebel groups it armed, to the consternation of local forces accustomed to a freer hand.[5] In September, CNN reported that CIA-funded arms were flowing to Syrian rebels.[6] In October, the CIA program expanded further, with paramilitary specialists deploying to Jordan to accelerate training.[7] By December, the existence of "secret" CIA training camps for Syrian rebels in Jordan was widely reported in the regional and international media.[8] Somewhere around this time, advanced anti-tank TOW missiles began to arrive.

These programs to arm and train Syrian rebels rarely satisfied their recipients and failed to compel serious peace talks. They did, however, produce exactly the negative results that the academic literature had predicted. Rebel groups were never satisfied with the level of support they received and frequently pursued interests at odds with those of their sponsors.

Insurgents fighting a brutal civil war showed little respect for human rights or democratic niceties. The selective arming of groups encouraged splintering and fragmentation, undermining efforts at a negotiated solution. When they did have some impact, their efforts were quickly counteracted by increased support by Russia, Iran, and Hezbollah. The result was, as expected, a far bloodier and more destructive war that produced neither victory nor negotiations. That this predictable outcome came to be cast as evidence of the costs of *not* arming rebels is testament to the willingness of the Syria policy community and the media to go along with a convenient political narrative.

The competition between allies that shaped every front of the new Arab wars was never more fully destructive than in Syria. US efforts ran in parallel with, but at a very different thrust than, Saudi, Qatari, and Turkish efforts. Saudi Arabia's Prince Bandar became the semi-public face of the Saudi mission to arm Syrian rebels.[9] Veteran Saudi officials such as Prince Turki al-Faisal explained their Syria policy in terms of the successful 1980s support for the jihad in Afghanistan, even if most Americans did not consider the shattered state, Taliban rule, and al-Qaeda haven, which that campaign produced a success to emulate. The Saudi program to arm the rebels began in early 2012, helping to tip the balance within the divided Syrian opposition towards armed insurgency and away from the diplomatic track.

Many American backers of arming the rebels such as Senators John McCain and Lindsey Graham saw the Saudis as a better bet than their own government.[10] They wildly overestimated Saudi competence, however. The Saudis could spread money and arms through their extensive networks, try to influence external powers through financial incentives, and flood the Arab media with supportive messaging. Like all other external players, they were bedeviled by severe limitations on their ability to control local proxies, limitations on local knowledge, unanticipated blowback, and offsetting countermoves by their rivals.

Once again, intra-alliance competition proved devastating. The Saudis were keen to bring down Asad and bleed Iranian assets, but were at least as concerned with competing with the Qataris and Turks for control over the rebellion. In July 2015, Saudi columnist Mishari al-Zaydi posed what he called "a frank question. Who are the states that want to overthrow Bashar Asad by force? Saudi Arabia, Turkey, and Qatar. The rest of the Arab states have mixed views."[11] And he was not so sure about Turkey.

Many others shared those doubts about Turkish policy. Turkey remained a cipher, host for most of the political and military institutions of the Syrian opposition along with the largest share of refugees, but also prone towards turning a blind eye towards unsavory dealings across its border. Indeed, it is unlikely that the insurgency would have lasted long without Turkish support. Turkey hosted the major Syrian opposition institutions, including both the Syrian National Council and the leadership of the Free Syrian Army, and served as the primary conduit for arms, funds, and humanitarian aid to reach rebel-controlled areas in northern Syria. Its long border with Syria remained largely uncontrolled for most of the Syrian crisis, allowing insurgent factions—including ISIS, al-Nusra, and other jihadists—to move people, goods, and weapons largely unimpeded. Since coming out hard against Asad in 2011, the Erdogan government was determined to deliver on the threat. Western officials were deeply worried by its cavalier attitude towards jihadist groups, however, and consistently identified Turkey as the key facilitator of their expansion in Syria.

Turkey's Syria policy was inevitably shaped by its prioritization of the Kurdish issue. As the aggressive policy towards Syria grew domestically unpopular, it became interwoven with domestic struggle over Erdogan's incipient authoritarianism and struggling outreach to his Kurdish citizenry. On May 28, 2013, Turkey would suddenly face its own "Arab Spring" moment when protestors filled Gezi Park in central Istanbul to protest a local commercial development. Erdogan, who had posed as the champion of popular mobilization in Egypt and Tunisia, now adopted the mask of the autocrat. His forceful repression of the protestors polarized Turkish politics, just as he sought to rewrite the constitution to facilitate a powerful presidency that he expected to soon occupy. In summer 2015, Erdogan would launch a military and political offensive against Kurds after the unprecedented electoral success of a Kurdish political party and the growing power of Syrian Kurdish armed groups.

These developments would have significant implications for Turkey's engagement with Syria and the broader Middle Eastern proxy war. Erdogan's Syria war was extremely unpopular at home, making it a liability during a critical election season. The greatest effects, however, involved Turkey's Kurds. The shift from uprising to war was proving bountiful for Kurds across the region. In Iraq, the Kurdish Regional Government (KRG) moved ever closer to independence from a dysfunctional and distracted Baghdad. In Syria, the Kurdish Democratic Unity Party (PYD) would emerge as a favored partner for the United States in its air campaign against the Islamic State. This rising Kurdish wave could hardly fail to impact a Turkey that had long been defined by its hostility towards Kurdish nationalism. Even as the US increasingly depended upon Iraqi and Syrian Kurds as ground troops against the Islamic State, Turkey launched offensive operations against the same groups.

Supporters of the Syrian insurgency drew very different lines dividing acceptable and unacceptable jihadist recipients of aid.[12] Supporters of the Saudi approach argued that their strategy aimed to sideline hard-line jihadists in favor of more moderate Islamist factions. This distinction was more for media consumption than anything else, though. Saudi Arabia had no interest in seeing democracy come to Syria (or anywhere else) and had very well-developed Islamist and tribal networks through which to distribute their material support.[13] Riyadh's conflict with Syrian jihadist groups came not because of any evident aversion to their ideology but because of their sponsorship by its rivals. They shied away from supporting the most extreme jihadists such as Jubhat al-Nusra and (later) the Islamic State, in part because they perceived such groups as threatening their own domestic security, and in part because Qatar and Turkey were already working those networks.

Qatar and Turkey infuriated the West with their willingness to work with those jihadist groups. Each maintained working relationships with the al-Qaeda affiliate Jubhat al-Nusra, despite its designation as a terrorist organization by the United States. Turkey would only second that designation in 2014, after a lengthy failed effort to convince al-Nusra to renounce its al-Qaeda affiliation in order to remain a viable recipient of support. Turkey was widely accused of purposefully leaving its border un-policed to allow easy passage to its rebel proxies and, inevitably, to the Islamic State. Even Kuwait was the target of an unusually public American rebuke and the terrorist designation of several of its citizens for the chan-neling of huge amounts of privately raised money to Islamist rebel groups.

Turkey's most potent ally, Ahrar al-Sham, was particularly divisive as a partner in the insurgency. The United States deemed Ahrar al-Sham a jihad-ist group beyond the pale. It based this assessment on a wide range of con-siderations, including Ahrar al-Sham's active cooperation with al-Nusra, its avowed Salafi-jihadist ideology, and its extreme sectarianism. Qatar and Turkey, along with Gulf Islamist networks, considered Ahrar al-Sham an acceptable, mainstream component of the rebellion and a legitimate recipi-ent of assistance.[14] Its combination of Salafism and military effectiveness made it one of the primary recipients of private donations from the Gulf.[15] In 2015, Ahrar al-Sham would become the core of the Saudi-backed Jaysh al-Fateh, without sacrificing either its jihadist ideology or its Qatari-Turkish ties. Despite these American reservations, in January 2016, the Saudi-backed Jaysh al-Islam leader Mohammad Alloush would become the lead rebel ne-gotiator at the United Nations–sponsored peace talks in Geneva.

Syrian rebel supporters frequently blame the United States for the Is-lamization of the insurgency, arguing that they never would have gone in this direction had the US intervened earlier and more forcefully on their side. Nothing in either Syrian reality nor comparative experience from Iraq, Libya, or Afghanistan suggests that this is true. The longer that such civil wars go on, the more likely that hardline groups will emerge to shape the violence at the expense of the one-time moderates. A better explanation for the radicalization of the Syrian insurgency would be the iron logic of pro-tracted civil wars, exacerbated by the promiscuous provision of money, arms and political support to extremist groups by external actors.

ESCALATING VIOLENCE

The arming of the rebels may have evened the playing field, but it most certainly did not reduce the killing or facilitate negotiations. Instead, the front lines reconsolidated, while violence ratcheted up to new, almost unbelievable levels. Casualty statistics, never especially reliable to be sure, tell a clear story. Early in the conflict, the victims were counted in the tens and hundreds, with almost all of them civilians dying at the hands of regime forces. This is the image of the war that continues to frame most media coverage and policy discourse.

But this changed as the rebellion militarized. Better-armed insurgents killed more and more regime soldiers, and regime-held areas of Aleppo or Damascus became fair game for rebel mortars or car bombs. Surely, had this not been the case, those funding the armed insurgency would have wanted their money back. Civilians were the primary victims of the war, but a very significant portion of the deaths came on the battlefield—on both sides. As of December 2013, the Syrian Observatory of Human Rights had confirmed more than fifty thousand deaths among regime fighters and just under thirty thousand rebel fighter deaths.[16] Those trends would continue. The most recent summary of confirmed casualties by the Syrian Observatory of Human Rights, in June 2015, documented the deaths of approximately forty thousand rebel fighters and thirty thousand foreign fighters aligned with jihadist factions (including ISIS alongside al-Nusra and others), against approximately fifty thousand regime soldiers and thirty-two thousand regime-aligned irregulars.[17] Asad's forces continued to be by far the greatest killers of civilians, but the overall death toll was less lopsided.

The increasing military capabilities of the insurgency caused a predictable escalation in the scale of devastation. While the insurgency captured new territory and inflicted far more damage on regime forces, it did not seriously threaten Asad's survival. When it did look like his control over crucial areas might be threatened, Hezbollah, Iran, Shi'ite militias from Iraq, and ultimately Russia stepped in to reinforce his positions and establish a new strategic stalemate. As critics of the insurgency strategy had long warned, each move to strengthen the rebels invited a countermove to reinforce the regime.

The escalating violence was accompanied by a troubling shift towards jihadist rhetoric and ideology. Massive fund-raising and support campaigns across the Gulf, and especially in Kuwait, were led by ambitious religious personalities and run through mosques and Islamic charitable societies. Leaders were eager to associate themselves with a popular cause such as Syrian children and refugees, and frequently sponsored telethons and charitable festivals. They feared losing control over the channels of funding to the Syrian rebels, however, and even more feared the potential blowback from radicalized Syrian factions.

They were right to be concerned, given the logic of an already exceedingly complex and frustrating proxy war.[18] These private fund-raising campaigns involved large-scale social mobilization and responded to a very different logic than did the regimes. Private fund-raisers could not be quite so cynical and strategic in manipulating flows of aid into rebel groups. The lines between these groups was in any case rather fluid. For instance, in its English-language presentations, the Free Syrian Army maintained a sharp distinction with the jihadist groups in order to remain a viable candidate for Western support. But in Kuwait, FSA commander Riadh al-Asaad moved comfortably between fund-raisers organized by hard-line Salafi preachers such as Hajjaj al-Ajmi, who would eventually be designated as supporters of global terrorism for their supporting Jubhat al-Nusra and Ahrar al-Sham.

The mobilizational campaigns initially tended to emphasize the generic suffering of the Syrian people and to focus upon providing humanitarian assistance. They rapidly took on sectarian overtones, with anti-Shi'a rhetoric and open calls for jihad mounting as the conflict intensified. As the uprising tentatively militarized in late 2011, some—though not all—of the fund-raising networks began to shift their attention to the armed groups. They did not always have crystal-clear visibility into realities on the ground, of course. Often, fund-raisers in the Gulf simply wanted to support groups which seemed effective, and, secondarily, which seemed to share their broad identity and ideology. Fighting groups shrewdly tailored their messaging to those incentives. Posting videos of battles and attacks was at least partly intended as a form of advertising to potential patrons, a way to prove that their money would be well spent on an effective fighting force. Given that most of the cash flowed through Salafi Islamist networks, it made sense as well for them to adopt Salafi identities to match their prospective donors.

While the ultimate destination of funds might have been obscured, these networks were not especially secretive.[19] Consciousness-raising was a key component of these campaigns, which meant a steady stream of media stories and social media postings about suffering Syrians requiring help. The fund-raising campaigns were highly public, spanning social media and mainstream media and involving regular public and private events. The Kuwaiti Salafist Nabil al-Awadhy was frequently the single most re-tweeted account dealing with Syria in the entire world.[20] In September 2013, former Kuwaiti parliamentarian Walid al-Tabtabaei posted a video to YouTube of himself fighting alongside the Free Syrian Army.[21] Prominent campaigners such as Shafi al-Ajmi and Hajjaj al-Ajmi posted photos on their Twitter feeds of their visits to the front lines. In 2012, Hajjaj al-Ajmi publicly claimed to have begun fund-raising for armed groups such as the Free Syrian Army and Ahrar al-Sham as early as April 2011.[22]

The preferences of potential Gulf donors interacted with realities on the ground in Syria in complex ways. There was a clear change in the composition, content, and network structure of Syria-focused social media between 2011 and 2013. Content produced by Salafis, for instance, focused on in-group solidarity, fund-raising appeals, and denunciation of other groups. Insurgents primarily worked within insular social media networks to highlight the power and ideology of their own group in order to attract external private and state support (including foreign fighters). Attention-grabbing videos became a currency of political competition between groups, as opposition factions with different interests, ideologies, and strategic visions competed to frame the message emerging from inside of Syria. Their use of social media often focused on distinct identity communities with less regard to how the content might be viewed by broader audiences. Where Western-focused activists might work hard to suppress evidence of anti-Shi'ite violence or rhetoric for fear of alienating Western potential sponsors, insurgent groups might seek to highlight the same content in order to attract support from anti-Shi'ite Salafi networks in the Gulf.

This is, at least, part of the reason that the insurgency palpably Islamized in this period. The extent to which the membership of these proliferating jihadist groups represented real convictions or cynical posturing is as difficult to judge as it is central to Western debates over arming rebels. Advocates of arming rebels essentially assumed that they grew beards to attract Islamist money and would shave them off if the West could offer a better deal. While not flattering to the rebels, this would at least solve the problem of the limited pool of prospective "moderates." If the Islamist fighters were (or had, over time, become) genuinely motivated by religious conviction, however, then no amount of Western support would buy their loyalty.

Gulf regimes began to clamp down on these fund-raising networks as the war ground on and the insurgency radicalized. This was only partly due to concerns about the effects on the ground or the radicalism of the recipients of aid. In part, the crackdown responded to growing American pressure. In late 2013, Treasury Department official David Cohen delivered highly unusual public criticism of Kuwait for "continuing to be a permissive environment for terrorist fundraising."[23] The appointment of prominent Syria campaign supporter Nayef al-Ajmi as justice minister in March 2014 prompted a sharp public complaint from Washington.[24] In October, Vice President Joseph Biden went even further, publicly blaming the Gulf states and Turkey for fueling the insurgency (he later backed down after diplomatic complaints, but the point had been made). State Department officials routinely raised the issue with their Gulf and Turkish counterparts as well.

American pressure would probably have had little effect had there not been other more local drivers of the crackdown. Some regimes palpably began to fear blowback in their own countries, and moved to restrict travel by their citizens to join the jihad. Saudi Arabia, Qatar, and the UAE placed restrictions on unofficial charitable donations for Syria. Saudi leaders launched multiple official campaigns to support humanitarian relief, but attempted to block private non-sanctioned campaigns.[25] In April 2013, the Interior Ministry warned against social media, mosque-based, and other non-official donation campaigns for Syrians.[26] Saudi Arabia's Mufti Abd al-Aziz Al al-Shaykh repeatedly praised the impulse to support Syrians, but warned against violating laws against donations through non-official channels.[27] Saudi officials frequently warned about the risks to well-intentioned citizens of unintentionally supporting terrorists.[28] Saudi Islamists chafed against the restrictions. In March, leading Islamist figure Salman al-Odeh publicly called for accountability, demanding to know where the millions of dollars raised through official channels had gone.

If other Gulf states would not permit social media-driven campaigns for Syrian groups, this created an opening for Kuwait-based personalities. As Hajjaj al-Ajmi declared in a 2012 interview, "I say to any Saudi who wants to donate for Syria that I am right here in Kuwait." Kuwait became the primary location for unfettered private donations from Arabs across the Gulf. Former Parliamentarian Falah al-Sawagh told the Kuwait newspaper *al-Qabas* in June 2013 that "the West and the United Nations have failed to support the people of Syria, but after the Muslim ulema called for a jihad of raising money to support fighters defending their people we collected 80,000 Kuwaiti dinar ($282,500) in only four hours."[29] In August 2014, Kuwait adopted stricter controls over charitable donations for Syria, with Minister of Social Affairs Hind al-Sabeeh establishing requirements for transparency on the origin and final destination of funds raised for Syria, and the Islamic Affairs Ministry shutting down all charitable campaigns inside mosques.[30] Several months later, the Kuwaiti government barred the "Syria Calls" campaign launched by the Syrian Support Campaigns Union as violating charity laws.[31]

The fund-raising campaigns for Syria also ran afoul of the Gulf's crackdown on the Muslim Brotherhood following Egypt's military coup. The leading Islamist supporters of the Syrian rebels were also prominent supporters of the Morsi government in Egypt. Many were extremely outspoken in their criticism of the coup, and after the Rabaa massacre in August, yellow four-finger avatars proliferated through Syria fund-raising social media accounts. This posed a real dilemma for the Gulf regimes, for whom these Islamist networks were vital to Syria, but a significant obstacle to Egypt.

Western publicists for the insurgency fought hard to sustain the image of moderate, secular rebels worthy of American support. This image was increasingly at odds with reality, however. The horrors of war made it difficult to sustain moderation, particularly when the regime shrewdly focused its military efforts on eradicating those factions most likely to be attractive to Western sponsors. Insurgencies do insurgency things. The concept of nice rebels made little sense in a brutal, multipolar civil war involving intermixed populations. Insurgent car bombs and mortar shells in regime-held populated areas were no less deadly than barrel bombs against civilians in rebel-controlled areas.

These truths could be muted, if not concealed completely, in part through the complicity of the journalists and activists who chose not to publicize them. Videos showing opposition atrocities tended to disappear, while those showing regime atrocities would be circulated through social media and form the raw material for "reporting" by journalists and analysts who could not directly access the battlefield themselves. Occasionally, material from one sphere would seep into the other, with devastating results to the image of the opposition. A video showing a US-backed rebel commander eating the lung of his vanquished opponent no doubt thrilled sectarian audiences in the Gulf but shocked Western audiences who had been conditioned to expect less barbarity from their moderate opposition figures.

Aleppo became ground zero for this grim reality. Syria's second city had largely avoided the war for its first year, as its Sunni business community had refused to join the uprising. Beginning in July 2012, however, armed groups began incursions into the city. Soon, the city was divided between rebel and regime forces. Each side routinely shelled the other, while battling block by block for advantage. On the rebel side, intense competition between groups consumed attention when battle lines stabilized. The carnage of Aleppo, still more accessible to journalists via Turkey than was Damascus, helped to introduce doubts about the nature of the insurgency.

THE RED LINE

September 2013 is the closest the United States ever came to intervening against Asad. Many in the region believed that it had been Obama's concerns about the November 2012 election that had prevented him from signing on to the obvious policy of overthrowing Asad by force. The new Secretary of State John Kerry publicly and privately endorsed more aggressive efforts on Syria, raising expectations of an American policy shift even higher.

Efforts to arm the opposition were by this point well underway. The Obama administration had formally announced that they would provide arms to the rebels on June 14, in response to reports of chemical weapons use by the Asad regime. On June 22, 2013, the Friends of Syria meeting in Doha pledged to "provide urgently all the necessary [military] material and equipment to the opposition on the ground."[32] The stated goal of this assistance was, once again, to create a balance of power on the ground that would allow the rebels to negotiate with Asad from a position of strength. Such an outcome never materialized, however, for familiar reasons. The rebels remained deeply divided, riven with internal factionalism and competition among their external sponsors. Asad and his foreign backers were able and willing to escalate in response to any increase in rebel capabilities, leading again and again to the rapid reversal of any tactical gains achieved through arming.

It was in this context that, on August 6, reports came in of a large-scale chemical weapons attack in the Damascus neighborhood of East Ghouta which killed some fourteen hundred people. The use of chemical weapons on this scale manifestly crossed the "red line" which President Obama had set a year earlier when explaining what might trigger a direct American military intervention in Syria's war. The violation of the red line was so severe and blatant that many observers immediately questioned whether it could have really been ordered by Asad, who had spent more than two years carefully calibrating his military strategy to avoid Western military action. Rumors flew that rebels and their regional backers, such as Turkey and Saudi Arabia, may have carried out a false flag operation, launching an attack on themselves masked as a regime assault, in order to finally force America into their war. A launch by a rogue Syrian regime officer, whether on his own initiative or in the service of a foreign intelligence agency, would make sense but no evidence has ever been offered in support of the theory. Intensive investigations failed to turn up substantial evidence for these possibilities, however, instead offering abundant support for Asad's culpability.

The Obama administration quickly began whipping up regional and international support for military strikes in retaliation for the chemical weapons attack. The regional powers who had been lobbying for such military action relentlessly for several years could barely restrain their enthusiasm, promising full participation in the campaign. The American public, especially Obama's liberal base, was rather less enthusiastic, despite the earnest efforts by Secretary of State John Kerry and the president to explain the need for a tightly limited military strike.

Still, once the evidence for a chemical weapons attack became undeniable, the United States began to gear up for war. The resulting spectacle was somewhat embarrassing to watch. White House officials who had spent years arguing against military action suddenly found themselves mouthing the very arguments that they had previously mocked. Kerry waxed poetic about Asad's perfidy, invoking Hitler and the need to confront genocide, but then reassured wavering supporters that the attacks would only involve "unbelievably small" pinprick air strikes. Obama worked to build public support with a series of speeches, but was clearly still deeply troubled by the likelihood of the attack beginning the rapid slide down a slippery slope into another Iraq.

War seemed inevitable until British Prime Minister David Cameron suffered a shocking defeat in the House of Commons, failing to secure parliamentary support for participation in the coalition. When Cameron's government failed to win parliamentary approval for joining the air strikes, after years of British campaigning for military escalation, it sent a powerful signal about the fragility of political support for what would likely be a long and difficult war. Obama had not forgotten Libya, which began with enthusiasm, then rapidly hemorrhaged political support before turning into both a political liability and a distressingly failed state.

The British defection sparked renewed contemplation at the White House. At the last possible moment, after consulting with his closest aides, Obama announced not the beginning of air strikes but his decision to first seek Congressional approval to ensure that any new war would command full national consent. His turn to Congress threw national politics into a frenzy. Congressional leaders, who had not been warned of this gambit, wanted little to do with what would be an unpopular war. It seemed quite possible that Obama, like Cameron, would lose this vote—which would be a major political defeat, to be sure, but would also give him an off-ramp from a war that he clearly wanted to avoid.

Before the proposition could be tested, however, Russia stepped forward with a proposal to allow international inspectors to strip Syria of its dangerous chemical weapons arsenal. Asad, with little choice given Russia's role, agreed. This allowed Obama a face-saving compromise and a real achievement. While clearly not the masterpiece of coercive diplomacy that administration officials would later claim, the chemical weapons deal did manage to address a major security concern without succumbing to an incredibly poorly conceived war. The Organization for the Prevention of Chemical Weapons would later receive the Nobel Peace Prize for its successful efforts to remove and safely destroy Syria's arsenal. Obama could present this outcome as an effective exercise of coercive diplomacy, with the threat of war accomplishing the primary goal of chemical disarmament. Few really believed this face-saving spin, though.

Obama's red-line diplomacy provoked a real crisis with America's Gulf allies and with much of the Syrian opposition. Chemical weapons had never been the issue for them. They wanted American military support for the overthrow of Asad. They could hardly believe the turn of events. They had believed that they had finally, after years of lobbying, forced the despised American president into their war against his better judgment and determined opposition. Years of Gulf diplomacy, spy craft, and military support had gone into this moment, only to have it snatched away at the last minute. Perhaps they simply could not believe that Obama had once again outmaneuvered them, or maybe they genuinely believed that a historic moment to remove Asad and set the region on a better course had been lost.

What followed was an eruption of rage with lasting implications. Saudis and Israelis alike speculated that Obama's failure in Syria removed their faith that he would follow through on military threats against Iran—and publicly warned of their intention to go it alone. Prince Bandar, always deeply at odds with the Obama administration, warned ominously of "major changes" in the US-Saudi relationship as a result of the perceived betrayal.[33]

While much of this public posturing was just the usual alliance politics, there were some real changes. The following month, Saudi Arabia proposed the formation of a unified Syrian rebel army trained outside the country to combat both Asad and the rising jihadist factions.[34] This would involve a key role for the Jaysh al-Islam (The Army of Islam), a new rebel coalition marketed as bringing together moderate Islamist factions against both Asad and the Islamic State, but actually including a range of unsavory Islamist factions and headed by the controversial Salafist Zahran Alloush.[35] While Jaysh al-Islam was supposed to be subordinated to the Western-backed Supreme Military Council headed by Salim Idriss, this never really materialized given the dysfunction of the opposition's political institutions. Bandar lobbied hard for the US to ease its restrictions on the transfer of antitank and antiaircraft weapons to the rebels, with more success on the former score than the latter.

The announcement of Jaysh al-Islam signaled a more public (if not substantively different) Saudi approach. It was perhaps partly meant to pressure the United States by acting unilaterally and showing a willingness to work with more extreme groups than Washington was comfortable with. The avowed goal was to build a substantial, unified rebel army that would not only topple Asad but also serve as the foundation for a new Syrian state. But the Saudi initiative only revealed yet again the pathologies associated with external support to the rebels. There were few pretences of moderation among these new proxies, many of which (like Alloush) had a history of extreme sectarian rhetoric and violent practice.

The new coalition challenged the existing Syrian opposition political institutions, prompting pushback from factions and personalities with vested interests in their continuation. As one of the best Syria analysts, Yezid Sayigh, pointedly noted, the various shuffling coalitions "reveal a competitive logic driven by the expectation of external funding that presages greater political polarization and deepening division." The Saudi approach created perverse incentives for groups on the ground, and undermined the carefully constructed opposition leadership. Channeling funding and weapons flows directly to rebel groups on the ground predictably undermined efforts to create institutionalized structures.[36]

Turkey and Qatar adapted as well. Turkey, after denying the United States access to its territory during the 2003 invasion of Iraq, became deeply involved in its proxy wars over the course of the 2000s. Turkey's greatest concerns in Iraq revolved around the evolving Kurdish proto-state in the Kurdistan Regional Governorate. Preventing the emergence of a Kurdish state had been a primary Turkish objective for decades. Its hostility to Kurdish political aspirations did not prevent Ankara from cultivating close relations with the KRG as part of its strategy against the Kurdistan Workers' Party (PKK). Several times over the previous decade, the Iraqi Kurds had allowed Turkish military incursions into its territory to strike PKK camps. Still, maintaining Iraqi territorial unity to prevent the creation of a Kurdish state remained Ankara's highest priority.

In the middle of the decade, Erdogan's government had aligned with Saudi Arabia and other external powers in backing the al-Iraqiya coalition led by Ayad Allawi to balance against Prime Minister Nuri al-Maliki.[37] After Allawi failed to unseat Maliki in 2010, Turkey shifted to a strategy of cultivating its own clients, particularly in northern Iraq. It succeeded in placing its key political ally, Osama Nujayfi, of the Mutahidun Party, in the vice presidency, which increased its power in Baghdad politics. Its influence on the inside was undermined by the alienation of the Iraqi Sunni community from the central government. Baghdad would soon be rocked by the eruption of a new Iraqi Sunni uprising intimately tied to Syria's war.

In early 2014, the Turks pushed to create an Islamist military coalition in northern Syria, which would be capable of acting as a more effective proxy force.[38] While it finally agreed to designate al-Nusra as a terrorist organization and exclude it from the coalition, after long enjoying a good working relationship with the al-Qaeda affiliate, it doubled down on its support for the powerful Salafi-jihadist faction Ahrar al-Sham. In coordination with Qatar, it pushed Ahrar al-Sham to moderate its rhetoric and disavow al-Nusra. It did not.

The United Nations convened new talks in Geneva in January 2014 to attempt to get a handle on the spiraling war. Few gave it much of a chance of succeeding. The talks were mostly an exercise in keeping some diplomatic process alive while awaiting more propitious conditions. The Syrian Coalition, riven by these external rivalries and wielding little influence on the ground, was barely holding itself together. The Gulf campaign against the Muslim Brotherhood in Egypt had ramifications for the Syrian opposition, where the Brotherhood remained strongly represented among the Coalition's leadership. The re-election of the Saudi-backed Ahmed Jarba led Riad Hijab and other key Qatar-backed leaders to withdraw from the Council in protest, though they later returned. Sayigh noted, "the National Coalition's reprieve during the Geneva talks also momentarily masked the extent of its incapacitation by renewed Saudi-Qatari competition for influence over the Syrian opposition."[39]

The problem was not only the divided politicians. The armed insurgents, flush with new Saudi and Turkish support, had no interest in making a deal, and key commanders had openly threatened violence against opposition factions that participated in the talks. In the end, they went along primarily to avoid a rupture with their Western backers, but had no intention of agreeing to anything short of Asad's unconditional departure. The Asad regime, having survived the "Red Line" crisis, felt confident enough in its survival to avoid painful concessions.

On April 14, 2014, Prince Bandar was relieved of his duties in Syria. His removal could not have come soon enough. His strategy of building an armed opposition had proven an abject failure, undermining American strategy while contributing to the radicalization of the insurgency and the uncontrollable spread of violence. Pouring guns and money into a fragmented insurgency had always been a fool's bet, and Bandar had played a dangerous hand badly. Competition with Qatar and Turkey had only made things worse, as had the tolerance of ever more radical jihadist groups within the framework of armed groups. The Syrian rebels were in poor shape when Bandar departed. Syria was in even worse shape—with virtually no possible path back from the abyss.

Grim headlines at this point suggested that Asad had effectively won. But this too was highly misleading. It reflected the overly close identification with and reliance upon information from the Syrian opposition; the tendency to draw unwarranted straight-line projections from recent events; and the impulse to overemphasize American policy as a causal factor. In fact, Syria remained trapped in a strategic stalemate.

Victory and defeat had little meaning here. Asad's regime continued to slowly degrade from within under the pressures of war, and the insurgency was morphing in disquieting ways. Civilians continued to suffer, refugees fled wherever they could find sanctuary, and the overall trajectory of the war had hardly changed at all. When the rebels advanced, Hezbollah and then Shi'a militias from Iraq stepped in.[40] When Asad advanced, Saudis, Turks, Qataris, or Americans rushed in new weapons to prevent rebel defeat. The effective strategic stalemate created by the modulating role of external powers would survive even the greatest shock of all to the system: the emergence of the self-styled Islamic State.

By the winter of 2013-14, Syria had settled into a devastating equilibrium between a radicalizing insurgency and an exhausted, externally-backed regime. The prospect of US military intervention, which by early fall 2013 had seemed inevitable, had faded. Most of Asad's chemical weapons had been removed by international inspectors, but the rest of his arsenal remained intact. Gulf and Turkish frustration over the aborted American air strikes had provoked ever more reckless support for anyone who might be able to hurt Asad, regardless of the radicalism of their jihadist ideology. Hezbollah and Iran had successfully buttressed the Asad regime against these enhanced military challenges. The refugee crisis continued to spread, as did virulent forms of sectarianism and Salafi-jihadism. Even the Jordanians had their hand in the "southern front," where the US had its most direct role as well.

As Syria's violence escalated and the prospect of any resolution faded endlessly in to the distance, Syria's neighbors were drawn ever more deeply in to the war. The sheer volume of refugees and internally displaced Syrians is virtually impossible to comprehend. More than half the population of Syria had been forced from their homes by 2015, with millions fleeing abroad and the rest seeking sanctuary in less-contested areas behind either regime or rebel lines. Turkey, Lebanon, Jordan, and Iraq together took in some 95 percent of the refugees, with some number of those eventually making their way onward into North Africa, the Gulf, or Europe. Armed men would often move back and forth across these borders, but, for the most part, the camps avoided the kind of overt war support role familiar from other civil wars involving massive refugee flows.

Lebanon, swamped by more than a million Syrian refugees, tried grimly to remain outside the conflict. This became complicated when Hezbollah intervened directly by force.[41] Hezbollah had long carefully cultivated a position as a legitimate Lebanese political party and the vanguard of military resistance to Israel. Involvement in the fighting in Syria put the organization at considerable risk. It had a limited pool of fighters to deploy and enjoyed none of the local advantages in Syria that it could use against Israeli incursions on its own territory. By the spring of 2013, it could no longer avoid getting involved, both at Iranian urging and to protect its own interests. The decisive intervention came in the town of Qusayr in April, when Hezbollah fighters took the lead in pushing back a rebel offensive close to the Lebanese border. Once in, Hezbollah discovered—like everyone else involved in the quagmire—that it could not as easily get out.

Hezbollah's entry into Syria and the rising jihadist domination of the Syrian insurgency increased the risks of conflict spreading into Lebanon. Fighting episodically erupted, along with occasional bombs exploding in Beirut, but Lebanon proved surprisingly resilient. With millions of refugees straining its resources, it was difficult to anticipate this resilience lasting forever.

Jordan was similarly overwhelmed with more than a million refugees. In sharp contrast to its treatment of Iraqi refugees in the previous decade, Jordan this time decided to create vast refugee camps to accommodate the massive flow of Syrians. Zaatari, in a forbidding desert close to the Syrian border, became one of the largest refugee camps in the world and the third largest city in Jordan. Other camps housed even more Syrians, but together contained only a fraction of the massive population flow. Syrians moved into the cities seeking housing and jobs, generating pressure on services and resources, and increasingly sparking conflict with locals.

Jordan played an ambivalent role in the unfolding war, as it sought to protect itself while pleasing the foreign sponsors on which it utterly depended. Jordan viewed Syrian events with extreme anxiety, fearing reprisals and refugee floods and the ramifications of the ever-growing strain on its resources. It publicly refrained from demanding Asad's ouster and consistently called for a negotiated political resolution to the crisis. At the same time, its heavy financial dependence on Saudi Arabia and political dependence on the United States constrained its ability to either side with Asad or stand to one side. It worked closely with the United States and Gulf militaries in building up the capacity of the southern front, hosting secret training camps for Syrian rebels and reportedly deploying its own special forces. It feared being targeted by Syrian agents, however, something that would be all too easy given the vast numbers of Syrians dispersed through the country. It would only expand its military role publicly when provoked by the barbaric murder of a Jordanian pilot participating in the air campaign against ISIS.

The greatest regional spillover from Syria would come not in Lebanon or Jordan, however, but in Iraq.

IRAQ AND THE SYRIAN CRISIS

The June 2014 seizure of Mosul by Sunni jihadists and the declaration of an Islamic State radically changed the politics of Syria's war and the global perspective on the Arab uprising. By establishing control over a vast swath of territory spanning two countries, and carrying out a horrific series of videotaped executions, ISIS brought the United States directly into Syria, and back into Iraq, in ways that the president had, up to that point, fiercely resisted. The Islamic State franchise quickly mutated and began to spread through other failed and failing states, inspiring a new generation of jihadists and showing an uncanny ability to drive the political agenda.

There are at least three popular theories behind the emergence of ISIS. The first is the one marketed by the Syrian rebels that the Asad regime intentionally created ISIS by releasing jihadists from prison early in the insurgency in order to undermine the rebellion. Asad hoped to create a self-fulfilling prophecy, the argument goes. He had claimed from the start that the rebellion was a thinly veiled jihadist insurgency, and by encouraging the jihadists to organize and metastasize, he sought to make his own prediction come true. Asad's forces thus directed their fire towards the secular insurgents while ignoring the jihadists. By this stratagem, he hoped to pose the world with a stark choice between himself and the jihadists, a choice he believed would rebound in his favor. The implication, of course, is that ISIS can only be defeated by overthrowing Asad.

The second theory, more popular with Asad supporters and critics of the Syrian rebels (two overlapping but distinct camps), is that ISIS was created by the Gulf states and Turkey as part of the anti-Asad campaign. This thesis points to the ideological similarities between Saudi Arabia and ISIS, and the large degree of support for its goals among the Saudi religious sphere. It also points to the unregulated and undiscriminating flow of money from Gulf states and private networks into the most extreme jihadist groups. Finally, it points to the open border with Turkey which facilitated the movement of people, money, and weapons into ISIS-controlled areas. The implication, then, is that Asad should be recognized as an ally in the shared struggle against ISIS and global terrorism.

The third theory moves beyond Syrian particularities to posit that ISIS is the culmination of trends within Islamism more broadly. This approach focuses (ironically) on the Darwinian evolution of jihadism over the last decade. Al-Qaeda's successes and failures provide the raw material for tactical and strategic learning. While Syria and Iraq were the location for this particular experiment, ISIS rests upon more than a decade of the cultivation of a dense ecosystem of jihadist networks, online communities, and accumulated grievances. From this perspective, the IS is a truly global phenomenon rather than a local one, and its power and novelty lie in its ideology and organization.

As with all stories, there is some truth to each of these. But each is potentially misleading. While Asad may well have seen the utility in the appearance of highly-publicized jihadists and done what he could to encourage it, creating such a movement was far beyond his capabilities. The ISIS-Asad theory is usually taken too far by those keen to distract accountability from the backers of insurgency. Asad did open his prisons in late 2011, allowing key jihadists to enter the field. He also tended to militarily prioritize fighting against the rebels rather than ISIS. Asad's prisoner release did matter, but the origins of ISIS actually lie with the reconstitution of the Iraqi insurgency, over which Asad had little sway. Asad's strategy of ignoring ISIS made good tactical sense, given the locations in which they were strong and their common targeting of other rebel groups. No conspiracy is needed to explain common strategic sense. ISIS was not Asad's proxy, no matter how much he might have benefited from its actions.

Nor is Gulf or Turkish money solely to blame, at least in terms of intentional policy. The question of whether Gulf regimes had supported ISIS received wide scrutiny, but largely missed the point. Without Asad's brutality, ISIS would never have had the opportunity to take root. At the same time, whether or not there was direct support the insurgency sustained by the Gulf regimes created the conditions within which ISIS could thrive. That insurgency was Islamized, decentralized, radical, and dependent—opening the door for a group which could claim to be more Islamic and more radical, but well organized and independent.

The emergence of the Islamic State should be placed within the context of the failure of the Arab uprisings, the unresolved Iraqi insurgency and the evolution of the Syrian insurgency.[42] ISIS emerged out of the ruins of Iraq and Syria, taking advantage of an environment almost engineered for its success. Its broader appeal was rooted in the failures of the Arab uprisings, a highly potent ideological mixture of Sunni grievance and thwarted Islamist ambition, and the intensely sectarian rhetoric promoted by Arab regimes. ISIS is a creature of the environment that both Asad and the insurgency shaped, of the failure of the Arab uprisings and of more than a decade of American military intervention and counterterrorism campaigns in the Middle East.

Attempts to attribute responsibility for ISIS to any one of these causes will be radically incomplete. For instance, many within the Syrian opposition trace the emergence of ISIS to May 30, 2011, when Asad opened up the prisons to release a wide range of Islamist prisoners. They view this prisoner release as an intentional gambit to flood the heretofore peaceful protest movement with violent jihadists who would ultimately show their true colors and justify his repression. There is no question that many of these released prisoners would play key roles in the formation of jihadist rebel brigades. These ex-prisoners included not only ISIS figures but also non-ISIS Islamists such as Ahrar al-Sham founder Hassan Abboud and Jaysh al-Islam commander Zahran Alloush. But, as was typically the case with the proxy war gambits by Arab regimes, events defied their easy control. Asad's prison gambit would not have produced ISIS without the entry into Syria by Iraqi insurgent remnants or the broader context of funds and fighters pouring into an increasingly jihadist insurgency.

The origins of ISIS lie in Iraq more than in Syria, but the Iraqi insurgency would never have rekindled as it did without the opening provided by the Syrian civil war. The Iraqi Sunni insurgency against the American occupation was originally stood up in 2003 by former Baathists who went to ground following the conquest of Baghdad. A wide range of often competitive insurgent factions would emerge to fight the occupation. Factions such as the Islamic Army of Iraq, the 1920 Revolution Brigades, and the Mujahideen Army combined Sunni nationalism with an Islamist orientation. Islamist societies such as Harith al-Dhari's Association of Muslim Scholars provided religious legitimacy. The insurgency against the United States and the new Iraqi government received broad popular support across the Arab world, including favorable media coverage from al-Jazeera and other pan-Arab television stations, for their resistance to American occupation. The US-backed Shi'a-dominated government targeted by the insurgency was increasingly framed by these factions as an "Iranian occupation." Syria emerged as a major transit and logistics point for the Iraqi insurgency, with weapons and men easily smuggled across the border. Syria, in the mid-2000s, saw little contradiction between its alliance with Iran and its facilitation of a Sunni insurgency challenging an Iran-dominated emergent Iraqi order.

Abu Musab al-Zarqawi's Monotheism and Jihad organization, which would soon earn the label of al-Qaeda's official Iraqi franchise, lay on the far end of this jihadist spectrum.[43] Zarqawi's AQI was both a part of the broader insurgency and a dangerous outsider to the nationalist jihadists at its center. Zarqawi's extreme sectarianism, rigid theology, and strategic use of extreme brutality put him at odds with the mainstream Sunni insurgency, leading Islamist scholars like Abu Mohammed al-Maqdissi and Yusuf al-Qaradawi, and even the central al-Qaeda leadership. Zarqawi focused on brutal attacks against Shi'a civilians, both for ideological reasons and with the strategic goal of provoking retaliation which would drag all of Iraq down into an ungovernable civil war. He had few friends and many enemies when he was finally killed by US Special Forces in 2006, but had put an indelible stamp on the course of the war.

Zarqawi's successors, Abu Ayub al-Masri and Abu Omar al-Baghdadi, were the first to declare an Islamic State of Iraq and to seek hegemony over the full spectrum of jihadist forces. This Islamic State of Iraq imposed a fierce regime over the territories it controlled, and made little secret of its intention to control the insurgency. The Islamic State badly overreached. Its harsh methods and naked ambitions triggered an avalanche of resistance from within Sunni ranks, with tribal leaders, local politicians, and then major national-jihadist factions turning against it. What came to be called "the Awakening" and conflated with the US "surge" led by General David Petraeus had its origins in the intra-Sunni political conflict triggered by the Islamic State's overreach, as well as by the desperate state of the war against the Shi'a triggered by Zarqawi's provocations.[44]

The temporary alliance between the United States and these Iraqi Sunni Awakenings eventually dealt a major defeat to the Islamic State of Iraq. Violence plummeted as local Sunni forces backed by US muscle retook control over their own areas. In 2010, Masri and Baghdadi were killed in a raid north of Tikrit. While much of the Islamic State of Iraq's senior leadership was killed and its operatives routed from their urban strongholds, it managed to sustain a low-level campaign of violence and to sustain enough of its network to reconstitute itself and prepare for later rounds. Even the ideologues of the jihadist forums acknowledged their failure, and some set out to conduct incisive "lessons learned" analysis, which would likely inform the strategies adopted by ISIS.[45]

It would get that chance largely because of the sectarian mismanagement of Iraqi politics by Prime Minister Nuri al-Maliki.[46] Iran had dominated the post-2003 Iraqi political order through a broad portfolio of political assets. Shi'a numerical advantages guaranteed power through democratic elections, particularly when the electoral rules (largely designed by the United States) incentivized sectarian voting. Iran had obvious close ties to Shi'a political parties such as ISCI (the Islamic Supreme Council for Iraq, formerly SCIRI, the Supreme Council for Islamic Revolution in Iraq), the Badr Corp militias, and Dawa (the party of Nuri al-Maliki, former Prime Minister Ibrahim Jaafari, and future Prime Minister Hayder al-Abadi). It had more tenuous relations with Muqtada al-Sadr's Mahdi Army. It also cultivated ties with a range of Kurdish and Sunni politicians, ensuring through multiple contact points that its interests would be protected. Iran's role created obvious challenges for the United States, which needed to coordinate its massive military and political presence with its primary regional rival. It also served as an excuse for Saudi Arabia and other Sunni-led Gulf states to avoid deeper engagement in Iraq, even when such a presence might have served as a check on Iran's diverse and intense activities.

. Maliki, who enjoyed both a close relationship with the United States and Iranian support, was the pivotal player in the politics of the "Surge"—and in degrading its aftermath. The US deal with the Awakenings had been predicated on American guarantees of their political interests in Baghdad and in the integration of their fighters into the Iraqi Security Forces. Maliki reluctantly agreed to these terms, but slow-rolled their implementation and rarely missed an opportunity to constrict Sunni opportunities. Feeling secure in power, he now felt little need to make the painful concessions which had been agreed under pressure. In the years following the decline in violence, Awakenings' fighters and leaders complained frequently of broken promises, undelivered payments, and lack of protection from insurgent retaliation.

In line with Iraqi public opinion, and evidently believing that he now had the power to survive on his own, Maliki refused to negotiate a Status of Forces Agreement which would have allowed US troops to remain in Iraq for the long term. Negotiations broke down over the question of guarantees against prosecution of American troops, but the issues ran much deeper: Obama was determined to deliver upon his promise to extricate America from Iraq, while virtually all Iraqi politicians and most of the public opposed the American presence. The departure of American troops in 2011 had far less significance to the subsequent breakdown than is usually claimed. Maliki's sectarian campaign had proceeded with tens of thousands of US troops still in the country, and it is unclear how a smaller residual force would have offered greater leverage. The Islamic State of Iraq's first moves into Syria's uprising came four months *before* American forces departed.

IRAQ'S SUNNI UPRISING

The Arab uprising also played a role in reigniting a Sunni insurgency. At first, the Arab uprisings seemed to skip Iraq. This was unsurprising, given the recent traumas of occupation and insurgency, as well as the ethnic and sectarian composition of the country. But the ongoing crisis of Sunni inclusion in Iraqi politics had never been meaningfully addressed, and Syria's uprising helped to catalyze these simmering grievances into open protest.[47] The Iraqi protestors presented themselves as inspired by the Syrian uprising, with popular social media accounts explicitly connecting the "Iraqi Revolution" to Syria's within a profoundly Sunni sectarian frame. The growing violence and devastation of Syria's war opened the door to the jihadists. Within six months of the outbreak of the Syrian uprising, the Islamic State of Iraq had sent operatives across the border to begin exploring the situation. The Syrian uprising did not only inspire new political energies and a heightened sectarian identity. The escalating Syrian insurgency opened the spigot of massive flows of weapons, money, and foreign fighters into an area separated from Iraq by only a nominal border.

In late 2012, an initially peaceful Sunni protest movement erupted over an Iraqi Security Force raid on the home of Deputy Prime Minister Rafi Issawi. Protests spread from Fallujah to Ramadi and across Anbar Province, offering a new political opening to Sunni forces, which had been marginalized in recent years—including, ominously, the Islamic State of Iraq. The protests began peacefully, but increasingly were marred by violence. Protestors were killed in clashes in Fallujah and Mosul over the first few months of 2013. A decisive turning point came on April 23, 2013, when Iraqi Security Forces unleashed considerable violence against the protest encampment of Hawija, near Kirkuk. A ferocious round of violence erupted in response, framed in manifestly sectarian terms. Rather than make concessions, the Iraqi military escalated, bombarding Fallujah and fighting in Ramadi. Those attacks drove Iraqi Sunnis noticeably back towards the insurgents and against the government, setting the stage for the dramatic events in Mosul. By the late spring of 2013, whatever window for political compromise might have existed had decisively closed, as Iraqi Sunni leaders across the spectrum opted for a strategy of renewed insurgency against a regime they had concluded was hopelessly sectarian and corrupt.

It remains unclear the extent to which the protest movement had been motivated by genuine political protest as opposed to a cover for the revitalization of a dormant insurgency.[48] Whether or not the protest encampments had been an insurgent gambit, the ISI was clearly well-prepared to take advantage of the remilitarization of the conflict. The former Islamic State had been busy in the previous couple of years, assassinating members of the Awakenings and middle leaders of the various armed factions. A dramatic prison break had freed a coterie of key insurgency leaders who would serve as the backbone for a rekindled insurgency.

As the Iraqi insurgency gathered momentum, it could do more to project power over the border in support of its preferred Syrian insurgency groups. Guns, money, and foreign fighters poured into Syria to fight Asad could easily move across the porous border into Iraq. What is more, the presence of an Iraqi safe haven would strengthen factions fighting in Syria which enjoyed a presence on both sides of the border, which could tilt the balance inside that insurgency towards such factions. Weapons captured or obtained in one theater—such as the massive quantity of US-provided arms seized when the Iraqi Army fled Mosul—could be moved to the other when needed. Maliki clearly saw these connections. His warnings against the arming of the Syrian insurgency were not solely due to Iranian policy, and certainly not because of supposed Shi'a solidarity (which, if true, would make it difficult to understand why he had taken his accusations against Asad's support for terrorists all the way to the Security Council in August 2009). Maliki saw how the intimate connection between the Iraqi and Sunni insurgencies could impact Iraq— but proved utterly unable or unwilling to recognize his own role in fueling the crisis.

The Islamic State of Iraq moved into the Syrian arena cautiously at first, and then more brazenly as the tide turned in the favor of Sunni insurgency in both theaters. Jubhat al-Nusra, the al-Qaeda franchise in Syria, grew very directly from the Iraqi insurgency and was initially under its direct control. Abu Mohammed al-Jolani and seven colleagues entered Syria from Iraq (not Asad's prisons) in August 2011 and began to establish the networks, which would soon become Jubhat al-Nusra.[49] The decision to form al-Nusra reportedly came in October 2011, and it officially announced its existence on January 23, 2012. On February 12, 2012, al-Qaeda leader Ayman al-Zawahiri spoke about Syria for the first time, calling on all able-bodied Muslims to travel to the "fields of jihad" in Syria.

The two organizations were closely tied together and embedded within the broader environment of Sunni Islamist insurgency. According to Lister, "[T]he Iraq-based ISI had agreed to provide approximately 50% of its budget to its new Syrian front [and] additional support provided by pre-existing Al-Qaeda financiers in the Gulf had begun to arrive via their own respective private networks."[50] Much of this Gulf money went to Islamist groups besides al-Nusra. This is a crucial point. Al-Nusra and ISIS were only a small part of a much broader jihadist tapestry, which emerged across Syria, and which subsisted in crucial ways through the uncoordinated, massive public campaigns to raise money and awareness sweeping through the Gulf. Many Gulf citizens channeling money through Kuwaiti charities likely only wanted to support Syrian children or support civilians suffering under the regime's siege. But once received, that money was disbursed into Syria through a variety of networks on often personal, idiosyncratic criteria. By early 2014, some of the regional powers had begun to recognize the dangers of the jihad they had helped to create. Fear of blowback terrorism at home led Saudi Arabia and others to now clamp down on travel to Syria and to try to regain control over online incitement and the flow of money. But those processes were by this point far too advanced to be easily controlled.

As the funding networks shifted in a more openly jihadist direction, this sent powerful signals to would-be recipients. Many of the funding networks which initially supported the Free Syrian Army shifted over time to financing jihadist organizations. It was not uncommon even in the summer of 2012 for FSA commanders to share a charity fund-raiser stage with Salafi-jihadists. Veteran, deeply rooted Muslim Brotherhood networks also got in on the Syrian fund-raising action, as reflected in the notorious "jihad conference" hosted by President Mohammad al-Morsi in Cairo and in the May 31, 2013 declaration by Yusif al-Qaradawi in Doha exhorting—in terms alarmingly similar to Zawahiri's—every capable Muslim to travel to Syria to join the battle.

Al-Nusra's link to the Islamic State of Iraq was not officially acknowledged in public until April 2013, to avoid repelling potential allies and to remain a viable recipient of funding from the Gulf. But it was not much of a secret. Tactics such as suicide bombing and its vocally articulated ideology clearly demonstrated its extremism, as did its tight integration into the broader jihadist online media platforms.

American officials quickly identified al-Nusra's relationship with its long-time Iraqi foes. The United States designated al-Nusra as a terrorist movement in December 2012 because of its clear connection to al-Qaeda. American allies such as Turkey and most Gulf states would not go along with this designation for several years, because they viewed the group as an effective fighting force against Asad. The American designation did little to stop al-Nusra's steady growth into one of the most powerful armed factions in the Syrian insurgency. It continued to be the beneficiary of large-scale external funding from Gulf-based donors, and also began to pioneer the seizure and operation of oil production facilities.[51]

Al-Nusra's steady growth was interrupted by two public interventions: an April 7, 2013 video release by Zawahiri urging jihadist unity and an April 8 statement by the Islamic State of Iraq's less well-known leader, Abu Bakr Baghdadi, confirming for the first time the relationship between the two organizations. Baghdadi's announcement that the ISI had become ISIS—the Islamic State of Iraq and al-Sham—seemed intended to assert the Iraqi organization's leadership over the increasingly powerful and autonomous Syrian branch. It backfired.

Jolani responded to Baghdadi shortly thereafter by asserting al-Nusra's autonomy. A private and public battle ensued between the backers of the two camps, leading to a formal split between the two organizations in May. Over the next few months, al-Nusra (along with other jihadist organizations such as Ahrar al-Sham) fought bitter campaigns against ISIS over control over Syrian territory which had been liberated from the regime. ISIS steadily gained ground, and, in January 2014, finally succeeded in driving its rivals out of Raqqa which would come to be named its Syrian capital. Zawahiri's urgent plea to restore jihadist unity went ignored.

And then came the fateful seizure of Mosul by only a few hundred IS fighters, which transformed both wars and decisively locked together the two theaters by establishing a single governance structure across what had once at least nominally been the Iraq-Syria border. Two divisions of the Iraqi Security Forces (ISF) simply dissolved, abandoning a major city to a small IS force. The dissolution of the ISF opened the door for reckless expansion through Sunni areas. The conquest was not simply military, of course—it could not have succeeded without the active cooperation of local Sunnis prepared to go along with ISIS against the hated Shi'a-dominated Iraqi government.

The fall of Mosul, as shocking as it genuinely was, was actually the culmination of a long sweep of Sunni defections to the Islamic State's alternative over the course of months.[52] Many local residents cheered the takeover, which they described as a "liberation" from the occupation by an Iranian-backed Shi'a regime. Those leaders likely expected that they would have the upper hand politically in the governance of their areas, and assumed that the Islamic State had learned since its miserable tenure in the mid-2000s, but would soon be cruelly disappointed on both counts.

ISIS BEYOND SYRIA AND IRAQ

The Islamic State terrorist spectaculars, from the beheading of journalists to the shocking murders of the French journalists of Charlie Hebdo, reversed a decade of progress against global jihadism. Anti-Muslim activists who had been sidelined for years suddenly reappeared at the center of European and American public discourse. The sudden resurgence of anti-Islam sentiment was fanned and fueled by political figures and media personalities keen to promote religious confrontation. Extremists on both sides shared an interest in erasing the vast majority in the middle. Pretending that most, if not all, Muslims were, in fact, extremist suited the interests of both the jihadists and their putative adversaries.

The Islamic State itself represented a novel, if not unique, model for the jihad. Instead of hiding in the margins of society and seeking opportunities to carry out terrorist attacks, the Islamic State sought to seize territory, declare the sovereignty of god, and govern like an actual state. It developed an elaborate bureaucracy designed to fill most of the functions of a modern state, such as education, taxation, basic services, and infrastructural maintenance. For finances, it relied primarily on the illicit sale of oil and plundered antiquities, the seizure of assets in territories under its control, and flows of funding from supporters abroad. Internally, it relied upon the messianic fervor of its members, while ruthlessly policing the population under its control.[53] How did this model travel?

Its spread was facilitated by a range of broad factors at the regional level. The American killing of Osama bin Laden had significantly weakened al-Qaeda's authority and legitimacy within the jihadist milieu. The Arab uprising, with its promise of peaceful democratic change and empowerment of moderate Islamist movements, challenged al-Qaeda's core political message. Ayman al-Zawahiri picked up the pieces and continued to fill bin Laden's organizational role, but lacked his predecessor's charisma or political stature. Its official affiliates remained active and dangerous, with notable advances in Syria, North Africa, and Yemen even as the central leadership struggled. But in a crucial transitional period in the course of the transnational jihad, there is no question that al-Qaeda was knocked back at least temporarily.

The fortunes of these evolving jihadist movements were intimately tied with the rise and fall of mainstream movements such as the Muslim Brotherhood. The jihadists found little support from their old Islamist rivals in power. Both Egypt's Morsi and Tunisia's Ghannouchi viewed al-Qaeda with profound hostility. The Muslim Brothers and al-Qaeda were competing for the same Islamic public, each offering radically different ideology, organization, and strategy. Mainstream Islamists had little fear that they would lose voters to secular liberals, but they did have to worry about Salafi challengers at the ballot box and jihadist challengers on the streets. While they were frequently attacked for doing too little to confront the newly public extremists, this had more to do with state weakness than with any tacit acceptance. They understood that the appearance of these jihadists badly hurt their efforts to present an acceptable face of Islamist rule, and there is little evidence of any private support which might contradict their public stances. The failure of the Muslim Brotherhood rebounded enormously to the advantage of jihadists, however. The 2013 military coup devastated the Muslim Brotherhood's organization and ideology, leaving behind a pool of potential recruits.

The Islamic State was superbly effective at using social media and mass media spectaculars such as mass beheadings to cultivate the impression of a rapid, unstoppable march towards conquest. In fact, the model did not travel especially well from its Syrian-Iraqi heartland.[54] The model for Islamic State provinces ("*wilayet*") involves fairly limited goals such as waging local battles and providing limited governance in liberated areas, framed potently by extremely energetic and focused media campaigns. While the declaration of new affiliates across the region made for an impressive map of an emergent caliphate, the reality hardly matched the grand ambition. The wilayet of the Islamic State were for the most part unimpressive, rebranded jihadist factions which enjoyed the status conveyed by the new identity while doing little more than carrying out familiar terrorist strikes from the margins. The primary exceptions were those groups fighting in particularly receptive environments, such as Egypt's Sinai Peninsula, where a long-running insurgency, minimal governance, and clumsy military repression provided strong foundations.

These local IS franchises did not need to have a major developed presence in order to have a disproportionate impact, however. Terrorist attacks could work in more traditional ways. In Tunisia, for instance, the March 2015 attack on a Tunis museum, and especially the gruesome June 26, 2015 terrorist attack which killed three dozen tourists at a beach in Sousse, had a devastating effect on the economy, effectively shutting down one of the transitional country's key industries. The Islamic State branding and social media presence magnified the impact of these terrorist attacks by placing them within the broader narrative of the Islamic State advance.

The greatest impact of ISIS came not on the ground but in its impact on the broader regional landscape. Its rapid rise and media savvy forced all other Islamist movements to respond, at a time when mainstream movements like the Muslim Brotherhood were already reeling from political failure and unprecedented repression.[55] Islamist movements of all stripes now needed to justify their policies and ideological choices to their own members and within the intensely competitive Islamist public sphere. For some, particularly within failed states or when facing severe repression, this meant emulation of the Islamic State's methods or rhetoric. For others, it meant differentiation in behavior and ideological denunciation. But by late 2014, no Islamist movement had the luxury of ignoring the IS movement any longer.

This would have long-term ramifications for the place of political Islam in the region's political landscape. The balance of power and ideas within the Islamist milieu tilted decisively at this point towards jihadism of various flavors, and against the patient political strategy which had been dominant for decades. Revenge, the absence of other options, and a frenzy of ideological argumentation all pushed towards the embrace of violence—whether through the Islamic State, al-Qaeda, or any of dozens of small new violent factions starting up their own local insurgencies.

The rise of the Islamic State and the Syrian stalemate posed a new set of strategic challenges to the regional powers which had been fighting over the aftermath of the Arab uprising. America's entry into Iraq and the endgame of the nuclear negotiations offered novel possibilities for cooperation with Iran. Turkey became increasingly concerned about the Islamic State and growing Kurdish ambitions. The Gulf states feared that the Islamic State could posed a threat to their own domestic security, and fretted over Iran's growing regional presence. This set the stage for the unusually assertive Saudi policy which soon would emerge following the Saudi royal succession.

| 8 |

THE SAUDI GAMBIT

I t was in this context, of Egypt's military coup and Syrian stalemate and the gory emergence of ISIS, that the United States accelerated its long-running but troubled diplomacy with Iran. The new diplomacy began with secret meetings in Oman and then proceeded into several highly public negotiating marathons. With Obama in the final two years of his presidency, it was clear to everyone that this was the last chance for such diplomacy. The possibility of such a deal hung over every aspect of regional politics. Gulf and Israeli leaders dreaded the possibility of Iran's rehabilitation and empowerment, and feared even more what such a change might imply for their own alliances with the United States. The Iran negotiations provoked a historically public spat between Washington and its regional allies, and palpably shaped the course of events in Syria, Iraq, and Yemen.

The convergence of negative trends across the region created a mutually reinforcing cycle of despair. The hopes of the activists for peaceful change had long since been crushed. The hopes of the regimes for decisive military and political victory had now too been crushed. What was left was a bitter, tight new politics waged in broken arenas by scarred and watchful combatants who manifestly lacked not only any idea of how to win, but also even a clear sense of what victory might entail. The coming phase would be shaped by the Islamic State, the final US-led push for a negotiated resolution of the Iranian nuclear challenge and an erratically muscular new Saudi foreign policy.

The three were intimately interrelated. As the Saudi columnist Khaled al-Dakhil observed, it was hardly a coincidence that Operation Decisive Storm was launched just a few days before the deadline for the nuclear talks.[1] The Iran nuclear deal also heightened the fears of regional ruling elites, forcing everyone to recalculate alliances and positions within a rapidly shifting regional order. ISIS reshaped the wars in Iraq and Syria and heightened fears of jihadist blowback across the region.

The fear of an impending, sudden increase in Iranian power, prestige, and resources led the Gulf states to partially close ranks, including a tentative reconciliation between Qatar and Saudi Arabia. This, in turn, meant a more aggressive policy in theaters such as Yemen and Syria—which all too predictably only created new threats and problems. Israeli and Saudi frustration with the United States, combined with the reality of their dependence on American military and political support, led to an erratic, often counterproductive foreign policy with extraordinarily toxic effects on the rest of the region. The Obama administration's greatest failure was that it could not restrain the Saudis and other regional allies from their terrible policy choices.

The long-expected death of Saudi Arabia's King Abdullah served as the gateway to this new period. The late king was smoothly replaced by his designated successor Salman, who, in turn, appointed the Washington-favorite Mohammed bin Nayef as crown prince and—more controversially—his little-known young son, Mohammed bin Salman, as deputy crown prince. Initially, as with the 2013 abdication of Qatar's emir, Gulf pundits rushed to assure everyone that little would change in Saudi policy with a new king. And, as with Qatar, this initial pundit and analyst consensus quickly proved mistaken. Saudi policy under Salman would change quickly. The new regime eased the regional crackdown on the Muslim Brotherhood, engaged in unusually public criticism of Washington, and—in March 2015—launched an exceptionally risky and ill-conceived war with Yemen.

Oman positioned itself as an unlikely mediator in this period, offering discrete opportunities for dialogue between the United States and Iran. In November 2013, Oman hosted and facilitated the secret meetings between American and Iranian officials, which paved the way for the negotiation of the nuclear agreement. Oman offered neutral ground for negotiations in Yemen, to the public fury and probable private relief of the Saudi-Emirati coalition. In October 2015, the Omani foreign minister became the first GCC official to meet with Bashar al-Asad since the descent into total war. This Omani role cut against the grain of regional escalation, provoking intense criticism of the famously inward-looking sultanate, but provided an essential service at a desperate time.

The final stages of diplomacy with Iran consumed most of the oxygen for regional diplomacy over several decisive months. In November 2013, Iran agreed to the Joint Comprehensive Plan of Action (JCPOA), an interim agreement designed to test the intentions of both sides while freezing Iran's program in place pending the conclusion of a final agreement. After intensive talks failed to deliver a final agreement by the original deadline of July 2014, the talks were extended. In March and April 2015, marathon talks in Laussane produced a framework agreement, but not a final one. With another deadline looming at the end of June, the negotiations reconvened in Geneva for a final, high-stakes round of talks. That deadline was extended repeatedly, until finally, on July 14, the parties to the talks announced a final agreement.

These negotiations represented a genuine, high-stakes turning point in regional order. The negotiators on both sides carefully refrained from tying the nuclear talks to broader regional issues, but it was impossible for a nuclear deal not to have ramifications more broadly. By the time of the signing of the JCPOA, much of the frantic lobbying over the deal was less about the deal itself—which even its critics would largely concede in private would be both a useful means for controlling Iranian nuclear ambitions and was highly likely to ultimately be agreed upon—than on the terms of the post-deal regional order. Israel and the Gulf states alike were determined to limit the possibilities for a broader reconciliation between the United States and Iran, and to maintain containment and confrontation of the state they deemed their primary enemy and most dangerous threat.

The American management of Israeli objections received enormous media coverage, with the theatrics of Netanyahu's controversial address to Congress dominating much political coverage. As important as this was, American efforts to convince its Gulf partners of the virtues of the deal and to ensure the continuity of the US-GCC alliance was more central to the issues on which this book focuses. On May 14, 2015, Obama convened an extraordinary summit at Camp David with the leadership of the GCC. While several Gulf leaders, including the recently annointed King Salman of Saudi Arabia, stayed away in protest, all sent top officials to hear out the American president. The official communiqué stated blandly that the "leaders underscored their mutual commitment to a US-GCC strategic partnership to build closer relations in all fields, including defense and security cooperation, and develop collective approaches to regional issues in order to advance their shared interest in stability and prosperity."[2] Such collective approaches had been in scant evidence over the previous four and a half years. They would almost immediately be put to the test in Yemen.

The diplomatic tension surrounding the new Iranian diplomacy intersected dangerously with the rising sectarianism surrounding the wars in Syria and Yemen. Sectarianism had been on the rise for at least a decade, driven by Iraq's civil war and by the regional confrontation between Iran and Saudi Arabia. The 2011 uprisings intensified and accelerated this sectarianism. The repression of Bahrain's uprising had been legitimated within a highly sectarian framework equating Shi'a political demands with Iranian subversion. The public campaigns in support of the Syrian rebels featured a relentless barrage of sectarian incitement, with such defamatory terms as "Safawi" (Safavid, equating them with the old Persian Empire) and "Ruwafidh" (Rejectionist, an ancient slur against Shi'ites) migrating from fringe web sites to mainstream media and extremely popular social media accounts. The regional sectarian wave could hardly fail to blow back upon domestic politics, especially in the Gulf. Bahrain remained deeply unstable, with the wounds of its sectarian repression festering without even the pretense of treatment. Even traditionally tolerant Kuwait, where Shi'a represented a sizable and powerful minority, began experiencing significant sectarian tensions.

These were exacerbated in the summer of 2015 by a series of carefully designed terrorist attacks on Shi'ite mosques in Kuwait and Saudi Arabia. The Islamic State claimed responsibility for these attacks. The attacks certainly fit with its extreme anti-Shi'ite ideology and with their strategic pattern of seeking to foment Sunni-Shi'a violence to destabilize targeted regimes. Kuwait largely rallied around their Shi'a citizens, rejecting the terrorist attacks. But in Saudi Arabia, the Islamic State had hit an open wound. Anti-Shi'ism was a foundational component of the Saudi system, deeply embedded in its government institutions and religious establishment, and large portions of the Saudi population likely sympathized with core components of the Islamic State's ideology. The Shi'a-dominated Eastern Province had been in a state of roiling protest for years.

THE WAR AGAINST THE ISLAMIC STATE

The rapid ISIS advance which brought it to the gates of Baghdad and Erbil finally triggered an American military intervention. In July, the Obama administration launched Operation Inherent Resolve, involving air strikes and arms supplies to Iraqi and Kurdish forces fighting ISIS, and the return of a small number of US military advisers and trainers to Iraq. It was designed to first block the IS advance, which it soon achieved. It then laid out a long-term strategy of containment in which IS would be steadily degraded through targeted air strikes, cutting off finances and the flow of new fighters, and the gradual recapture of territory by US-trained and equipped local forces.

The United States found few real Arab allies in this war, however. While the UAE, Jordan, and other Arab states ostentatiously joined the initial wave of air strikes, this soon passed. By the second half of 2015, the Arab states were conducting virtually no sorties over Syria or Iraq. They simply did not see the Islamic State as their highest priority. The war in Yemen, launched in March, consumed an ever-growing share of Gulf military attention and hardware. The Gulf states viewed Asad, not the Islamic State, as the core of the problem and objected to efforts to refocus rebel energies away from Damascus. They also had little interest in coming to the defense of the Iraqi government, which they viewed as an Iranian ally not worth protecting. The United States thus fought the war against the Islamic State largely alone and with local partners found among Iraqis and Kurds, despite its large formal coalition.

The Obama administration played this hand well. It used conditionality effectively, by withholding all but the most essential assistance to Iraq until the removal of Maliki as prime minister. This was not simply a matter of personal spite. American diplomats had long since concluded that Maliki represented a major driver of the Iraqi insurgency and the dysfunction of the Iraqi state. His paranoid style and sectarian posturing created a toxic political atmosphere which had alienated the Sunni leadership, which would be essential to any meaningful political strategy against ISIS. Removing Maliki did not magically solve Iraq's vast political dysfunction, but it was a necessary step.[3]

The US-led intervention in Iraq crystallized one of the many contradictions of the unfolding regional map. The move against ISIS meant, in practice, renewed support for an Iraqi government and security forces viewed in sectarian terms by most Sunnis in Iraq, Syria, and the Gulf. ISIS very effectively framed its campaign in terms which commanded quite broad support from across the Arab world, emphasizing Sunni grievances and effective resistance to Iran.[4] For just one of countless examples, the Kuwaiti Salafi Hajjaj al-Ajmi, a key fund-raiser for Syrian jihadist insurgents, denounced "the moves by America and Iran to confront the Iraqi revolution."[5] In a region polarized along sectarian lines, the Iraqi government—and not only Maliki—was tagged as Shi'ite and considered an Iranian ally, if not a proxy.

The Popular Mobilization Forces (Hashd) called by Grand Ayatollah Ali Sistani to defend Baghdad were seen in even more overtly sectarian terms as a Shi'ite mobilization against Sunnis. Widely publicized abuses against Sunnis by these Shi'a militias inflamed these prejudices. While most of these players despised and feared ISIS, they remained virulently hostile to Maliki and the Shi'a-dominated Iraqi political order which the US had mobilized to defend. They were even more horrified by the tacit collaboration between the US and Iran in the defense of Baghdad, given Iran's pride of place in the demonology of the Syrian insurgency. How could the United States side with Iran in Iraq and be taken seriously as supporting the Syrian insurgency against Iran's ally in Damascus?

Inside of Syria, the air strikes and training missions were carefully targeted at ISIS and not at Asad, but extended to other jihadist groups despite their alignment with the more moderate opposition. The targeting of al-Nusra proved especially controversial with the Syrian insurgency and their Arab and Turkish backers, most of whom now viewed al-Qaeda as an acceptable partner against Asad. Efforts to train and equip Syrian forces which would pledge to fight ISIS but not Asad were doomed from the start. That is not unique: no such arming mission would be likely to decisively change the strategic stalemate. Still, the efforts to build a Syrian rebel army failed spectacularly even on their own terms.

A key crucible of this emerging campaign came with the determined defense of the Kurdish city of Kobani which had been surrounded by IS forces and seemed certain to fall. Weeks of sustained US air strikes and airlifted weapons reversed the tide, and ultimately delivered the first highly public defeat to the Islamic State. The enormous amount of military attention to this one battle makes sense primarily in terms of the centrality of narrative and optics to these new wars. ISIS generated enormous power from its online media juggernaut, spreading terror with its horrific videos while projecting an air of confident inevitability through its prolific online posturing. The coalition victory in Kobani was the first clear setback for ISIS since it first captured public attention. This broke the perception of their invincibility and inevitable victory, and established a template for coordinated warfare with local forces and US air support.

It also created new problems of its own. The Peshmerga's victory unleashed a new round of expectations that the Kurdish moment had arrived. Intensive lobbying campaigns pushed for the US to directly arm the

Kurds rather than going through Baghdad, and to finally support the creation of a Kurdish state. This provoked both Turkish and Iraqi fears, leading to countervailing moves by these key allies.

When the ISIS campaign stalled outside of Baghdad and Erbil, the urgency of the campaign inevitably flagged. Kurdish politicians returned to their endless jockeying for power and lobbying for external support. Iraqi politicians walked away from the promises of political change made under such extreme duress—at least until an exceptional Shia-dominated protest movement which erupted in 2015 provided an opening for new Prime Minister Abadi to introduce a package of major political reforms.

The war soon settled into a stalemate in which ISIS steadily lost ground, fighters and resources but grimly held on. The Shia-dominated Iraqi government's enthusiasm for extending the war into Sunni areas quickly flagged, while the behavior of the Shia militias likely reinforced Sunni acquiescence to ISIS rule. ISIS slowly lost territory, but proved resilient, digging in to its vital territory and opportunistically advancing where opportunities presented themselves. The American bombing campaign alternated between Syrian and Iraqi targets, while attempting to retrain Iraqi security forces. The Iraqi forces eventually retook Tikrit, and a few months later, Baiji, but plans to move into Ramadi stalled and Mosul itself seemed far out of reach. The coalition plan was for the slow degradation of the Islamic State, not its rapid destruction.

External players became ever more visibly central to maintaining the Syrian equilibrium as the war ground on. When Asad had been in danger, Hezbollah, Iran, and Iraqi Shi'a militias had escalated their presence. Iran dramatically increased its own direct role in the war, as Asad's military wore down. The Iranian Revolutionary Guard Corps's General Qassem Soleimani moved from the shadows into the spotlight, with his photos from the ground in Syria posted regularly to social media. As the IRGC increasingly assumed a direct role in planning and executing the war, growing numbers of Iranian officers died in combat. The ranks of the pro-regime forces were supplemented by Iraqi Shi'ite militias and volunteers, reinforcing the sectarian framing of the war as well as its transnationalization.

When the regime forces advanced, Turkey, Qatar, and Saudi Arabia momentarily overcame their differences to sponsor the formation of a new jihadist-dominated alliance, Jaysh al-Fateh. But once again, the escalated support for the insurgency did not help. Jaysh al-Fateh's advance, along with advanced US talks with Turkey over the possible creation of a no-fly zone, likely then prompted Russia to intervene in the regime's defense. The fact that it needed to deploy its own personnel and warplanes to achieve this limited objective is suggestive of the regime's deep manpower and resource problems, but also shows that the stalemate could nonetheless continue for quite a long time.

Advocates of arming the insurgency frequently complained that the plans would have worked if only Russia, Iran, or Hezbollah had not stepped in. This is transparently nonsense. Any strategy which did not anticipate such countermoves was fundamentally flawed. Competitive interventions by the backers of each side had been built into Syria's war since almost its inception. Saudi Arabia, Qatar, Turkey, Russia, Iran, the United States—all of them would continue to ensure that the war would take its deadly toll until those outside backers decided to opt instead for a negotiated solution.

Meanwhile, the Syrian rebels struggled to find a place amidst a struggle redefined by the ISIS war. Their fundamental objective remained the overthrow of the Asad regime. They tended to hate ISIS, which they largely viewed as Asad's creation and pawn. They viewed the other jihadist groups, including al-Nusra, as vital components of the armed insurgency—a view only occasionally challenged and more generally encouraged by their Turkish or Gulf backers. Saudi Arabia took the lead in seeking to create a rebel coalition which would include all forces, including the FSA and jihadists, arrayed against both Asad and ISIS. These efforts repeatedly stumbled against the enduring reality of a highly fragmented insurgency divided by real ideological differences, competing funding streams, and highly localized zones of control. The emergence of ISIS had captured the attention of the US-led coalition and squeezed the non-ISIS rebels between an expanding Islamic State and a resilient regime. In his final State of the Union Address, in January 2016, President Obama tellingly named ISIS the top foreign policy threat facing the United States and his leading priority.

Again and again, new coalitions were announced to much fanfare from media aligned with a particular network, only to fade away. Saudi and Emirati media trumpeted the creation of the Army of Islam and the November 2014 formation of a Revolutionary Command Council, but nothing much came of them. Analysts hyped the potential for a southern front, where tight Jordanian supervision of the border and the relative absence of ISIS might allow for an effective proxy army, but the campaign faded quietly away. The American train-and-equip mission, bringing carefully vetted fighters out of the country for advanced training, ended in humiliating fashion when the fighters were summarily taken captive and relieved of their weapons by al-Nusra upon entering Syria. Moves to arm Kurdish fighters after their successes in Kobani and in the KRG ran into opposition from Turkey and from Arab fighters suspicious of Kurdish intentions.

The new Saudi posture would be seen in Syria with the May 2015 formation of Jaysh al-Fateh (Army of Conquest), the fruits of a temporary Qatari-Turkish-Saudi convergence on a strategy of arming an even more extreme Islamist coalition. Jaysh al-Fateh was built around the Salafi-jihadist Ahrar al-Sham and maintained very close working ties to al-Nusra. Armed with a significant flow of advanced weapons from their momentarily aligned sponsors, Jaysh al-Fateh won a series of surprising victories in the north, capturing Idlib and advancing in Latakia and other key regime areas. The fact that this alliance was dominated by jihadists such as the al-Qaeda affiliate Jaysh al-Nusra and other slightly less extreme jihadist groups such as Ahrar al-Sham reinforced American concerns, but did not seem to overly concern its regional sponsors or the pro-rebel analysts impressed more by their effectiveness than by their ideology. But their advance bogged down after an infusion of direct Iranian military assistance, and the strategic stalemate settled back into place.

Each potential or real international escalation provoked a countermove. In September 2015, the US and Turkey finally agreed on American use of the Encirlik airbase for its war with ISIS. But this advance was quickly reversed by the Turkish assault on the PKK, a savage terrorist attack in Ankara, and the rapid deterioration in the political scene. In October 2015, Russia entered the war to great fanfare by launching a barrage of air strikes primarily directed against the rebel groups threatening Asad. In response, Saudi Arabia, with American support, dramatically increased its shipment of advanced weaponry, including antitank missiles, to the rebels. And the stalemate continued.

YEMEN AND OPERATION DECISIVE STORM

While Syria's and Iraq's wars ground on, the Saudis would dramatically open up a new front in the regional war: Yemen.

State authority and security in Yemen had rapidly deteriorated over the course of 2013-14 as the political stalemate continued. Armed skirmishes broke out across several fault lines. The Houthis fought against Islah-affiliated Islamists, while Hirak southern secessionists fought with the Yemeni army. AQAP seized considerable territory, while unidentified forces (often blamed on Saleh) escalated attacks on oil pipelines and infrastructure. Through all of this, the UN's Jamal Benomar continued to doggedly pursue a National Dialogue, which would provide the foundation for a legitimate new Yemeni constitution which might finally put its fractured pieces back together.

That process ended abruptly in September 2014, when Houthis swept down from northern Yemen into the capital Sanaa and seized power. President Hadi, placed under house arrest, announced his resignation as president, but then rescinded the resignation after his escape to Aden. Hadi evocatively described the Houthi takeover of Sanaa not only as an attempted coup but also as identical to the ISIS seizure of Mosul.[6] He blamed the Houthi advance on the support of Iran, an argument widely shared by the GCC leaders who had backed Hadi's government. The Houthis continued their advance far beyond their natural home, seizing Aden too. Hadi barely escaped and was smuggled into exile in Riyadh. The carefully managed Yemeni transition lay in tatters. Saudi Arabia took in Hadi and defended his legitimacy as Yemen's president, vowing to resist the Houthi advances.

How did the Houthis end up in Sanaa? There was far more to it than simple Iranian expansionism. The Houthi coup, as it came to be termed in much of the Arab media, followed directly from a series of long-recognized fatal flaws in the GCC transitional framework. The amnesty granted to Ali Abdullah Saleh left him free to scheme against his successor, a role he played with customary ruthlessness and brilliance. The National Dialogue over federalism posed a direct threat to Houthi core interests. And the exclusion of protestors and youth voices undermined popular consent to the Hadi government.

The nearly year-long National Dialogue, led by UN Representative Jamal Benomar, made real efforts to include Yemen's many stakeholders and constituencies, and involved frequent, long consultative sessions. In contrast to the hastily arranged 2012 presidential election, the National Dialogue was an extended, sincere effort to construct a consensus around a long-fragmented Yemeni polity. When it reached its decision point in January 2014, it had made significant process on a wide range of difficult issues. The timeline stipulated one year for the implementation of the recommendations, setting January 2015 as a critical deadline.

But it had failed to resolve one key issue of contention: Hadi's determination to establish a new regional federal structure for Yemen. Hadi reportedly believed that such decentralization would be the best way to break Saleh's networks of patronage, and, secondarily, to respond positively to Houthi and southern complaints of domination from the center under Saleh.[7] In practice, the federal provisions seemed to threaten the autonomy and resources of the provinces. The proposed new federal regions divided the constituencies of the Hirak and the Houthis alike, while creating the conditions for the central government to exploit oil revenues and to divide potential opponents. The proposed National Dialogue framework intersected with local and regional interests in ways which should by now sound familiar. The old elite which had grown wealthy and powerful under Saleh worried about any changes which might threaten their privileges. This made them easy prey for the machinations of Saleh, who was keen to prevent Hadi from consolidating his authority over a new institutional structure. Saleh himself retained vast wealth and a network of associates spanning the Gulf (and the globe), which could underpin a challenge to the shaky new Yemeni government.

The Houthis took a dim view of calls for their disarmament. As the Crisis Group succinctly summarized their views in the spring of 2014,

"With their foes...determined to violently halt the peaceful spread of their ideas, they insist on retaining their weapons, at least for now, to prevent a state controlled by their enemies from crushing them."[8] This is the same logic which motivated Libya's Revolutionary Brigades, Syria's armed opposition, and other similarly positioned groups. In the months following the conclusion of the National Dialogue, the Houthis expanded their position on their home by winning a series of battles against the Yemeni army and local competitors. They also attracted some degree of political support beyond their local base by positioning themselves as avatars of discontent with the machinations of the traditional Yemeni elite. They had unequivocally rejected the November 2011 GCC agreement, which granted immunity to Saleh, a position popular with many revolutionaries.

Their expansion increased hostilities with an alarmingly wide range of Yemeni political actors. It also set off warning lights in Riyadh, still fuming from its humiliating defeat at Houthi hands in 2009. Talks between Abd al-Malik al-Houthi and President Hadi in April 2014 went nowhere. The Saudis were fiercely opposed to any suggestion of compromise. Riyadh had always viewed Yemen as well within its sphere of influence (whether or not Yemenis agreed), but now increasingly viewed it within the wider regional arena as part of the struggle with Iran.

For the Saudi agenda to succeed, however, the Houthis needed to be stripped of their revolutionary identity and successfully framed as a Shi'ite movement backed by Iran. Only that would allow Riyadh to assemble not only a regional coalition, but also a viable grouping of Yemeni forces, ranging from the Islah movement to southern secessionists, in support of their "legitimate" president. Saleh's efforts on this front had always failed, but by 2014, in the shadow of Syria and the coming nuclear deal, the regional context had changed dramatically and sectarian labels had become far harder to escape.

Whatever the case, in March, a coalition led by Saudi Arabia began a major military campaign against the Houthis under the American-style tagline "Operation Decisive Storm." This campaign was driven in part by the shocking events on the ground in Yemen. It was also, to some degree, an extension of the UAE-Egyptian cooperation on air strikes against Libya, which some Gulf officials viewed as a successful test run for a viable test of a model of effective Arab action and the construction of a joint Arab force, discussed at the March 2015 Arab Summit.

But it was also intimately related to the Iran nuclear agreement. The Lebanese journalist Ghassan Cherbel tellingly tagged it "Operation Restore Balance."[9] Gulf officials viewed it as essential to respond to the potential nuclear deal by demonstrating power and resolve elsewhere against Iran's regional aspirations—and, crucially, to compel the United States to demonstrate its support for the campaign as a signal to Iran of its continued commitment to the Gulf alliance. As the well-connected Saudi pundit Nawaf Obeid explained, "Ever since the Obama administration embarked on its disastrous policy of rapprochement with Iran, Saudi Arabia has been working to establish a new defense posture whereby it can use its own military assets—not those of traditional allies like the US, UK or France—to defend its interests. Thus, when Iran attempted to overthrow the democratically elected government in Yemen, a key ally of Riyadh, Saudi-led forces were deployed."[10]

The media component to this war bears attention. Saudi Arabia fully mobilized its formidable media assets to support the campaign, with al-Arabiya in particular broadcasting a ceaseless barrage of positive news and opinion. Many Saudi journalists embraced their role supporting the campaign rather than as neutral observers. For instance, in April, the leading Saudi journalist Daoud Shriyan observed that "from the start Decisive Storm has faced propaganda from regional media supportive of the Iranian project. How can we respond to these lies?"[11] The notion that the media's role might not be to support the government's war was not even raised.

The air campaign diverted most of the GCC participation from the ISIS campaign and devastated Yemen's cities. It nonetheless soon proved inadequate. Month after month of air strikes and naval blockade created mounting humanitarian catastrophe but little political or military progress. Recognizing the need for manpower, the coalition reached out to multiple potential sources of troops. Saudi Arabia worked assiduously to mobilize the tribal and personal networks which it had cultivated over decades in order to put together sufficient local forces to fight and then to control liberated territory.

Egypt seemed to many in the Gulf the obvious source of an effective ground force, but Cairo deflected requests about entering the Yemen war. While Saudis argued that Egyptians should be the most eager to join their war, Egyptians did not seem to agree. The calls for Egyptian participation in the Yemen war provoked an unusually sharp public divide in the Sisi-era political elite. While the military regime understood well the extent of its dependence on its UAE and Saudi backers, it faced considerable public skepticism about a military role in Yemen. The historical memory of the disastrous Egyptian war in Yemen in 1962-67 had long hovered in the back of the Egyptian national narrative. Terrible memories of Egyptian conscripts dying pointlessly in Yemen's mountains had scarred a generation, albeit with little public commemoration or acknowledgment. It was not common in the tightly controlled and highly nationalist post-coup media to see headlines as openly critical of Sisi as those which began appearing about Yemen.

The timing of the GCC pressure on Egypt to join the Yemeni war could not have been worse. Egypt's uneasy rulers were facing deep political instability, an escalation of the long-running insurgency in the Sinai, the collapse of next-door Libya, and a troubling growth of low-level attacks and assassinations in Cairo itself. Even worse from an Egyptian perspective was the inclusion of the Muslim Brotherhood-affiliated Islah movement in the Saudi Yemen war coalition, and the general easing of Saudi hostility to the Brotherhood under King Salman. The well-connected Saudi journalist Abd al-Rahman al-Rashed ominously grumbled about Egyptian reticence towards the Yemen war: "Egypt is big but it should remember that it needs regional friends."[12] With Egyptian forces not forthcoming, the coalition turned to the Sudan. President Omar Bashir was happy to offer some ten thousand troops to serve as peacekeepers, presumably in exchange for Gulf help in easing his international isolation. The role of an indicted war criminal did not seem problematic.

In early August, the Saudi-led coalition scored its first major victory by establishing a foothold in Aden and facilitating the temporary return of the Hadi government to Yemeni soil. In a major departure for its traditional military policy, the UAE landed some three thousand of its own forces for the battle, and then left a substantial presence in place to police the newly liberated territory. Accounts of a delirious reception by grateful Adenis and the flying of Emirati flags were eerily reminiscent of the Libyan welcome for Qatari forces in early 2011.[13] Few who remembered Qatar's Libyan trajectory could be optimistic about the enduring popularity of the UAE's presence in Yemen.

Advancing towards Sanaa proved every bit as challenging as critics of the war had warned. Despite the cheerful parade of propaganda about impending victory, the reality was that the Saudi coalition's advances stalled. Liberating Aden from a widely hated Houthi occupation was one thing, but moving into contested or Houthi-controlled areas of Yemen was far different. To compensate, the coalition escalated its air strikes, causing tremendous damage to little evident military purpose. The humanitarian toll of the Saudi-led campaign was daunting indeed—and put a stark spotlight on Saudi rhetoric about Syria, for those who cared to draw the comparisons.

By September, it was obvious to a growing number of thoughtful Saudis and Emiratis that the war had bogged down into a quagmire. The independent-minded Emirati political scientists Abd al-Khaleq Abdulla, in the course of defending the war, acknowledged that many had come to "warn against an unwinnable war in the poor, unstable and sharply divided tribal Yemen, where a military victory is a mirage. Even if the UAE and the Saudi-led coalition liberate Sana'a and the legitimate government is restored to power, the military victory comes at an unbearable human cost and a bitter political defeat."[14]

This is the way of quagmires. It is always easier to get in than it is to get out, and the Saudis were now discovering yet again ancient lessons about the limits of military power.

| 9 |

WHERE DO WE GO FROM HERE?

As I write these words in January 2016, the prospects for the Middle East have rarely looked more grim. The wars in Syria, Iraq, Libya and Yemen continue to rage without a viable political solution in sight. Terrorist attacks associated with the Islamic State regularly claim new victims across multiple continents. Leading figures in Egypt's newly elected Parliament openly scoffed at the January 25, 2011 revolution, while the country's prisons groaned with political prisoners. Syrian refugees continued to spread out across the world in a desperate search for any kind of normal life.

The next president, whoever he or she might be, is going to face difficult decisions about the American role in this new Middle East. Even if the Iran nuclear deal manages to take hold, the temptation will be to go back to business as usual, rebuilding traditional alliances and increasing the use of military force. But the region has not gone back to the way it was, and will not any time soon. Arab regimes have not even begun to deal with the underlying problems which drove the 2011 uprising, and most of those problems have gotten worse. The wars afflicting the region will not be resolved any time soon, and their impact will continue to be felt for many years to come. Few if any of America's traditional allies share its aspirations for the region, and conflict between them will likely continue.

Navigating the complexities of this rapidly evolving Middle East will require thinking carefully about how and why things went so wrong. The story told in these pages is a genuinely tragic one, because it did not have to be this way. The Arab uprisings offered a real opportunity for the consolidation of new democratic systems which might finally be responsive to the unmet needs of their citizens. The unity, enthusiasm, and nonviolence of the crowds which filled the streets in early 2011 offered a tangible rebuttal to a generation of propaganda about their political immaturity, sectarian divisions, and inherent radicalism. The grim warnings of Arab dictators that the choice was between either them or the Islamist mobs evaporated in that surge of popular enthusiasm.

The traumas of the last few years have crushed many hopes and restored damaging old narratives. The idea that demands for political change can only end in the abattoirs of Iraq, or that only Islamist radicalism lurked behind the cheerful faces of protesting crowds, seemed fanciful in 2011 and obvious by 2015. Regimes which were the object of popular fury and disdain in 2011 now bask in popular acclamation. The barrier of fear, so forcefully shattered in 2011, has been rebuilt. The idea that Islam and the West were doomed to violent confrontation had largely faded by 2011 but has now returned in even more virulent forms. Americans who were allergic to anything to do with military intervention in 2011 now seem enthusiastic for even a ground war against the Islamic State. Obama's efforts to "change the mindset which got us into war" are a likely casualty of the region's calamities.[1]

This book's account of the new Arab wars offers a different way of making sense of the current regional situation. Put bluntly: the Arab uprisings have not failed; the Arab regimes have not restabilized and are not the solution; more forceful intervention would not have saved Syria; the failure of the Muslim Brotherhood does not validate anti-Islamist views; and the Islamic State does not represent real Islam, but the challenge of jihadism will persist long after its state is destroyed.

Here's why, and what it means for the United States:

THE ARAB UPRISING IS NOT OVER

Almost everyone today agrees that the Arab uprising has failed. Tunisia's ability to sustain a shaky consensus on democratic institutions can hardly compensate for the shattered remains of Egypt's paradigmatic revolution, the violently collapsed states in Yemen, Libya, and Syria, or the brutally constituted autocracy across much of the rest of the region. If democracy was the goal, then it has manifestly not been achieved. But while consolidated democracy would be the best outcome by far for the popular uprisings in the Arab world, there was always far more to the Arab uprisings.

Time and scale matter here. The protest wave of early 2011 should not be seen as a sudden eruption out of nowhere, which faded as quickly as it appeared. Instead, it should be seen as just one especially visible moment in a decades-long process of the rewiring of regional politics. The decade before 2011 had been shaped by the astonishingly rapid spread of information and communications technology and the visible erosion of governance and state capacity. Increasingly empowered and impatient youth of all ideological trends pioneered new forms of protest, completely rewriting the script of public politics in the process.

The 2011 uprising was shocking because of its size and success, but was otherwise completely within the scope of these long-term trends. I have tried to capture this trend with the image of a sea break against a rising tide. Year after year, the tide of protest came in higher only to be repelled by the wall of authoritarian regimes. In 2011, the tide finally overwhelmed the seawall. While most observers were shocked at the breach, since the seawall had always in the past proven adequate, few had been unaware of the fact of the rising tide. But the metaphor does not end with the initial flood. The surge into the streets of the capital cities had awesome power to destroy but resisted anyone's control. The floods could not easily be diverted into the canals of institutionalized democracy. The architects of the seawall certainly did not give up on their dreams of power. Over time, the tide receded, leaving behind damaged streets and shattered dreams, and new, stronger seawalls were constructed. But the metaphor still isn't over, as long as the rising waters continue to gather power beyond those hastily constructed walls.

That is where we are today. The protest wave is over, but the conditions which drove it have only strengthened. The Arab regimes have largely destroyed the hope for meaningful democratic change, and the failures of transitional regimes have badly degraded popular enthusiasm for democratic institutions. The regimes have done less than nothing to address the underlying grievances behind the Arab uprisings, however. In many ways, conditions are now worse: economies struggling with low oil prices and collapsed tourism, ruling coalitions narrowing, repression tightening. Meanwhile, the transformations in information and communication technology, and the radically new expectations and competencies of young Arab citizens, continue their relentless expansion.

Lebanese #youstink protests and Iraqi protests for reform show that the spirit of Arab Spring is far from dead. Egyptians and others have perhaps retreated to safe spaces to lick their wounds, rethink, and cultivate alternative discourses, but there seems little doubt that at some point discontent with the new military regime will spill back into the streets. The veteran Jordanian journalist Hilmi al-Asmar recently argued that the Arab Spring "will return very soon and will be more intense and more organized." The campaign against the uprisings, he argued, carried within it the seeds of its own failure: "the fierce repression by the enemies of the Arab spring will actually cause it to reappear...clamping down on freedom and violating dignity to suppress demands for change will only make those demands more powerful."[2]

That sounds right. It is abundantly clear that no Arab state has come close to solving any of the problems which drove the uprisings in the first place—and in most cases, have made them worse. When the new uprising does explode, however, it will likely be different this time. Sectarianism is far more deeply entrenched now, and uprisings will likely identify along Sunni or Shi'a lines rather than a single public confronting undifferentiated regimes. Democracy has been discredited, which means that it will not likely be a consensus rallying cry for the next round of uprisings. There will be no Muslim Brotherhood in place to enforce discipline among Islamist sectors of the population. The bloody repression by regimes such as Bahrain's or Egypt's probably means that the next uprising will be far more focused on revenge, far less peaceful, and far less tolerant of allowing members of the old regime to hang around with impunity.

ARAB REGIMES ARE NOT THE ANSWER

The failure of the Arab uprisings and the resurgence of Arab authoritarianism has brought with it a strong urge to return to the old regional status quo. Western policy debates for the most part center around rebuilding the old alliances which have come under such strain. With hopes for change frustrated, prudence suggests retreating to what works. In the Middle East, this means doubling down on partnerships with "moderate" Arab autocracies in pursuit of stability. This will have predictably negative consequences, producing neither stability nor more amenable partners.

America's passive-aggressive approach to the authoritarian resurgence will prove deeply problematic. Accommodating Egypt's coup or Saudi Arabia's war in Yemen may have seemed prudent in the short term, but will come back to haunt Washington down the road. The challenge posed to the American-backed regional order will likely be even more direct, with less latitude for Washington to attempt to finesse the contradiction between its normative aspirations for Arab democracy and the reality of its alliances with anti-democratic regimes.

Arab autocrats today project an air of confidence, which should convince nobody. In fact, they are badly overextended, hypernationalist, more repressive, and paralyzed in the face of mounting crises. Most Arab regimes are just barely hanging on. Their increased violence and repression of critics should be seen as a sign of their weakness, not their strength. Many face mounting domestic insurgencies which their repression only seems to fuel. None have viable plans to confront their mounting economic crises. The unlimited financial resources which allowed the Gulf regimes to protect themselves and bail out their allies are rapidly being drained by domestic spending commitments, expensive foreign wars and massively increased arms spending, and a collapsed price of oil. And no matter how quiescent publics currently appear, they have proven repeatedly that they are ready to explode at a moment's notice.

The insecurity felt by today's Arab regimes helps to explain both their harsh internal repression and their frenetic regional policies. Saudi Arabia and other regional powers intervene recklessly in Egypt, Libya, Syria, and Yemen out of both fear and opportunity. They certainly seek to take advantage of the prostrated countries around them, pursuing influence and power within their weaker neighbors in time-honored fashion. But they are also driven by profound, existential fear: fear of how their rivals might exploit those same opportunities, fear of the potential blowback from the regional crises on their own thrones, fear of abandonment by the West, fear of their own people. Such a toxic combination of existential fear and political opportunity rarely produces wise policies. It has not here.

It has become increasingly apparent that America has no real allies in the Middle East. America shares no values with the monarchies of the Gulf or nationalist military regimes like Egypt's. Nor does it share a diagnosis of the region's problems or even core national interests. There are certainly high degrees of military cooperation and intelligence sharing, political coordination, and protestations of eternal friendship. But if "alliance" entails some basic shared values, interests, and policy preferences, then it is hard to find any American allies in the Middle East beyond utterly dependent Jordan. Nor does the United States have any strong sector of Arab societies with which it shares such bonds of identity, interest, or values. Decades of imperium and intervention have produced a region where America is despised by both regimes and publics alike.

Over the last five years, leading Gulf states and Israel objected to and actively undermined virtually every dimension of American policy towards the region. Where the United States hoped to usher in genuine democracy in Egypt, the Gulf states subverted democracy and financed the military coup which ended it. Where the US hoped to incorporate mainstream Islamists like the Muslim Brotherhood, the Gulf states sought to destroy it. Where the US hoped to negotiate a nuclear agreement with Iran, the Gulf states and Israel viscerally opposed it and tried to defeat it. Where the US sought to demilitarize the Syrian conflict and find a negotiated agreement, the Gulf states poured weapons into the war zone. Where the US hoped to see serious negotiations towards an Israeli-Palestinian two-state solution, Israel fiercely opposed it and the Gulf states could hardly be bothered to care.

This has largely been blamed on the Obama administration. But the real problem lies with the allies. Obama has proven to be a forceful, skilled, and even obstinate negotiator on these issues, refusing to give in to the enormous pressure exercised by Saudi Arabia, the UAE, and Israel to give in to their preferences on core issues such as Syria, Egypt, Iran, and the Muslim Brotherhood. His strength has frustrated them, and their advocates in the American policy community, to no end. But if Obama did not lose these bargaining problems, he also didn't win. The president simply did not have the power to compel these regimes to support its strategy, or even to punish them for systematically undermining his policies. The next US president will likely rush to "repair" these alliances. Expect a January 2017 declaration that "America is back," early high level visits to Israel and Arab allies, and a show of force in a symbolic theater such as Syria. But after those early theatrics, the new President and the allies who so eagerly anticipated his or her inauguration will soon find that the problems in the alliance went far beyond Obama.

The Iran nuclear agreement will be at the center of this recalibration. Initially, the deal was predictably met by escalated confrontation across the region as leaders in both Washington and Tehran hastened to prove to their own people and their regional allies that they had not capitulated. The ratification and implementation of the nuclear agreement led not to immediate comity but to heightened hostility. It is entirely possible that this will solidify into a modified regional cold war, with the arms control agreement hived off from enduring political confrontation. This would satisfy Israel and the Gulf states, please the Beltway consensus, and probably work for Iran's leaders.

But it would also be a historic missed opportunity. Over the longer term, the nuclear deal offers the prospect of a more fundamental rewiring of the regional order in which Iran is incorporated into the broader American-structured security architecture. The model for such a regional restructuring should be the Camp David Accords, in which Egypt did not simply make peace with Israel but was deeply embedded into the American-led regional order. But American allies view such a rapprochement not as an opportunity but as an existential threat. That such a prospect of conflict de-escalation and peaceful diplomatic engagement is viewed as so deeply threatening by American allies is a rather damning indictment. It will be the task of the next American president and a new generation of Iranian and Arab leadership in the very near future to configure this new regional order.

INTERVENTION WOULD NOT HAVE SAVED SYRIA

The conventional wisdom now holds that the Obama administration's failure to act in Syria has been as devastating as the Bush administration's invasion of Iraq. Obama's supposed passivity in the face of Syria's collapse is presented by Arab and American analysts alike as the fatal stain in his legacy. There is no question that Syria has become one of the greatest political, strategic, and human catastrophes of modern days. With a quarter million dead and more than ten million displaced, Syria will haunt the region for decades. But American non-intervention was not the problem, and if it does ultimately intervene directly this will only create new problems.

The proximate cause of the catastrophe was, without question, that Bashar al-Asad's regime chose to respond to a popular uprising with massive, bloody violence. The decision to employ any level of violence to retain power was not inevitable, but was certainly highly likely given the nature of the regime. The atrocities which followed have been painstakingly documented by Syrian activists and humanitarian NGOs, and if there is any justice in the world (a very much open question), this evidence will someday form the basis for substantial war crimes prosecutions. There have been many such campaigns of state brutality over the years, but few have been so thoroughly recorded on smartphones, disseminated on social media, and thrust firmly in the face of a horrified humanity. Asad and his regime bear full responsibility for the initiation of Syria's apocalypse, and they should never be allowed rehabilitation into the international community.

Those atrocities did not unfold in a strategic vacuum, however. It is easy to understand why Syrians decided to take up arms in self-defense in the face of such a brutal, sustained military assault on their communities. The arming of the uprising and its transformation into an insurgency created an entirely different political, strategic, and moral situation. The militarization of the insurgency played into Asad's hands politically, solidifying his support at home among those communities terrified by the rebels and guaranteeing external support for his military posture. The arming of the insurgency dramatically increased the level of violence in all directions, shattering state and society with untold human consequences. The turn to insurgency and the flood of external support for these armed groups inevitably opened the door to jihadists, warlordism, and a devastating strategic stalemate. There should be an accounting for those who advocated an insurgency strategy in Syria knowing perfectly well that it could not hope to succeed. Their claim to the moral high ground is one of the great mythologies of the last four years. They knowingly pushed for a strategy guaranteed to produce enormous human suffering and with little chance of success, in the hopes of forcing the United States into a war that Obama was determined to avoid.

Obama was right to avoid this intervention. Perhaps his greatest sin in the eyes of the Washington consensus was to have learned the lessons of Iraq. He understood deeply that American military power could not solve the region's conflicts and that limited intervention would only pave the way to ever-escalating demands for more. Obama saw through the sophistry of the interventionists and impatiently dismissed their ill-conceived suggestions. He refused to buy the carefully marketed illusions of an organized moderate opposition or easily enforced no-fly zones or safe areas. He understood the iron logic of the slippery slope from limited intervention to full-scale quagmire, and would pay the political costs to avoid that fateful path.

Ironically, perhaps the best window into what might have happened had America intervened against Asad is the fate of Obama's actual intervention against ISIS. Operation Inherent Resolve, launched in June 2014, involved a major air campaign, significant arming of and tactical support for local forces on the ground, and a wide Arab and international coalition. It had some real successes, halting the Islamic State's advances in Iraq and slowly reversing its territorial gains while steadily degrading it through sanctions and air strikes. But American power did not deliver immediate victory. And when it did not, it invited incessant pressure for escalation.

Syria is a historic catastrophe, but it was not one of America's making. If anything, the Obama administration did too much and not too little. By staking out a position that Asad must go, Obama created expectations which shaped political and military behavior on all sides. By failing to restrain allies from arming the opposition early in the crisis, Washington watched seemingly helplessly as the disaster it had predicted unfolded inexorably. By then joining the campaign of arming rebels, it helped to entrench the strategic stalemate without gaining significant leverage over the opposition or defeating the regime. By threatening war in August 2013 and then stepping back at the last minute, it achieved the worst of all worlds. By making public promises for political cover, it raised expectations which were inevitably frustrated at great cost to American credibility and prestige. In almost all instances, the US and the region would have been better served by a more, not less, restrained American policy towards Syria.

But for all America's failings, the real responsibility for Syria's apocalypse lies with Asad and with the regional powers which facilitated the war. Iran and Hezbollah enabled Asad's atrocities before stepping in directly to fight his war. Saudi Arabia, Qatar, and Turkey poured weapons into the opposition with little regard to the implications. The price for their willingness to wage a regional cold war on Syrian soil has been paid in countless lives destroyed and the deep destabilization of the Levant.

ISLAMIST EXTREMISM IS ONLY GOING TO GET WORSE

The failure of the Arab uprisings and the emergence of the Islamic State has revitalized a critique of Islamist movements which had fallen into disrepute. For these critics, Egypt's disastrous transition revealed the true essence of the Muslim Brotherhood as a totalitarian cult set on imposing radical Islamist views. The Islamic State, for its part, represents something authentic about not just Islamism but Islam itself. The viral concept of a "clash of civilizations" has metastasized and infected public discourse.

The Muslim Brotherhood certainly failed to govern Egypt, but its incompetence does not merit the sweeping conclusions about its perfidy, which are being so aggressively marketed by analysts and Arab regimes alike. The Brotherhood's hierarchical, insular organizational structure served it well for surviving Mubarak's authoritarianism, but proved tragically ill-adapted to the demands of a chaotic, highly polarized transition. But it was not a terrorist organization. It was a strategic competitor to Salafi-jihadist groups like al-Qaeda, with a distinct ideology, organization, and political strategy. Mohammed el-Morsi's brief presidency reveals the yawning divide between the Brotherhood's worldview and the preferences of large, powerful segments of Egyptian society, but little about the Brotherhood's true essence. Blurring the lines between very different Islamist trends will squander a decade's analytical progress.

That Muslim Brotherhood is gone, however. The 2013 Egyptian coup and the subsequent repression have shattered the Brotherhood's organization and discredited its ideological claims and political strategy. Young Muslim Brothers have turned out not to be the robotic dupes portrayed by their critics. They have responded to the repression in a variety of ways, some retreating from politics altogether and others turning to violence in an array of new, small organizations. What Muslim Brother today could be convinced that democratic participation is a viable political strategy? The options have been effectively narrowed to apolitical social outreach or violent insurgency, leaving no middle ground for the large pool of Islamist-minded youth who would prefer peaceful participation in society and politics. The firewall which the highly organized, strategically-minded Muslim Brotherhood once offered against jihadism has been shattered. This is not a victory against jihadism. Quite the contrary. The desolation of the Muslim Brotherhood has created a vast pool of potential recruits for jihadist groups and removed their most powerful competitors.

Even more dangerous is the revitalization of the actual extremists and the collapse of the best available strategies for containing them. Obama's 2009 Cairo speech had articulated a powerful counter-vision in which Muslims and the West shared a common civilization, an alternative given substance by his push to include the Muslim Brotherhood and other Islamist groups within democratic politics. Arab regimes opposed this approach not because it couldn't work, but because it could—but would require concessions to democratic inclusion which they were simply unprepared to make. Arab regimes viewed the rise of the Brotherhood following the Arab uprisings as profoundly threatening not because of its Islamism but because they feared any popular challenge to their rule. Fanning the fear of Islamism was as basic a survival strategy for regimes like Egypt's as was sectarianism in the Gulf.

With the possibility of democratic inclusion in ruins, bin Laden's vision of a world of necessary, essential conflict between Islam and the West looks more compelling. The ironies are as painful as they are evident. Jihadists and their enemies alike share a common interest in denying the possibility of coexistence and moderation for the world's Muslims. This vision has always failed because it is fundamentally untrue. Al-Qaeda's strategic problem was that the overwhelming majority of the world's Muslims rejected its vision in both theory and practice. The events of the last few years have rescued this strategy from the abyss into which it had fallen. The crushing of the Muslim Brotherhood has decimated the primary player occupying that Islamist mainstream. The regime-fueled polarization between Islamists and their enemies across the region has reinforced al-Qaeda's strategy in every particular. The Islamic State and its emulators have galvanized hostility towards Islam in the West. It has never been more urgent for a renewed American and global strategy designed to prevent this reckless spiral into a clash of civilizations.

The Islamic State as a territorial entity in Syria and Iraq will likely not have a long life. But the model and the idea it represents will likely continue to metastasize and adapt to survive in new conditions. There will be no possibility of meaningfully addressing the challenge of jihadism without addressing the core failures of governance which fuel popular discontent. Stronger states may be desperately needed to fight military campaigns against the Islamic State, especially in failed state zones like the Sinai, Libya, or Yemen. But ultimately, Arab regimes are the problem and not the solution.

Even as the Islamic State struggled in its Syrian and Iraqi stronghold, affiliated and sympathetic individuals and movements took their jihad farther afield. The Islamic State took advantage of Libya's anarchy to seize a foothold in Sirte, from which they would prove difficult to uproot. The IS claimed terrorist attacks in Tunisia and Yemen, and in the fall of 2015 took responsibility for the bombing of a Russian jetliner departing Egypt. Most shockingly of all, the IS claimed to have organized two spectacular terrorist attacks in France, including the murder of the staff of the satirical magazine *Charlie Hebdo* and a massacre in the heart of Paris. The IS could be contained territorially, but the ideas of global jihad would not be so easily blocked.

THE LEGACIES OF THE NEW ARAB WARS

The new Arab wars described in this book will be shaping the region's politics for decades to come. The reassertion of state power against the popular mobilization of 2011 has created new, less stable, and more violent forms of Arab autocracy. None of the popular grievances which drove the Arab uprisings have been addressed, and most of those problems have grown worse. The trashing of the transitions has closed the door to some of the most promising possibilities for escaping this predicament. Egypt's military coup shattered that political system for a generation, with effects still being felt far beyond its borders. The prospects for the region in the coming years are grim indeed.

The region's proxy wars have shattered states and generated a level of human tragedy which will take generations to comprehend. Syria's apocalypse has displaced more than ten million people. Hundreds of thousands have fled to Europe, while millions suffer in refugee camps along the border and even more search for safety within Syria's borders. Libya's civil war has driven hundreds of thousands more people to seek refuge in Europe or in neighboring states. Yemen's war has created many more hundreds of thousands of refugees and a state of famine. An entire generation of children will grow up knowing nothing but displacement, death, and fear. Why would they ever contemplate reconciliation or abandon thoughts of revenge? Any strategy to rebuild the Middle East must offer them such hope.

The wars have entrenched dangerous new forms of sectarianism and extremism which will prove far more difficult to dispel than they were to spread. Sectarian and local hatreds are partly a result of the violence itself. It is difficult to escape primordial identities when one's family is being slaughtered in their name. Worse, those hatreds and polarizing identities have been actively encouraged by state-backed media and by newly empowered social movements. The cynical entrepreneurs of sectarianism have found this polarization to be useful for generating power, raising money, and winning support for their political causes. They may believe that they can ratchet those hatreds back down when they are no longer useful. But there is little reason to believe that they will be able to control the forces they have unleashed.

The Arab uprisings have galvanized this catalog of horrors, but all are rooted in the political order shaped by decades of Arab autocracy. The sectarianism, extremism, and social polarization of today's Arab politics were not created by the protestors who took to the streets to demand the overthrow of their regimes. They were created by those regimes. Small wonder, then, that the response by wounded regimes has been to double down on despotism and proxy war, while fanning the flames of sectarianism and social polarization. Relying on these Arab regimes to fix what has gone wrong with the Arab uprisings is foolish beyond compare. It is also, naturally, the policy which the United States is likely to pursue in the coming years, until it is once again surprised by the inevitable explosions to come.

There will be no return to stability. The Arab uprisings of 2011 were only one episode in a generational challenge to a failed political order. Protesters won some battles in 2011, and regimes won them in the following years. Many of the conflicts, especially Syria's and Yemen's, had no winners at all. There will be more rounds of upheaval, more state failures, more sudden regime collapses, more insurgencies, and more proxy wars. There is little which the United States, or any external power, can do at this point to fundamentally alter the trajectory of this unfolding struggle. America can be more or less directly involved, paying a greater or lesser share of the costs, but it will ultimately prove unable to decide the outcome of the fundamental struggles by Arabs over their future. Neither more military intervention nor catering to the preferences of Arab autocrats will re-establish American control over this Middle East. America would be better served to consolidate its retrenchment from the region and invest its support not in its brutal regimes but in those Arabs seeking a more democratic future.

Acknowledgments

This book has been painful to write. The shattering of the hopes and dreams unleashed by the Arab uprising of 2011 has left far too many friends, contacts, colleagues and inspirational figures of those dizzying days dead, imprisoned or in exile. I hope that this book helps to make sense of what went wrong in order to get it right next time.

Writing this book would not have been possible without the consistent support of some extraordinary people and institutions. I would not have been able to finish this book had I not had the opportunity to step down as director of the Institute for Middle East Studies after six excellent years. I would like to thank former Dean Michael Brown for his consistent support for my work at George Washington University, and especially for approving my research sabbatical. I would also like to thank Nathan Brown for taking over as IMES director, Shana Marshall for holding down the fort as associate director, Kate Getz for doing everything, and the entire hardworking staff.

This book reflects my immersion in the phenomenal community of scholars which has come together around the Project on Middle East Political Science. This initiative has wildly exceeded my hopes and aspirations since its launch in 2009. I would like to thank the Carnegie Corporation of New York, the Henry Luce Foundation, and the Social Science Research Council for their consistent support of POMEPS. I would also like to thank the POMEPS steering committee and advisory council for their efforts on behalf of the initiative, as well as the more than three hundred scholars who have contributed to its workshops and publications. And, above all, I would like to thank my amazingly talented and hardworking colleagues at POMEPS who have made everything happen: Maria Kornalian, Mary Casey, Cortni Kerr, Lauren Baker, and Stephanie Dahle.

My thinking for this book has also been greatly enriched by my opportunity to edit and write for the Washington Posts's Monkey Cage. I am proud to be a part of this great experiment in real time political science which has so significantly improved and enriched public discourse on policy issues. Hundreds of scholars have contributed their research insights, and I have learned from them all. Thanks to John Sides, Henry Farrell, Erik Voeten, Joshua Tucker, Kim DiYonne, Laura Seay, and all the other contributors to the Cage.

I joined the Carnegie Endowment for International Peace as a nonresident senior associate just as I began the final stage of drafting the book. I would like to thank William Burns for the invitation to join the outstanding team of Middle East scholars in Carnegie's Middle East Program. I'd also like to thank Michele Dunne and Marwan Muasher for their enthusiastic welcome to the program, and their patience as I hunkered down to write. My gratitude also goes out to all my colleagues at the Center for a New American Security, which hosted me as a senior fellow for six crucial years. And, finally, I'd like to thank Sheldon Himmelfarb and Anand Varghese of the United States Institute of Peace for shepharding the "Blogs and Bullets" initiative over more than half a decade, and my colleagues Sean Aday and Deen Freelon for their rigorous and thoughtful partnership in that program.

I'd like to thank several editors who have been endlessly supportive of my work over the years. Gideon Rose at *Foreign Affairs* has repeatedly reached out at exactly the right time to encourage me to pull together my thoughts into a concise argument. Jeffrey Isaac of *Perspectives on Politics* is a fiercely passionate intellect who has constantly pushed me to engage more deeply with politics and political science. I can not thank Clive Priddle of Public Affairs enough for believing in this book and helping me to shape its ideas, and the incredibly efficient Public Affairs team for making it happen.

I can not even begin to list all the scholars, colleagues and friends whose efforts have shaped my thinking about the trajectory of the Arab uprising. I would like to thank all of them, and for fear of leaving somebody out name none of them. You all know who you are. Thanks.

I'd like to thank Kendrick Lamar for being Kendrick Lamar.

Readers of *The Arab Uprising* may recall the pivotal role played in its crafting by Jack, my faithfully annoying dog. I woud like to thank, I suppose, Jack and his brother Wilson for ensuring that I never sleep past 5:00am and have had many, many opportunities to think about the Middle East while walking them around the neighborhood. This time around, I would like to give Jack all the credit for whatever is good in this book and blame Wilson for the rest.

Finally, my deepest and most heartfelt gratitude goes always to Lauren, Sophia and Alec. My fondest memory of the writing of this book is that while finishing penultimate draft, I left Paris a day early so I could be a part of Sophia's first softball tournament championship. This book, like everything I do, would have been impossible without my family's love, companionship and support, and it is dedicated to them.

Notes

PREFACE

1. John McCain, Joe Lieberman and Lindsey Graham, "The risks of inaction in Syria," *The Washington Post*, August 5, 2012.

2. Marc Lynch, "Reflections on the Arab uprising," *Washington Post* November 17, 2014.

CHAPTER 1

1. Arab Barometer, second wave (2011) and third wave (2013); all data publicly available at http://www.arabbarometer.org.

2. Abd al-Rahman al-Rashed, "The Yemen war is connected to Syria," *Al-Sharq al-Awsat* April 13, 2015.

3. Dalia Mogahed, "Arabs doubt benefits of the uprisings," September 12, 2012, http://www.gallup.com/poll/157400/opinion-briefing-arabs-doubt-benefits-uprisings .aspx

4. All Arab Barometer data, here and cited elsewhere in the book, is available at http://www.arabbarometer.org/.

5. For an excellent discussion of how such regional cold wars operate, see Gregory Gause, *Beyond Sectarianism: The New Middle Eastern Cold* War (Washington, DC: Brookings, 2013).

6. Steven Heydemann, "Mass politics and the future of authoritarian governance in the Arab world," in *POMEPS Studies 11 The Arab Thermidor* (August 2014).

7. Robert Springborg, "The role of militaries in the Arab Thermidor" and Yezid Sayigh, "Militaries, civilians and the crisis of the Arab state" in *POMEPS Studies 11 The Arab Thermidor* (August 2014).

8. Roy Gutman, "Biden continues to apologize; first Turkey, now UAE," last modified October 6, 2014; http://www.mcclatchydc.com/news/nation-world/world/middle -east/article24774259.html

9. Wael Qandil, "The International Organization for the Counter-Revolution," Al-Araby al-Jadeed, September 3, 2014 (Arabic).

10. Patrick Seale, *The Struggle for Syria: A Study in Post-War Arab Politics, 1945-1958* (New Haven: Yale University Press 1987); David Hirst, *Beware of Small States: Lebanon, Battleground of the Middle East* (New York: Nation Books, 2010).

11. Laurent Louer, *Transnational Shia Politics: Religious and Political Networks in the Gulf* (Oxford University Press 2012); Toby Matthiesen, *Sectarian Gulf: Bahrain, Saudi Arabia, and the Arab Spring That Wasn't* (Palo Alto, CA: Stanford University Press, 2013).

12. Col. Hassan Mustafa, acting commander of Division 30, quoted by Borzou Daragahi, Buzzfeed, "Moderate Syrian Rebels Say They May Not Be Doing Well But Are Very Much Alive," October 7, 2015; http://www.buzzfeed.com/borzoudaragahi/syrian-rebels-say-they-may-not-be-doing-well-but-are-very-mu#.abLQJn0m9

13. Palestinian Center for Policy and Survey Research, Palestinian Public Opinion Survey 57, September 2015; http://www.pcpsr.org/en/node/619

14. Khaled al-Dakhil, "Is Israel or Iran the enemy?" *al-Hayat,* April 3, 2015; Daoud Shriyan, "Is Israel or Iran the enemy?" *al-Hayat* April 7, 2015.

15. Marc Lynch, "Calvinball in Cairo," *Foreign Policy*, June 12, 2012.

16. Personal interview, Rached Ghannouchi, Tunis, 8 November 2014.

17. Frederic Wehry, *Sectarian Politics in the Gulf* (New York: Columbia University Press 2014).

18. Nathan Brown, *When Victory Is Not an Option* (Ithaca: Cornell University Press 2012).

19. Carrie Wickham, *The Muslim Brotherhood* (Princeton: Princeton University Press 2013); Marc Lynch, "Winter in Cairo," *Democracy: A Journal of Ideas* 29 (2013); Shadi Hamid, *Temptations of Power* (Oxford University Press 2013).

20. Will McCants, "A New Salafi Politics," *POMEPS Studies 2 The New Salafi Politics* (2012).

21. Louisa Loveluck, "Planting the seeds of Tunisia's Ansar al-Sharia", and Aaron Zelin, "Know your Ansar al-Sharia," *POMEPS Studies 2 The New Salafi Politics* (2012).

22. See Leah Farrall, "How Al Qaeda Works," *Foreign Affairs* (2012); Dan Byman, "Al-Qaeda's Affiliates: Asset or Burden?" *Studies in Conflict and Terrorism* (2015).

23. Daveed Gartenstein-Ross and Tara Vassefi, "Perceptions of the 'Arab Spring' Within the Salafi-Jihadi Movement," *Studies in Conflict and Terrorism 35,* no.12 (2012).

24. On the relationship between al-Qaeda and Ansar al-Sharia Tunisia, see Daveed Gartenstein-Ross, "Tunisian jihadism and the Sousse massacre," *CTC Sentinel*, October 2015.

CHAPTER 2

1. The best account of this labor activism is found in Joel Beinin, *Workers and Thieves: Labor Movements and Popular Uprisings in Tunisia and Egypt* (Palo Alto, CA: Stanford University Press 2015).

2. Quoted by CNN, January 29, 2011. http://www.cnn.com/2011/WORLD/meast/01/29/egypt.middle.east.reaction/

3. Sean Yom, "Jordan's New Politics of Tribal Dissent," *Foreign Policy,* August 7, 2012.

4. Adria Lawrence, "Morocco's resilient protest movement," *Foreign Policy,* February 20, 2012.

5. POMEPS Brief 15, "Kuwait's Moment of Truth" (November 2012).

6. Ra'id al-Jamali, "Oman, Kind of Not Quiet," *Foreign Policy*, November 7, 2012.

7. See the essays collected in POMEPS Studies 11: The Arab Thermidor (August 2014), and the Steve Heydemann and Reinoud Leenders chapter in *The Arab Uprisings Explained*, edited by Marc Lynch (New York: Columbia University Press 2014).

8. Abd al-Bari Atwan, "Grim scenarios for Libya," Al-Quds al-Arabi, February 21, 2011 (Arabic).

9. David Roberts, "Qatar, the Ikhwan, and Transnational Relations in the Gulf," in *POMEPS Studies 7: Visions of Gulf Security* (March 25, 2014).

10. Toby Mathiessen, "The sectarian Gulf vs. the Arab Spring." *Foreign Policy*, October 8, 2013; and see the collected essays in *POMEPS Studies 4: The Politics of Sectarianism,* edited by Marc Lynch (November 18, 2013).

11. On these variations, see Jason Brownlee, Tarek Masoud, and Andrew Reynolds, *The Arab Spring* (Oxford University Press 2014); Sean Yom and Gregory Gause, "The Resilience of Monarchs in the Arab Spring" *Journal of Democracy 2012*; and Marc Lynch, ed., *POMEPS Studies 3: The Arab Monarchy Debate* (2012).

12. Stephen Day, *Regionalism and Rebellion in Yemen* (Cambridge University Press 2012).

13. Gregory Johnsen, *The Last Refuge: Yemen, Al-Qaeda and America's War in Arabia* (New York: W.W. Norton, 2014).

14. Peter Salisbury, "Federalism, conflict and fragmentation in Yemen," Report published by *SaferWorld,* October 2015.

15. April Alley, "Yemen changes everything . . . and changes nothing." *Journal of Democracy 24,* no. 4 (2013).

16. As quoted in the Bahrain Independent Commission of Inquiry report, p. 77.

17. Ala'a Shehabi and Marc Owen Jones, *Bahrain's Uprising: Resistance and Repression in the Gulf* (London: Zed Books 2015); Toby Matthiesen, *Sectarian Gulf* (Palo Alto, CA: Stanford University Press 2013)

18. BICI report, p. 93.

19. Justin Gengler, *Group Conflict and Political Mobilization in Bahrain and the Arab Gulf: Rethinking the Rentier State* (Bloomington: Indiana University Press 2015)

20. Tareq al-Homayed, "To those who could compare Syria to Bahrain," *Al-Sharq al-Awsat,* June 13, 2011.

CHAPTER 3

1. https://twitter.com/senjohnmccain/status/3331878099.

2. Lindsey Hilsum, *Sandstorm: Libya in the Time of Revolution*, (New York: Penguin Books, 2012), p. 212.

3. Dennis Ross quoted by *Politico*, March 23, 2011.

4. Michael Barnett, *Dialogues in Arab Politics* (New York: Columbia University Press 1994).

5. Kristian Coates Ulrichsen, *Qatar and the Arab Spring* (Oxford University Press 2014).

6. Fred Wehrey, "Is Libya a proxy war?" *Washington Post* October 24, 2014. http://www.washingtonpost.com/blogs/monkey-cage/wp/2014/10/24/is-libya-a-proxy-war/

7. Beth Dickinson, "A Gun Runner's Lament," *Foreign Policy* September/October 2015,

8. Bardu, "The Corridor of Uncertainty," p. 36; Peter Cole and Umar Khan, Chapters three and four, in *The Libyan Revolution and its Aftermath,* edited by Peter Cole and Brian McQuinn (London: Hurst Publishers 2015), 66

9. Cole and Khan, 68-69.

10. David Roberts, "Qatar and the Muslim Brotherhood: Preference or Pragmatism?" *Middle East Policy 21*, no. 3 (2014): 84-94.

11. Roberts, 2014.

12. Hilsum, 199.

13. Hugh Roberts, "Libya and the Recklessness of the West," *London Review of Books*, September 22, 2012; Roberts, "Who Said Qaddafi Had to Go?" *London Review of Books*, November 17, 2011.

14. Christopher Chivvis, *Toppling Qaddafi: Libya and the Limits of Liberal Intervention* (Cambridge University Press 2014).

15. Fred Wehrey, "The hidden story of airpower in Libya (and what it means for Syria)." *Foreign Policy*, February 11, 2013.

16. Hilsum, 215.

17. Peter Cole and Umar Khan, Chapters three and four, in *The Libyan Revolution and its Aftermath,* edited by Peter Cole and Brian McQuinn (London: Hurst Publishers 2015), 71.

18. Wehrey, in Cole and McQuinn, 113-15.

19. Hilsum, 220.

20. Cole and Khan, 81.

21. Quoted by Stephen Sotloff, "Why the Libyans have fallen out of love with Qatar," *Time*, January 2, 2012.

22. Colum Lynch, "Libyan opposition leaders rule out major role for international peacekeepers." *Washington Post*, August 29, 2011.

23. For a detailed analysis, see Christopher Chivvis and Jeffrey Martini, "Libya after Qaddafi: Lessons and Implications for the Future" (RAND 2014).

24. Ben Fishman, "Could Libya's Decline Have Been Predicted?," *Survival,* 57:5 (2015): 199-208.

25. Kristina Kausch, "Foreign Funding in Post-Revolution Tunisia," FRIDE Working Paper 2013.

26. Youssef Cherif, "Tunisia's Elections Amid a Middle East Cold War," *Atlantic Council*, October 22, 2014.

27. Zeinab Abou el-Magd, "The Egyptian Republic of Retired Generals," *Foreign Policy*, May 8, 2012; Shana Marshall, *The Egyptian Armed Forces and the Remaking of an Economic Empire* (Carnegie Endowment for International Peace, April 15, 2015).

28. Mara Revkin, "Egypt's injudicious judges," *Foreign Policy*, June 11, 2012.

29. Marc Lynch and Steven A. Cook, "U.S. Egypt Policy Needs a Big Shift," *New York Times*, November 30, 2011.

30. Stephen Day, "Can Yemen be a nation unified?" *Foreign Policy*, March 14, 2013.

31. Holger Albrecht, "Consolidating Uncertainty in Yemen," *Foreign Policy*, February 22, 2013.

32. Danya Greenfield, "Overcoming the Pitfalls of Yemen's National Dialogue," *Foreign Policy*, March 18, 2013.

33. Stacey Philbrick Yadav, "Best Friends Forever for Yemen's Revolutionaries?" *Foreign Policy*, March 19, 2013.

34. Laurent Bonnefoy, *Salafism in Yemen: Transnationalism and Regional Identity* (Oxford University Press 2012).

35. April Longley Alley, "Triage for a Fragmenting Yemen," *Foreign Policy*, October 31, 2012.

CHAPTER 4

1. David Makovsky, "Silent Strike," *The New Yorker*, September 17, 2012.

2. Steve Heydemann and Reinoud Leenders, "Popular Mobilization in Syria," *Mediterranean Politics 17*, no. 2 (2012): 139-159.

3. See interview with Bashar al-Asad, *Wall Street Journal*, January 31, 2011.

4. For insight into Asad's perception of the Arab uprising, see David Lesch, *Syria: The Fall of the House of Asad* (New Haven: Yale University Press 2012), chapter 3.

5. As quoted in Crisis Group, "Light at the End of the Tunnels? Hamas and the Arab Uprisings." Middle East Report No. 129, 14 August 2012.

6. Steve Heydemann and Reinoud Leenders, "Authoritarian Adaptation", in *The Arab Uprisings Explained*, edited by Marc Lynch (New York: Columbia University Press 2014).

7. For details, see Human Rights Watch, "Torture Archipelago" (July 2012).

8. Wendy Pearlman, "Emotions and the Microfoundations of the Arab Uprisings," *Perspectives on Politics 11*, no. 2 (2013).

9. See Marc Lynch, Deen Freelon and Sean Aday, "Syria's Socially Mediated Civil War" (US Institute for Peace 2014).

10. For an example of the critical discussion, see Bashir al-Baker, "The Syrian Ikhwan between taqiyya and a fatal mistake," *Al-Akhbar*, June 9, 2011.

11. "Qaradawi condemns atrocities against protestors in Syria," Gulf News March 26, 2011.

12. Marc Lynch, Deen Freelon, and Sean Aday, "Syria in the Arab Spring," *Research and Politics 1* (2014).

13. Emile Hokayem, "The Gulf States and Syria," *USIP Peace Brief 116* (September 30, 2011).

14. Khaled Hroub, "Where are the Arabs on Syria?" *Al-Ittihad (UAE)* July 15, 2011.

15. Leila Fadel, *Washington Post*, July 8, 2011.

16. Azmi Bishara, "Thoughts on the Syrian revolution," *Al-Jazeera,* June 15, 2011.

17. Oraib al-Rentawi, "The Syrian Intifada and the question of arming," *Al-Dustour* (Jordan) 11 June 2011.

18. Crisis Group, "Light at the End of the Tunnels? Hamas and the Arab Uprisings," *Middle East Report No. 129* (August 2012).

19. Mauricio Constantino and Kristian Gleditsch, "Fresh carnations or all thorn, no rose? Nonviolent campaigns and transitions in autocracies," *Journal of Peace Research 50*, no. 3 (2013): 385-400; Erica Chenoweth and Maria Stephan, *Why Civil Resistance Works: The Strategic Logic of Nonviolent Conflict* (Columbia University Press 2011).

20. Peter Harling and Sarah Birke, "Beyond the Fall of the Syrian Regime," *Middle East Report* (online), February 24, 2012 http://merip.org/mero/mero022412; for a similar argument, see my February 2012 Center for a New American Security report, "Pressure Not War."

21. See interview with Ghalioun posted to All4Syria.com, October 6, 2011.

22. Abd al-Rahman al-Rashed, "The armed revolution in Syria has begun" *Al-Sharq al-Awsat*, October 2, 2011.

23. Yasin al-Haj Saleh, "Back to the discussion of militarization of revolution," *al-Hayat*, May 10, 2012.

24. For a discussion, see Bassam Haddad, "Syria's Stalemate," *Middle East Policy 19*, no. 1 (2012).

25. Stephen Starr, *Revolt in Syria: Eye-Witness to the Uprising* (Columbia University Press 2012), p. x.

26. Yassin Haj al-Saleh, "The Revolution and Weapons"—Al-Jamhouryia Center for Studies, May 18, 2012; accessed version on All4Syria.com.

27. For example, see Jeffrey White, *Asad's Armed Opposition: The Free Syrian Army.* Washington Institute for Near East Policy, November 30, 2011.

28. Liz Sly and Karen DeYoung, "Syrian rebels get influx of arms with Gulf neighbors' money," *Washington Post*, May 12, 2012.

29. For instance, see Neil MacFarquhar, "After a Year, Deep Divisions Hobble Syrian Opposition" *New York Times* February 23, 2012.

30. http://www.joshualandis.com/blog/opposition-fails-to-unify-more-call-for-intervention-the-arab-league-first-political-defections/

31. Ghalioun quoted by BBC, March 1, 2012.

32. Abd al-Bari Atwan, "Syria and the Yemen model," *al-Quds al-Arabi*, June 12, 2012.

33. Quoted in Agence France Press, "Syrian Opposition Invited to Tunis Conference," February 19, 2012.

34. See *Al-Arabiya*, February 24, 2012.

35. Ian Black and Julian Borger, "Gulf states warned against arming Syria rebels," *Guardian*, April 5, 2012.

36. Anne-Marie Slaughter, "How to Halt the Butchery in Syria," *New York Times*, February 23, 2012.

37. Hussein Ibish, "Of course it's not too late in Syria," *The Daily Beast*, June 17, 2013.

38. Human Rights Watch, "We've Never Seen Such Horror: Crimes Against Humanity by Syrian Security Forces" (June 1, 2011); Human Rights Watch, "In Cold Blood: Summary Executions by Syrian Security Forces and Pro-Regime Militias" (April 9, 2012); Human Rights Watch, "By All Means Necessary: Individual and Command Responsibility for Crimes Against Humanity in Syria" (December 15, 2011).

39. United Nations Human Rights Council, Report of the independent international commission of inquiry on the Syrian Arab Republic A/HRC/21/50, 15 August 2012

40. Faisal al-Qassem, *Al-Sharq*, May 12, 2012 via http://all4syria.info/Archive /41849

41. "Syria's Mutating Conflict," International Crisis Group Middle East Briefing 33 (April 10, 2012).

42. See Syria's Mutating Conflict, 9.

43. For example, see Aysegul Aydin and Patrick Regan, "Networks of Third Party Interveners and Civil War Duration," *European Journal of International Relations* 18 (2012).

44. Marc Lynch, "Pressure Not War," Center for a New American Security, February 2012.

45. James Fearon, "Syria's Civil War," in *POMEPS Studies 5: The Political Science of Syria's War* (December 2013).

46. Kathleen Gallagher Cunningham, "Actor Fragmentation and Civil War Bargaining," *American Journal of Political Science*, 2013.

47. David Cunningham in *POMEPS Studies 5: The Political Science of Syria's War* (December, 2013).

48. "Against the Hopes of Stathis Kalyvas and Laia Balcells," in *POMEPS Studies 5: The Political Science of Syria's War* (December, 2013); on the question of the impact of arms transfers, see Matthew Moore, "Selling to Both Sides: The Effects of Major Arms Transfers on Civil War Severity and Duration," *International Interactions* 38 (2012): 325-47.

49. Steve Heydemann, "Managed Militarization," *Foreign Policy*; Tamara Wittes, testimony to the Senate Foreign Relations Committee http://www.brookings.edu/research /testimony/2012/04/19-syria-wittes

50. Tariq al-Homayed, "Iran feeling its defeat in Syria," *al-Sharq al-Awsat*, July 22, 2012.

51. Abd al-Rahman Rashed, "The rivalry towards Damascus," *al-Sharq al-Awsat*, July 29, 2012.

52. Hussein Hayder, "The end is near," *al-Hayat*, July 19, 2012.

53. Rania Abouzeid, *Time*, 2012; Gaith Abdul-Ahad, "How to Start a Battalion (In Five Easy Lessons)," *London Review of Books* 35, no. 3 (February 21, 2013).

54. Hassan Hayder, "Don't wait for America," *al-Hayat*, July 27, 2012

55. Yusif al-Kuwilit, "Supporting the Syrian revolution is a necessary choice," *al-Riyadh*, as reprinted by *al-Arabiya*, July 22, 2012.

CHAPTER 5

1. Abd al-Aziz al-Suwaygh, AA/al-Medina.

2. Mara Revkin, "Egypt's injudicious judges," *Foreign Policy*, June 12, 2012.

3. Nathan Brown, "Cairo's judicial coup," *Foreign Policy*, June 14, 2012.

4. Michael Wahid Hanna, "Blame Morsi," *Foreign Policy* July 8, 2013.

5. Dina Rashed, "What Morsi could learn from Anwar Sadat," *Foreign Policy*, August 14, 2012.

6. Jamal Khashoggi, "Iran and its neighbors.. and the Muslim Brotherhood," *al-Hayat*, August 11, 2012.

7. Abd al-Rahman al-Rashed, "The Syria battle between Egypt and Saudi," *al-Sharq al-Awsat*, May 2, 2015.

8. Mishari Zaydi, "The tears of Putin and Nasrallah," *al-Sharq al-Awsat*, July 20, 2012.

9. Marc Lynch, "Trashing Transitions: The Media After the Arab Uprisings," *Journal of Democracy*, October 2015.

10. Ben Hubbard and David Kirkpatrick, "Sudden improvements in Egypt suggest campaign to undermine Morsi," *New York Times*, July 10, 2013.

11. Transcript available at http://arabist.net/blog/2013/2/11/the-us-ambassadors-speech.html

12. Transcript available at http://egypt.usembassy.gov/pr061813a.html

13. Adel Iskander, "Tamarod: Egypt's Revolution Hones its Skills," *Jadaliyya*, June 30, 2013. http://www.jadaliyya.com/pages/index/12516/tamarod_egypts-revolution-hones-its-skills

14. David Kirkpatrick, "Recordings suggest Emirates and Egyptian military pushed ousting of Morsi," *New York Times*, March 1, 2015; Alain Gresh, "Shadow of the army over Egypt's revolution," *Le Monde Diplomatique*, August 2013; Sheera Frenkel and Maged Atef, "How Egypt's rebel movement helped to pave the way for a Sisi Presidency," *Buzzfeed*, April 15, 2014; Mike Giglio, "Cairo Conspiracy," *The Daily Beast*, July 12, 2013.

15. FM Sameh al-Shoukry's remarks as reported in *al-Ahram*, October 4, 2015 http://english.ahram.org.eg/News/152017.aspx

16. Yasir Abu Hilala, "The Gulf supports Sisi and Sisi supports Bashar?" Al-Ghad 8 September 8, 2013.

17. Stephane Lacroix, *Awakening Islam* (Cambridge: Harvard University Press, 2012).

18. Stephane Lacroix, "Saudi Arabia's Muslim Brotherhood predicament," in *POMEPS Studies 7: Visions of Gulf Security* (March 25, 2014).

19. Marc Lynch, "Gulf Islamist dissent over Egypt,":*Foreign Policy*, August 18, 2013,

20. Quoted by Lacroix, "Saudi Arabia's Muslim Brotherhood predicament."

21. On Nayef, see Guido Steiberg, "The Gulf States and the Muslim Brotherhood," in *POMEPS Studies 7: Visions of Gulf Security* (March 25, 2014).

22. Abo el-Fotoh interviewed in *Al-Shorouk*, July 21, 2014.

23. Ashraf el-Sharif, "The Muslim Brotherhood and the Future of Political Islam in Egypt." Carnegie Endowment for International Peace (October 2014).

24. Personal interviews with two Muslim Brotherhood online administrators, London, June 2015.

25. Ibrahim Houdaiby, "The Muslim Brotherhood in Transition," *Mada Masr*, March 18, 2015, http://www.madamasr.com/opinion/politics/muslim-brotherhood -transition; Eric Trager and Marina Shalaby, "Egypt's Muslim Brotherhood Gets a Facelift," *Foreign Affairs*, May 20, 2015.

26. Mohammad Abu Rumman, "The Muslim Brotherhood . . . and the Suicide of the Peaceful Solution," *Al-Araby al-Jadid*, July 12, 2015.

27. Mokhtar Awad, "Egypt's Escalating Insurgency," Carnegie Endowment for International Peace October 2015.

CHAPTER 6

1. The definitive account of these events is David Kirkpatrick, "A Deadly Mix in Benghazi," *New York Times*, December 28, 2013.

2. Jassem Boudi, "War on Kuwaiti Soil," *al-Rai*, June 14, 2013.

3. For the strong case that the pursuit of rapprochement with Iran drove Obama's regional policy, see Michael Scott Doran, "Obama's Secret Iran Strategy," *Mosaic Magazine*, February 2, 2015.

4. Thomas Bass, "How Tunisia is turning into a Salafist battleground," *The Atlantic*, June 20, 2013.

5. Quoted by Loveday Morris, "Uprising in Tunisia as regime critics is murdered," *The Independent*, February 6, 2013.

6. Quoted in Monica Marks and Kareem Fahim, "Tunisia moves to contain fallout after opposition figure is assassinated," *New York Times*, February 6, 2013.

7. Amel Bouebakeur, "Islamists, secularists and old regime elites in Tunisia: Bargained competition," *Mediterranean Politics* (2015).

8. On the National Dialogue, see Daniel Brumberg, "Could Tunisia's National Dialogue model ever be replicated?" *Washington Post* October 12, 2015.

9. "Divided We Stand: Libya's Enduring Conflicts," *International Crisis Group Middle East/North Africa Report 130* (September 14, 2012).

10. "Trial by Error: Justice in Post-Qaddafi Libya," International Crisis Group Middle East/North Africa Report 140 (April 17, 2013).

11. "Holding Libya Together: Security Challenges After Qaddafi," International Crisis Group Middle East/North Africa Report 115 (December 14, 2011).

12. Ali Zeidan interviewed by Christiane Amanpour, CNN, March 24, 2014.

13. Fred Wehrey, "Libya's Revolution at Two Years: Perils and Achievements," *Mediterranean Politics* (2013).

14. Hanspeter Mattes, "Rebuilding the National Security Forces in Libya," *Middle East Policy* 21, no. 2 (2014).

15. Karim Mezran and Eric Knecht, "Libya's Fractious New Politics," *The Atlantic Council,* January 9, 2013.

16. Karim Mezran, "Deepening polarization in Libya, no agreement in sight" *Atlantic Council* February 5, 2014.

17. Fahmy Howeydi, "Lift your hands from Libya," *Al-Jazeera,* January 20, 2015.

18. For an excellent overview, see "Algeria and Its Neighbors," *International Crisis Group Middle East Report 164* (October 12, 2015).

19. Quoted in "Algiera and Its Neighbors," 19.

20. Wehrey, "Is Libya a proxy war?" *Washington Post,* October 24, 2014.

21. Hilmi Nimnim, "Egypt and Libya and Qatar," *al-Masry al-Youm* April 15, 2014.

22. Hisham al-Shalwi, "Libya… and the road to a coup," al-Jazeera, September 18, 2013.

23. Jon Lee Anderson, "The Unraveling," *The New Yorker,* February 23, 2015.

24. David Kirkpatrick, "In Libya, a coup. Or perhaps not." *New York Times,* February 14, 2014.

25. Chris Stephen, Ian Black and Spencer Ackerman, "Khalifa Haftar: renegade general causing turmoil in Libya," *The Guardian,* May 22, 2014.

26. "Libya faces chaos as top court rejects elected assembly," Reuters, November 4, 2014.

27. Missy Ryan and Hassan Morajea, "In Libya, trying to make one government out of two,": *Washington Post,* September 18, 2015.

28. For a detailed discussion, see Daveed Gartenstein-Ross and Nathaniel Barr, *Dignity and Dawn: Libya's Escalating Civil War* (International Center for Counter-Terrorism, February 2015).

29. Fahmy Howeydi, "Another reading of the crisis in Libya," al-Jazeera, January 9, 2015.

30. Hisham Allam, "Sisi between the Nasser of Syria and the Sadat of Gaza," *al-Masry al-Yom,* August 3, 2014.

31. Ali Abu Yassin, *Al-Araby al-Jadeed,* February 27, 2015.

32. Khalil el-Anani, "Sisi's calculations in Libya," *al-Araby al-Jadeed,* February 21, 2015.

33. Yezid Sayigh, "The mirage of Egypt's regional role and the Libya temptation," *al-Hayat,* March 5, 2015.

34. Badar Shafa'ie, "Sisi and the intervention in Libya," *al-Araby al-Jadeed,* February 19, 2015.

35. Fahmy Howeydi, "The Emirati air strikes on Libya," *al-Shorouk*, August 27, 2014.

CHAPTER 7

1. Mark Hosenball, "Obama authorizes secret support for Syrian rebels," Reuters, August 1, 2012.

2. David Cloud and Raja Abdulrahim, "U.S. training Syrian rebels; White House 'stepped up assistance'," *Los Angeles Times*, June 21, 2013; Julian Borger and Nick Hopkins, "West training Syrian rebels in Jordan," *Guardian*, March 8, 2013.

3. C.J. Chivers and Eric Schmitt, "Arms Airlift to Syria Rebels Expands, With C.I.A. Support." *New York Times*, March 23, 2013.

4. Adam Entous, Julian Barnes, and Siobhan Gorman, "U.S. Begins Shipping Arms for Syrian Rebels," *Wall Street Journal*, June 26, 2013.

5. Adam Entous, "Covert CIA mission to arm Syrian rebels goes awry," *Wall Street Journal*, January 25, 2015.

6. Barbara Starr and Leslie Bentz, "Official says CIA-funded weapons have begun to reach Syrian rebels," CNN, September 12, 2013; Ernesto Londono and Greg Miller, "CIA begins weapons delivery to Syria rebels," *Washington Post*, September 11, 2013.

7. Greg Miller, "CIA ramping up covert training mission for Syria rebels," *Washington Post*, October 3, 2013.

8. For example, see Phil Sands, *The National*, December 8, 2013.

9. Steven Clemons, "Thank God for the Saudis," *The Atlantic*, June 23, 2014.

10. Adam Entous, Nour Malas and Margaret Coker, "A Veteran Saudi Power Player Works to Build Support to Topple Asad," *Wall Street Journal*, August 25, 2013.

11. Mishari Zaydi, "Is Erdogan with us?" *al-Sharq al-Awsat*, May 10, 2015.

12. Rania Abouzeid, "Syria's secular and Islamist rebels: Who are the Saudis and the Qataris arming?" *Time*, September 18, 2012.

13. On tribal networks, see Hassan Hassan, "Tribal bonds strengthen Saudi hand in Syria," *The National*, February 16, 2012.

14. Sam Heller and Aaron Stein, "The trouble with Turkey's favorite Syrian Islamists," *War on the Rocks*, August 18, 2015; Sam Heller, "Ahrar al-Sham's Revisionist Jihadism," *War on the Rocks*, September 30, 2015.

15. Elizabeth Dickinson, *Playing With Fire: Why Private Financing for Syria's Extremist Rebels Risks Igniting Sectarian Conflict at Home* (Brookings Institution, December 4, 2013).

16. Erika Solomon, "Syria death toll hits nearly 126,000: monitoring group," Reuters, December 2, 2013.

17. http://www.syriahr.com/en/2015/06/320000-people-killed-since-the-beginning-of-the-syrian-revolution/

18. Ben Hubbard, "Private Donors' Funds Add Wild Card to War in Syria," *New York Times*, November 13, 2013.

19. Suhaib Anjarini, "The unknown role of Kuwait's salafis in Syria," *Al-Akhbar*, March 21, 2014.

20. Marc Lynch, Deen Freelon and Sean Aday, "Syria's Socially Mediated Civil War," USIP 2014.

21. As reported in *Al-Quds al-Arabi*, September 6, 2013.

22. Hajjaj al-Ajmi interview published at http://www.syria2011.net/t33021-topic

23. *Washington Post*, September 21, 2013.

24. David Weinberg, "Kuwait's Embattled Justice Minister Part of a Bigger Terror Finance Problem," *The National Interest*, April 10,2014; and Weinberg, "New Kuwaiti Justice Minister Has Deep Extremist Ties," *The National Interest*, January 16, 2014.

25. "Saudi Arabia bans donation campaigns for Syrians," *Al-Arabiya*, May 29, 2012.

26. *Al-Sharq al-Awsat* 10 April 2013.

27. Remarks by Mufti Abd al-Aziz Al al-Shaykh, as reported in *Akhbaar 24*: February 26, 2014 and December 18, 2013.

28. "Saudi Arabia: warnings against supporting terrorism under the argument of donations for Syria," *Al-Arabiya*, December 18, 2013.

29. Quoted in "Donation campaigns for arming the Syrian opposition," *al-Qabas*, June 26, 2013.

30. "Kuwait steps up controls on Islamic charities," *The National*, August 5, 2014.

31. "Syria calls fundraiser illegal," *Kuwait Times*, November 4, 2014.

32. Yezid Sayigh, "What will the Friends of Syria do after arming Syria's rebels?" Carnegie Endowment for International Peace, June 28, 2013.

33. Angus McDowell, "Saudi spy chief, architect of Syria policy, replaced," Reuters April 15, 2014.

34. Yezid Sayigh, "Unifying Syria's Rebels: Saudi Arabia Joins the Fray," Carnegie Middle East Center, October 28, 2013.

35. Ian Black, "Saudi Arabia to spend millions to train new rebel force," *The Guardian*, November 7, 2013.

36. Yezid Sayigh, "Unifying Syria's Rebels," *Carnegie Middle East Center*, October 28, 2013.

37. Aaron Stein, "Turkey Weakness in Iraq Tied to Weakness in Nujaifi," *Atlantic Council*, May 26, 2015.

38. Aaron Stein, "What Idlib takeover means for Turkey," Al-Jazeera, April 5, 2015.

39. Yezid Sayigh, "The Syrian Opposition's Bleak Outlook," *Carnegie*, April 17, 2014.

40. Andrew Terrill, "Iran's Strategy for Saving Asad," *The Middle East Journal* 69, no. 2 (2015): 222-236.

41. Marisa Sullivan, "Hezbollah in Syria," *Institute for the Study of War* (April 2014).

42. Charles Lister, *The Syrian Jihad* (Hurst 2015), offers the best overview of where the IS fits in this full jihadist spectrum.

43. Joby Warrick, *Black Flags: The Rise of ISIS* (Random House, 2015).

44. For more detail, see Marc Lynch, "Explaining the Awakening," *Security Studies* 20 (2011), and Steven Biddle, Jeffrey Friedman and Jacob Shapiro, "Testing the Surge: Why Did Violence Decline in Iraq in 2007?" *International Security* 37 (2012).

45. Marc Lynch, "Al-Qaeda's Counter-Counterinsurgency Manual," *Foreign Policy*, March 17, 2010.

46. Zaid al-Ali, "Maliki has only himself to blame for Iraq's crisis," *Washington Post*, June 26, 2014.

47. Crisis Group, "Make or Break: Iraq's Sunnis and the State," *Middle East Report No. 144* (August 14, 2013).

48. See Kirk Sowell, "Iraq's Second Sunni Insurgency," *Current Trends in Islamist Ideology* (August 9, 2014).

49. See Lister, *The Syrian Jihad*, chapter 4.

50. Lister, *The Syrian Jihad*, p. 55 of typescript.

51. Alleged Gulf financial supporters of al-Nusra are named in a series of terrorist designations by the US Department of the Treasury.

52. Crisis Group, "Iraq's Jihadi Jack in the Box," *Middle East Briefing 38* (20 June 2014).

53. For evaluations of the Islamic State as a state, see Quinn Mecham, "How much of a state is the Islamic State?" *Washington Post*, February 5, 2015.

54. Aaron Zelin, "The Islamic State model," *Monkey Cage,* January 28, 2015; on the social media dimension, see J.M. Berger and Jessica Stern, *ISIS: The State of Terror* (2015).

55. Khalil al-Anani, "The ISIS-ification of Islamist politics," *The Washington Post*, January 30, 2015.

CHAPTER 8

1. Khaled al-Dukhkayl, "Operation Decisive Storm and the Nuclear Deal," *al-Hayat*, April 12, 2015.

2. Statement available at https://www.whitehouse.gov/the-press-office/2015/05/14/us-gulf-cooperation-council-camp-david-joint-statement

3. See the essays collected in *POMEPS Brief 24 Iraq Between ISIS and Maliki* (July 2014).

4. See Kirk Sowell, "The Islamic State's Eastern Frontier: Ramadi and Fallujah as Theaters of Sectarian Conflict," *Perspectives on Terrorism 9*, no. 3 (2015)

5. Marc Lynch, "How Arab backers of the Syrian rebels see Iraq," *Washington Post*, June 18, 2014.

6. Fahmy Howeydi, "Two Crises in Yemen," *al-Shorouk,* September 22, 2014.

7. See Salisbury, 2015, p. 11.

8. "The Houthis: From Sadaa to Sanaa," *International Crisis Group Middle East Report 154* (June 10, 2014).

9. Ghassan Cherbel, "Operation Restore Balance," *al-Hayat,* March 26, 2015.

10. Nawaf Obaid, "The liberation of South Yemen proves Saudi Arabia's power is growing," *The Telegraph,* August 26, 2015.

11. Daoud Shriyan, "Counter-Propaganda to Decisive Storm," *al-Hayat,* April 5, 2015

12. Abd al-Rahman al-Rashed, "Are Saudi relations with Egypt being trashed?" *al-Sharq al-Awsat,* April 5, 2015.

13. Yarislov Trofimov, "UAE takes the lead in leaderless South Yemen," *Wall Street Journal,* August 30, 2015.

14. Abdulkhaleq Abdullah, "Why the UAE is fighting in Yemen,":*Gulf News,* October 12, 2015.

CHAPTER 9

1. For the fullest articulation of Obama's ideas, see his remarks to American University, August 5, 2015, available at https://www.whitehouse.gov/the-press-office/2015/08/05/remarks-president-iran-nuclear-deal

2. Hilmi al-Asmar, "Waiting for the second campaign of the Arab spring," *al-Araby al-Jadeed,* 3/24/15.

Index

Marc Lynch is professor of political science and international affairs at George Washington University, where he is the director of the Institute for Middle East Studies and of the Project on Middle East Political Science. He is also a nonresident senior fellow at the Center for a New American Security, and a contributing editor at the Monkey Cage blog for The Washington Post. He is the co-director of the Blogs and Bullets project at the US Institute of Peace. He formerly launched and edited the Middle East Channel on ForeignPolicy.com. His most recent book, The Arab Uprising: The Unfinished Revolutions of the New Middle East, was called "the most illuminating and, for policymakers, the most challenging" book yet written on the topic, by The Economist. His other books include Voices of the New Arab Public: Iraq Al-Jazeera, and Middle East Politics Today, selected as a Choice Outstanding Academic Book, and State Interests and Public Spheres: The International Politics of Jordan's Identity. Follow him on Twitter @abuaardvark.

PublicAffairs is a publishing house founded in 1997. It is a tribute to the standards, values, and flair of three persons who have served as mentors to countless reporters, writers, editors, and book people of all kinds, including me.

I. F. STONE, proprietor of *I. F. Stone's Weekly*, combined a commitment to the First Amendment with entrepreneurial zeal and reporting skill and became one of the great independent journalists in American history. At the age of eighty, Izzy published *The Trial of Socrates*, which was a national bestseller. He wrote the book after he taught himself ancient Greek.

BENJAMIN C. BRADLEE was for nearly thirty years the charismatic editorial leader of *The Washington Post*. It was Ben who gave the *Post* the range and courage to pursue such historic issues as Watergate. He supported his reporters with a tenacity that made them fearless and it is no accident that so many became authors of influential, best-selling books.

ROBERT L. BERNSTEIN, the chief executive of Random House for more than a quarter century, guided one of the nation's premier publishing houses. Bob was personally responsible for many books of political dissent and argument that challenged tyranny around the globe. He is also the founder and longtime chair of Human Rights Watch, one of the most respected human rights organizations in the world.

• • •

For fifty years, the banner of Public Affairs Press was carried by its owner Morris B. Schnapper, who published Gandhi, Nasser, Toynbee, Truman, and about 1,500 other authors. In 1983, Schnapper was described by *The Washington Post* as "a redoubtable gadfly." His legacy will endure in the books to come.

Peter Osnos, *Founder and Editor-at-Large*